THE

NEWS

THE ANNENBERG FOUNDATION TRUST AT SUNNYLANDS

Institutions of American Democracy

Kathleen Hall Jamieson and Jaroslav Pelikan, *Directors*

Other books in the series

*Schooling in America: How the Public Schools Meet the Nation's Changing Needs*
Patricia Albjerg Graham

*The Most Democratic Branch: How the Courts Serve America*
Jeffrey Rosen

*The Broken Branch: How Congress Is Failing America and How to Get It Back on Track*
Thomas E. Mann and Norman J. Ornstein

# LOSING
## THE
# NEWS
### THE UNCERTAIN FUTURE OF THE
### NEWS THAT FEEDS DEMOCRACY

## ALEX S. JONES

THE
ANNENBERG FOUNDATION TRUST
AT SUNNYLANDS

THE ANNENBERG
PUBLIC POLICY CENTER
OF THE UNIVERSITY OF PENNSYLVANIA

OXFORD
UNIVERSITY PRESS
2010

# OXFORD

UNIVERSITY PRESS

Oxford University Press, Inc., publishes works that further
Oxford University's objective of excellence
in research, scholarship, and education.

Oxford  New York
Auckland  Cape Town  Dar es Salaam  Hong Kong  Karachi
Kuala Lumpur  Madrid  Melbourne  Mexico City  Nairobi
New Delhi  Shanghai  Taipei  Toronto

With offices in
Argentina Austria Brazil Chile Czech Republic France Greece
Guatemala Hungary Italy Japan Poland Portugal Singapore
South Korea Switzerland Thailand Turkey Ukraine Vietnam

Published by Oxford University Press, Inc.
198 Madison Avenue, New York, New York 10016

www.oup.com

First issued as an Oxford University Press paperback, 2010

Oxford is a registered trademark of Oxford University Press

Library of Congress Cataloging-in-Publication Data
Jones, Alex S.
Losing the news : the uncertain future of the news that feeds democracy / Alex S. Jones.
p. cm.— (Institutions of American democracy)
Includes bibliographical references and index.
ISBN 978-0-19-518123-4 (hardback : alk. paper)
978-0-19-975414-4 (paperback : alk. paper)
1. Journalism—Political aspects—United States.
2. Journalism—Economic aspects—United States.
3. Journalism—Objectivity—United States.
4. Journalistic ethics—United States.
I. Title.
PN4888.P6.J66 2009
071.3—dc22    2009018385

1 3 5 7 9 8 6 4 2

Printed in the United States of America
on acid-free paper

FOR
SUSAN

Alice: "Would you tell me, please, which way I ought to go from here?"
Cheshire Cat: "That depends a good deal on where you want to get to."
—Lewis Carroll, *Alice's Adventures in Wonderland*

# CONTENTS

CHAPTER 7
Newspapers on the Brink

CHAPTER 8
The New News Media

CHAPTER 9
Saving the News

*Index*

## ACKNOWLEDGMENTS

The origin of this book was an invitation to write it from Kathleen
Hall Jamieson and Geneva Overholser in their capacity as coedi-
tors of *The Press,* a part of the American Institutions of Democracy
series of books published through a partnership of Oxford University Press and the Annenberg Foundation Trust at Sunnylands.
*Losing the News* is also part of that series and a complement to *The
Press,* which is a collection of scholarly essays that examine the history, identity, roles and future of the American press.

Their confederate in conceiving what became *Losing the
News* was Tim Bartlett, who was the book's first editor at Oxford
University Press and was instrumental in framing what it should
be. When Tim left Oxford, it passed into the extraordinarily
capable hands of David McBride, who has been its principal
guide and editor. But it has also been encouraged and enabled
by an array of people at Oxford who believed it had an important message and have been enormously forbearing and supportive throughout. I especially wish to thank Niko Pfund,
Oxford's academic and trade division publisher, for his commitment to seeing that the book was published well, and Keith
Faivre, Sarah Russo, and Steve Dodson for their special efforts
on my behalf.

I am grateful to friends who read the manuscript and offered
guidance and corrections: Tom Patterson, Steve Oney, Nancy
Palmer, John Carroll, Dan Okrent, Dudley Clendinen, Fred

Schauer, Floyd Abrams, Nicco Mele, Camille Stevens, and Laurel Shackelford, whose rigor saved me many times.

My superb associates at the Joan Shorenstein Center on the Press, Politics and Public Policy at Harvard University's Kennedy School of Government, and Walter Shorenstein, the center's principal benefactor, have been my allies throughout.

I am also most grateful to Kathy Robbins and David Halpern, my agents, who were my allies from the start and contributed their counsel as well as their editorial wisdom.

It is important also to thank some particular people who inspired me along the way: Arthur Gelb, Joel Fleishman, Eugene Patterson, my late grandmother, Edith O'Keefe Susong, and my parents, John M. and Arne Jones.

Throughout the making of *Losing the News,* I have had the support of family and friends too numerous to mention, but who are most appreciated and loved. They bolstered me in some dark days and were essential.

I wish also to say that I have drawn strength from my fellow journalists, who share many of my concerns, if not always my views. You are my colleagues.

Finally, I thank Susan Elizabeth Tifft, who is my first and last reader, my trusted editor, my boon companion and friend, and my beloved wife.

# PROLOGUE:THE CRISIS

My best moment as a journalist took place in January 1986, around 3 A.M. in a hotel room that reeked of cigarette smoke and was littered with half-eaten sandwiches and abandoned glasses of watery iced tea. I was in the Hyatt Hotel in Louisville, Kentucky, and for five days had been working on a story about why the Binghams, the town's most famous family, had abruptly decided to sell the newspapers that had made them Kentucky's first citizens. Family strife had prompted the sudden announcement of the sale of the *Courier-Journal* and the *Louisville Times*, and I had immediately caught a plane to Louisville to cover the story for the *New York Times*. My beat was the press itself.

The collapse of the Bingham empire was big news because the *Courier-Journal* was regarded as perhaps the nation's finest and most honored regional paper. It was also a catastrophe to the nation's dwindling number of newspaper-owning families, who had looked at the Binghams as a model of success and determination to remain independent of chain ownership.

From my perspective, it was also a great *story*, and, after writing two fast articles, I'd fought with my editor in New York for the chance to stay in Louisville to report and write a longer, more penetrating account of what had happened to this family. My editor was reluctant because I had been at the *Times* for only two years. He had a far more seasoned person in mind for the job, but I fought for it and managed to persuade him to give me my chance. For five days I interviewed frenetically, talking to everyone I could reach who might shed light on why this family had come apart. At night I wrote and rewrote a piece that eventually swelled to more than 6,500 words, which was practically novelistic by *Times* standards. I sustained myself with sweet tea and Marlboros and worked almost around the clock.

And I got lucky. The Binghams were willing to speak to me, and I happened to catch Barry Bingham Sr., a man not given to psychological self-analysis, at a moment in which he was uncharacteristically candid about himself and his family. He spoke of the untimely deaths of two sons and the deepening strife among his other three children that led to his decision to sell. And he talked of how the family's culture of reserve had meant that the anger smoldered and grew without the honest confrontations that might have cleared the air. I interviewed him in his office on the day after he announced his decision to sell, after his surviving son had denounced him. He seemed stunned and sad. Perhaps, he said, the family might have been "much better off if we'd been a more Latin-type family with a lot of outbursts, tears, screams and reconciliations. But that has not been the way any of us operates."

The article was to appear on the front page of the *Times*'s Sunday business section, which was printed on Friday night. My deadline was Thursday, and in the silent, early hours of Thursday morning I pushed the button that sent the final section of the piece to New York by the cumbersome computer technology of the day.

And then I called my wife, Susan Tifft, who was a writer at *Time*, awakening her in our New York apartment. I was unable to contain myself. I declared to my sleep-muddled spouse, "I *know* it's the best thing I've ever done." Though it may be a cliché to say it, my heart was soaring. I had done my best. And I knew— I *knew*—that what I had created was going to make that special connection, was going to grab people and compel them to read it to the very end. I felt that I had learned what had happened and why it had happened, and that I had done the family justice, told their story honestly, and done it well.

I recount that moment because I feel it important to say that I love being a journalist and believe that journalism offers such transporting moments. They are rare, but I think most journalists could tell a similar tale of the time they knocked it out of the park. We don't get paid much, and this is a major part of our reward system. I felt that I had honored the journalistic traditions and standards that I had been brought up to believe in—of fairness and objectivity and accuracy. And I had also told a riveting story that illuminated something of value to many who read it.

It was a story with particular resonance for me because I am in the fourth generation of a newspaper-owning family in Greeneville, Tennessee, and I knew the secret prides and anxieties that go with being in the clan that owns the local newspaper. My family still owns and operates the *Greeneville Sun,* circulation about 15,000, where my father is publisher and my two brothers and brother-in-law go to work every day. I felt that my own history had helped me understand the Binghams in a special way, and that I had done right by them. The article I wrote had no villains, only a very human set of protagonists and a tragic ending. I later won a Pulitzer Prize for the article, but I cherish that night in Louisville amid the dirty ashtrays more than the Pulitzer.

The kind of news that I believe in is in trouble, and this is a problem that must engage us all, as it affects us all. I have practiced almost every kind of journalism: small newspapers and a big metro paper, radio, television, books, magazines, and, more recently, journalism on the Web and in academia. I feel I have been stewing in journalism my entire life, because "the paper"— as we always referred to the *Greeneville Sun*—was like a demanding but beloved family member from earliest memory. I am, at heart, a newspaperman, and undoubtedly come to the news crisis of today with the bias that comes from knowing the pungent smell of thick printers' ink and the frenzy of a newsroom at deadline. I am an aficionado of newspaper movies, my favorite being *Deadline-USA*, a 1952 melodrama with Humphrey Bogart as managing editor of the *Day*, a metropolitan paper on the verge of extinction. Its bickering owners are about to sell to a competing paper, which would then shut it down to kill the competition. But the *Day* is on the trail of one final big story. At the climactic moment, set amid roaring presses, Bogart is on the phone with a racketeer who has just told him, "Print that story, you're a dead man." Bogart holds the phone toward the deafening presses and then bawls into it, "That's the press, baby. The press! And there's nothing you can do about it. Nothing!" And while it's true that the racketeer can't stop the story, the final scene shows the *Day*'s lights going out to the accompaniment of a dirge-like musical phrase from "The Battle Hymn of the Republic": "his truth goes marching on."

While *Deadline-USA* is a newspaper romance, it is one with a spiky truth that was well understood in 1952: newspapers—indeed, almost all news organizations—may have a mission, but they are also businesses, with all that implies. That harsh reality is on gaudy display today as all traditional news organizations are trying to find ways to transform themselves so as to survive in a digital world. The Internet has blown the economic model of traditional journalism sky-high, and the rush to find a new model that will provide profits is prompting both innovation and relentless cost cutting, especially at newspapers. The cost of failing to make that transformation is the death of the organization, but the cost of survival is potentially as deadly to the journalistic mission. The succession of stories about shrinking newsrooms has been both depressing and almost numbing. I could read many articles about newsroom layoffs with sadness and gloom, but without a sense of panic. But then something happens that says it may well be time to panic. That moment for me came when I heard a friend's voice on my voicemail saying, "Rex has lost his job. He's very low. Call him."

I left the *New York Times* after nine years in 1992 to write a book. Rex Seline and I had been there together, and I had come to admire his expertise as an editor, and also his cool, unflappable intelligence. We had stayed in touch over the years. He referred to himself as a "lifer," meaning he was committed to newspaper journalism and in it to stay. Rex came from Lincoln, Nebraska, and got a BA in journalism at the University of Nebraska, where he was editor of the *Daily Nebraskan*. He loved newspapers and went up the ranks from part-time copy editor at the *Omaha World-Herald* to the *Rochester Democrat and Chronicle* to the *Dallas Times Herald*, and then arrived at the *Times* in 1984, about two months after I got there. He was originally a copy editor, but his talent was apparent and he soon was given bigger editing responsibilities. In 1990, he became executive business editor of the *Miami Herald*, and four years later went to the *Fort Worth Star-Telegram* as business editor. It was a typical, successful newspaper career, moving to steadily bigger jobs with more responsibility. Eight years ago, he became the *Star-Telegram*'s managing editor for news, supervising coverage of Fort Worth and the state of Texas, the business desk, and also the national/foreign desk. Along the way he and his wife, Becky, had two children, whom he tried—largely in vain—to make into rabid Red Sox fans, like their father.

He is serious about journalism, and would sometimes call to chew over ethical dilemmas, always with an eye on making sure he and his paper were on the side of the angels. He was determined to do his journalistic work honorably and well because he was an idealist—or perhaps a romantic—about journalism. He wasn't on a soapbox about it, but his work mattered to him a lot and it was recognized by his peers. For instance, in 2004 he became president of the Society of American Business Editors and Writers. But he also lived a family man's life and was chairman of the staff-parish relations committee at the Arborlawn United Methodist Church. His alma mater chose him as the Outstanding News-Editorial Alumnus for 2006, and he expected, eventually, to finish his career at the *Fort Worth Star-Telegram*.

The *Star-Telegram*, with a circulation of more than 200,000, is roughly the 45th largest newspaper in America, smaller than Denver or Kansas City but larger than Cincinnati and Richmond. It is of a size that has made it highly profitable for many decades, and it competes effectively with the *Dallas Morning News*, its much larger neighbor. The paper was family-owned until 1974, when the Carter family sold to Capital Cities Communications. Cap Cities acquired ABC and was then itself bought by Disney, which had no interest in newspapers and sold the *Star-Telegram* to the Knight Ridder newspaper chain in 1997. In 2006, disgruntled shareholders, unhappy with Knight Ridder's bottom line, forced the sale of the company, and, in a burst of optimism, McClatchy Newspapers purchased several of the papers, including the *Star-Telegram*. McClatchy is considered probably the most public-spirited and news-oriented newspaper chain in the nation, and has had a reputation of being satisfied with profit margins that were somewhat below those demanded by the industry's most avaricious chains. The papers purchased by McClatchy were considered to be in safe hands in what was already a difficult time.

But McClatchy's purchase of the newspapers, with its huge attendant debt, has proved to be a bottom-line disaster for the company. The flight of advertisers to the Internet was compounded by the general advertising malaise created by the recession, and 2007 brought the second-worst decline in newspaper advertising in half a century. For many papers, 2008 was worse. With McClatchy stock plummeting, the company pulled the plug on spending. And so, in late April of 2008, Rex was told that his job was to be eliminated in a round of newsroom staff reductions that eventually reduced the workforce by at least 55. Others have since left, and their positions have not been filled. All told, just over 25 percent of the newsroom disappeared. Abruptly, at 51 and after a 30-year newspaper career, my friend was out. And he fears his life as a newspaperman is over for good.

When I heard the news, I felt with a shudder that a corner had been turned for the nation's news media—not because of the loss of Rex Seline personally, but because a company with the pride and commitment to quality of McClatchy had felt forced by economic pressure to strip itself of people of the caliber of Rex Seline. It is not fat or excess that is now being shed, but the day-to-day stalwarts that are the greatest strength of newspapers and other news organizations. When the Rex Selines of news get thrown overboard, the seas are boiling and the ship may well be foundering. Should that happen, truth will be in shorter supply, and that would be a terrible blow to us all.

I believe that journalism is important. That it matters. For over a century, Americans have had as a birthright a remarkably good—though far from perfect—core of reported news that is as essential to our freedom as the Constitution itself. But the times we live in trigger an unsettling cascade of questions about journalism and news. If taken seriously, these are difficult questions. Some are moral or ethical ones. Others are thorny for other reasons. What, indeed, is *happening* to the news at this time of tumultuous technological change? Does it matter that newspapers seem to be in free fall? Is objectivity the best model for American journalism in a new era that prizes the individual voice? Is media concentration a menace or a red herring? Is traditional journalism *really* essential to democracy? What exactly *is* honorable journalism? Such questions are at the center of this book, which is an effort to explain the curious story of news, a tale that has come down laced with mythology and misconceptions. The book's focus is the values of journalism at a time when those values are increasingly viewed as obsolete or unaffordable in a media world turned upside down by digital technology. My purpose is also to try to see over the horizon to where news might go from here, or at least to ponder our choices.

The book is not intended for people seeking fresh ammunition with which to bash the press from the left or from the right. News is like government itself—endlessly subject to criticism, and with few defenders. But also like government, news can be good and bad; it can do its job well or let us down. And usually, like government, it does some of both. This is not a book about media bias, but about the uncertain fate of serious news itself.

News—or something that looks like it—will exist in the future, of course. There will be, through the Web, a torrent of news and opinion. But high-quality news is expensive to produce, and in ever shorter supply. One hopes that the *New York Times* and the *Washington Post* will endure, but two great general interest news organizations are not enough. The best reporting before the Iraq War is widely viewed to have been not by the *Times* or the *Post,* but by the what was then the Knight Ridder Washington bureau.

The profit squeeze has wreaked havoc on newsrooms and especially decimated the Washington-based press corps covering government on behalf of citizens back home. For instance, in 2006 Washington-based reporters for the *San Diego Union-Tribune* won a Pulitzer Prize for exposing the corruption of Congressman Randal "Duke" Cunningham—a story that would almost certainly not have come to light without their investigation. Now that bureau has been shuttered, along with a host of others. The future promises an abundance of what might be considered *commodity news*, which is to say plain vanilla news that is generated by a few news companies and sold cheap, like mass-produced fast food. Far less certain is whether *high-quality* news will be part of the daily life of any but the wealthy and the powerful—especially when it comes to local and state coverage. An analysis in 2009 of reporting strength in the nation's state legislatures by *Governing* magazine detailed the wholesale abandonment of statehouse reporting by the nation's news organizations. Government at the state level often has the most impact on people's lives, and it is also where corruption flourishes without a watchdog press.

The word "crisis" is hackneyed in journalism and should be treated with great skepticism—a reporter's virtue. Nevertheless, to my mind there *is* a genuine crisis. It is not one of press bias, though that is how most people seem to view it. Rather, it is a crisis of diminishing quantity and quality, of morale and sense of mission, of values and leadership. And it is taking place in a maelstrom of technological and economic change. The Internet and digital technology have sent the news business into a frenzy of rethinking, an upheaval of historic proportions whose outcome is much in doubt. Things that are precious may well be lost or terribly damaged, and new things that are marvelous will certainly emerge. What is sure is that the old media world is being transformed—collapsing, in some respects—and the new media world will be different, for better and worse. The chips that had been in orderly piles in front of a few players are now scattered all over the floor, and everyone in the casino is scrambling to grab a handful. Tom Brokaw likens it to "the second big bang," a stupendous media explosion in which some things are burning up and no one knows which of the swirling fragments will ultimately support life.

Optimists about the future of news are dazzled by the glories of the digital age and a democratization of news fueled by the Internet. They generally view those who express concern as self-interested sentimentalists clinging desperately to a disappearing media environment or as Luddites who are too old-fashioned to plunge into an exciting new world.

Pessimists see a frightening new order in which serious professional news reporting will be replaced by talk, advocacy, spin, trivia, and out-and-out propaganda. They see a world in which the news diet for most of the nation will be comparable to living on potato chips and beer, and a typical news story will be what fits on a cell phone screen. Despite the thrilling innovations in news taking place, they are alarmed by the dispiriting erosion of what has been the kind of news that made the press an institution of American democracy.

I like to think of myself as a realist, but not a cynic or a doom-sayer. An inchoate free-floating anxiety about the news is abroad in our nation, and I certainly share that. Many people are worried, but aren't sure what they should be worried about. The issues are bewildering, the values involved are often contradictory, and the technological landscape seems to change by the hour. This book aspires to clarify what is happening to news and why, to look frankly at news values, and to lay out the important choices that will shape the future. One thing is certain: the revolution in news now taking place will be critical to defining what kind of a nation we become in the years ahead.

# LOSING

### THE

# NEWS

CHAPTER ONE

# THE IRON CORE

*Unfortunately, that meant we had to offer buyouts to some very talented people.*

—Brian Kelley, editor of *U.S. News & World Report*, quoted
by Washington.com after the magazine eliminated its
investigative unit for economic reasons.

IMAGINE A SPHERE OF PITTED IRON, GREY AND IMPERFECT like a large cannonball. Think of this dense, heavy ball as the total mass of each day's serious reported news, the iron core of information that is at the center of a functioning democracy. This iron core is big and unwieldy, reflecting each day's combined output of all the professional journalism done by news organizations— newspapers, radio and television news, news services such as the Associated Press and Reuters, and a few magazines. Some of its content is now created by new media, nonprofits, and even, occasionally, the supermarket tabloids, but the overwhelming majority still comes from the traditional news media.

This iron core does not include Paris Hilton's latest escapade or an account of the Yankees game or the U.S. Open. It has no comics or crossword puzzle. No ads. It has no stories of puppies or weekend getaways or recipes for cooking great chili. Nor does it include advice on buying real estate, investing in an IRA, movie reviews, or diet tips. There is nothing wrong with any of these things. Indeed, pleasant and diverting stories are far more appealing to most people than the contents of the core, which some find grim, boring, or riddled with bias.

It has no editorials and does not include the opinions of columnists or op-ed writers or political bloggers. These things are *derived* from the core. They are made possible because there *is* a core. Their point of departure is almost always information gleaned from the reporting that gives the core its weight, and they serve to spread awareness of the information that is in the core, to analyze it and interpret it and challenge it. Opinion writers pick and choose among what the core provides to find facts that will further an argument or advance a policy agenda. But they are outside the core, because they almost always offer commentary and personal observation, not original reporting.

Inside the core is news from abroad, from coverage of the war in Iraq to articles describing the effort to save national parks in Mozambique. There is news of politics, from the White House to the mayor's office. There is an account of a public hearing on a proposal to build new ball fields and an explanation of a regional zoning concept that might affect property values. There is policy news about Medicare reform and science news about global warming. There is news of business, both innovation and scandal, and even sporting news of such things as the abuse of steroids. An account of the battle within the local school board about dress codes is there, along with the debate in the state legislature over whether intelligent design should be taught as science. The iron sphere is given extra weight by investigative reports ranging from revelations that prisoners at the county jail are being used to paint the sheriff's house to the disclosure that the government is tapping phones without warrants as part of the war on terror.

What goes into this cannonball is the daily aggregation of what is sometimes called "accountability news," because it is the form of news whose purpose is to hold government and those with power accountable. This is fact-based news, sometimes called the "news of verification" as opposed to the "news of assertion" that is mostly on display these days in prime time on cable news channels and in blogs.

Traditional journalists have long believed that this form of fact-based accountability news is the essential food supply of democracy and that without enough of this healthy nourishment, democracy will weaken, sicken, or even fail.

For more than a century, this core of reported news has been the starting place for a raucous national conversation about who we are as a people and a country. Just as the Earth is surrounded by a blanket of atmosphere, so too is this core enveloped by a thick layer of talk and opinion. The conversation—which seems more like an endless family squabble—takes place on editorial pages and in letters to the editor, in opinion columns and on Sunday morning talk shows, on *The O'Reilly Factor* and the radio programs of Rush Limbaugh and Don Imus, in blogs on the Internet and press releases, over dining-room tables, beside water coolers and in barrooms, in political cartoons and on *The Daily Show with Jon Stewart.*

And in-jokes. In his first ten years as host of *The Tonight Show,* Jay Leno told over 18,000 political jokes, almost 4,000 of them about Bill Clinton. But for each of Leno's political jokes, the starting point was something from the core. The core also feeds the entertainment industry, which has its own powerful voice in the national conversation. The quasi-news programs on television, such as *Today* and *20/20,* look to the core for ideas and inspiration. Some pure entertainment programs, such as *The West Wing,* come directly from the core, and even the silliest of sitcoms and nastiest of hip-hop lyrics are often linked to it in some murky way. No matter where the conversation about public affairs takes place, it is almost always an outgrowth of that daily iron cannonball.

The biggest worry of those concerned about news is that this iron core is in jeopardy, largely because of the troubles plaguing the newspaper business. It is the nation's newspapers that provide the vast majority of iron core news. My own estimate is that

85 percent of professionally reported accountability news comes from newspapers, but I have heard guesses from credible sources that go as high as 95 percent. While people may *think* they get their news from television or the Web, when it comes to this kind of news, it is almost always newspapers that have done the actual reporting. Everything else is usually just a delivery system, and while resources for television news have plunged and news on commercial radio has all but disappeared, the real impact on iron core news has been from the economic ravaging of newspapers.

Until now, the iron core of news has been somewhat sheltered by an economic model that was able to provide extra resources beyond what readers—and advertisers—would financially support. This kind of news is expensive to produce, especially investigative reporting. And there are indications that a lot of people aren't really interested. In the media economy of the future, cold metrics will largely determine what is spent on news. The size and quality of the iron core will be a direct reflection of what the audience for it will economically support. Demand will rule, and that may well mean that, as a nation, we will be losing a lot of news. There will be a bounty of talk—the news of assertion—but serious news, reported by professional journalists, is running scared.

Inside the core, there is a hierarchy of news, each type important in its own way. The first tier could be thought of as bearing witness. This is no small service to democracy, and is the meat and potatoes of accountability news in that it lets citizens know the fundamentals of what is happening in their world and in the corridors of power. Much of the headline news, both of the White House and around the world, is the act of journalists bearing witness to events. Firsthand coverage of disasters such as Hurricane Katrina and of wars in Afghanistan and Iraq are examples of this kind of bearing-witness journalism at its most challenging. Similarly, the reporter who tells you what happened at the mayor's press conference or at the school board meeting is bearing witness. Being a reliable surrogate for the public—the nation's eyes and ears—is most of what goes into the core, and it is also the most straightforward form of journalism. The burden for the reporter is to tell it straight and get as much of the truth as is possible.

But bearing witness is frequently not enough—indeed, not nearly enough for important issues. It opens the door to the second tier of core journalism, which can be thought of as "following up." Good journalists rarely stop with bearing witness. That is the point of departure for the second step of finding out what more is to be known and answering the all-important question "why?"—seeking reasons that often are not apparent at the moment of bearing witness. This is the journalism that requires being able to stay with a story rather than simply visit it and then move on to the next thing. It means listening to the mayor's press conference and then finding out what was behind the decision or policy that was announced. It is staying with the war rather than parachuting in, doing a quick report, and leaving on the next plane. It is sometimes simply being able to confirm what seemed to be the truth at the moment of bearing witness, but may have been a selective representation. It requires time to follow up, and it demands—and in turn creates—expertise and sophistication about what is being reported.

Next up the hierarchy of core news is what might be called "explanatory journalism," which takes even more time and expertise. This is the product of boring deeply into a subject, speaking to sources, unearthing data, gathering facts, and mastering complexity. It is the kind of reporting that compares the confusing options for older Americans as they try to choose between prescription plans and that examines—without prejudice—the evidence for and against the reality of global warming and presents the result in a form that is illuminatingly fair-minded. It could be thought of as following up on steroids, and if following up takes effort and dogged curiosity, explanatory journalism takes deeper knowledge and expertise, and even more time.

Finally, at the top of the reporting chain, is investigative reporting. This is the toughest kind of journalism because it not only takes time and great expertise, it must be done in the face of efforts to keep information secret. Inherent in the concept of investigative reporting is that it is news that someone with power does not want the public to know. Often, it starts with a reporter simply bearing witness. In perhaps the most celebrated example, in 1972 Bob Woodward was a low-level metro reporter at the *Washington Post*, on the job for only nine months, when five men broke into the Democratic National Headquarters in the Watergate complex and got caught wearing rubber surgical gloves and carrying fancy bugging equipment and $2,300 in cash. Both Woodward and another metro reporter, Carl Bernstein, worked on the first-day page-one story, along with eight other *Post* reporters, and they didn't even get a byline. But they then attacked the story like wolverines, and the *Post* won a Pulitzer Prize for Public Service for its coverage of the Watergate scandal. As Alicia Shepard points out in her article "The Myth of Watergate, Woodward and Bernstein," the story released a deluge of reportorial energy as the nation's best news organizations competed for scoops. The *Los Angeles Times* was first to get one of the burglars on the record in a hard-hitting interview. In his book *Richard Nixon, Watergate and the Press*, Louis Liebovich said that within six months of the break-in, the *Post* had produced 201 staff-written stories, but the *New York Times* had published 99 and the *Los Angeles Times* 45. Important investigative work was also done by the *Washington Star, Time, Newsweek,* and CBS. The aggregate of their work was the fruit of thousands of man-hours by talented reporters, and it took every bit of that commitment by news organizations to finally force the truth to emerge.

Compare that investigative blitzkrieg with investigative coverage of the Bush administration, which seemed tepid and even hapless. To my mind, one of the best investigative reporters in the country is Seymour Hersh, who won a Pulitzer in 1970 for exposing the My Lai massacre. Nearly 40 years later, he has broken story after story in the *New Yorker* ahead of the major news organizations. For instance, it was Hersh who, in 2006, revealed that the Bush administration was preparing plans for an air strike against Iran, including the possible use of nuclear weapons. His reporting has often been greeted with denials by authorities, but has also usually proven to be on target. "What it takes is time and money," says Hersh of the crucial ingredients for investigative reporting, and also a willingness from a publisher to support investigations that don't get anywhere. "I strike out one time in three," he said. Hersh, who is in his 70s and still blisteringly passionate about exposing lies and deception, has astonishing sources, a result of being able to work at his specialty for decades. And he is dismayed at the current lack of support for investigative reporting, which he blames on editors and owners, not reporters.

The problem is financial. Building the relationships and trust that generate high-stakes investigative reporting requires a news organization's patient support. A skilled investigative reporter can cost a news organization more than $250,000 a year in salary and expenses for only a handful of stories. Single projects can sometimes take months or even years. A few years ago, the *Los Angeles Times* allowed three reporters to work for three years, one of them virtually full-time, on a story that resulted in exposing a glaring bit of unexpected evil. The series, which was entitled "Guardians for Profit," told of how predatory opportunists manipulated the system to get themselves legally appointed guardians of elderly people without the victims' knowledge or wish. These vulnerable seniors had no close family, but did have assets, and their new "guardians"—with the law behind them—were able to take over their lives and plunder at will. The multipart series rocked Los Angeles and prompted a severe tightening in laws involving appointed guardianships. But the series cost hundreds of thousands of dollars in salaries and expenses.

This kind of reporting also often means incurring legal risks and igniting the wrath of powerful interests, which is one reason there is so little of it on the Web. The economic muscle of a major news organization, with lawyers and libel insurance, is all but essential. While it does not make up the greatest quantity of core reporting, it is the weightiest reporting of all when it comes to accountability. In the changing news economy, each form of core news is in jeopardy of shrinking in proportion to how expensive it is to produce, which will mean that investigative, explanatory, and follow-up news stand to get hit hardest. But even bearing-witness news—especially if it incurs significant expense, such as foreign reporting—is facing a bleak prospect. The hollowed-out iron core of the future may well be mostly a compendium of the simplest, cheapest kind of bearing-witness news, generated by a corps of general assignment reporters whose job is to fill a quota of publishable copy rather than to cover a beat with depth. News staffs are shrinking, and the most experienced and highly paid reporters and editors are usually the target. As they leave the journalistic ranks, the iron core steadily hollows out.

If there is an emblem of what is happening to the iron core, it is the wrenching recent history of the *Los Angeles Times*. The paper was founded in 1881 and purchased a few years later by its first editor, a former Union Army officer named Harrison Gray Otis. Journalistically, it was a labor-bashing promotional vehicle for the city's developers, and, in a notorious incident, the paper was bombed in 1910 in the midst of a struggle with labor unions and 21 people were killed. The two accused union leaders, who were defended by Clarence Darrow, eventually pleaded guilty, but there has been an enduring accusation that they were framed. When Otis died in 1917, the paper was taken over by his son-in-law, Harry Chandler, who, in turn, was succeeded by his son Norman in 1944. Throughout these decades, the paper was aggressively behind the local pro-growth power structure, and earned a reputation as one of the nation's most mediocre big-city newspapers.

The paper passed to Norman's son, Otis, in 1960, and he proved to be a shock. Big and handsome, with a playboy image as a skier, surfer, and bodybuilder, Otis was also ambitious for the family newspaper and for the next 20 years raised the *Times* from an embarrassment to recognition as one of the nation's best papers. A fierce competitor and prideful Californian, he wanted Los Angeles to have a paper as great as the ones in Washington and New York, and he was willing to spend the money to hire first-rate reporters and editors and then let them do their jobs. The paper added scores of people to the news staff, aggressively went after international coverage, and won four Pulitzers in the first decade of Otis's tenure as publisher. Among journalists it was jokingly called "the velvet coffin"—people had to be carried out because the pay and benefits were so good. For instance, first-class travel was provided for any reporter traveling more than 1,000 miles on assignment. The paper's profits increased with the quality—and with the times, which were very good for newspapers. The *Times* expanded coverage into the area around Los Angeles, beefed up its Washington bureau, and started a national edition to put the paper on the desks of the Eastern establishment to showcase the paper's good work. These ventures were journalistically glorious, but very expensive.

By the mid-1990s, Otis had been largely phased out of power, and the other members of the Chandler family were pressing for greater profits. They wanted someone with a tougher approach to the bottom line. In 1995 day-to-day control of the paper passed to Mark Willes, a former president of General Mills. Willes quickly became known within the paper as "the cereal killer," a reference to his seeming disdain of the paper's mission and his statements that suggested newspapers were no different than brands of cereal. Willes's tenure came to a crashing end in 1999 when word leaked out that he had authorized a revenue-sharing arrangement with the Staples Center, a new sports arena, for a special section. The problem was that the section was portrayed as independent reporting, but was written by journalists who found that they had been effectively working for advertisers. Such a breach of journalism ethics prompted a rebellion in the newsroom and roused Otis himself to denounce Willes. By then, the other members of the Chandler family were pressing for a sale, and in 2000 the Tribune Company of Chicago, Illinois, a more bottom-line corporation that owned the *Chicago Tribune* and other papers, acquired the Times Mirror Company, of which the *Los Angeles Times* was the crown jewel, albeit one that needed a surge of new leadership after the Staples Center scandal.

That fall, the newsroom was heartened to learn that John Carroll, one of the nation's most respected editors, was to take the news helm. The Tribune Company had chosen Carroll, until recently the editor of the *Baltimore Sun,* because of his stature in the newspaper fraternity and his proven record of inspiring great journalism. Carroll was not averse to cutting excess, and he recognized that the *Times* had fat. But he also believed that its profit margins of around 20 percent should be sufficient, and that the value of one of the nation's great newspapers was its reputation for fearless and high-quality journalism. In the news world, the *Los Angeles Times* was ranked with the *New York Times, Washington Post,* and *Wall Street Journal.* These four were in a class of their own, and all the others, good as they might be in their own domain, were a clear tier down.

When Carroll arrived to take over the *Times* newsroom, he found an enterprise of vast potential, aching to be led. "The fact that they'd rebelled openly against Staples told me all I needed to know about their ethics," Carroll recalled. If anything, Carroll was a bit dazzled by what he found. As he told *Los Angeles Magazine,* "It was my first week, and somebody said, 'Can you say a few words at the [*Times*] book festival? I thought it would be in a church basement with a few people, but it was a production, like the Oscars. I had a drink in the glorious L.A. evening, and I thought how wonderful this was."

At first, Carroll found working with Tribune Company a pleasure. There was some judicious cutting, but nothing onerous. That changed in 2003 with the appointment of Dennis FitzSimons, an executive from the company's broadcasting side, to be Tribune's CEO. To his disappointed shock, Carroll came to view the Tribune Company executives to whom he reported as an alien species who regarded his efforts to talk about the paper's mission with condescension. He resisted the cutbacks in personnel and coverage that the Tribune Company was insisting upon, to Chicago's mounting irritation. Carroll believes in public service and tried to invoke responsibility to the community as an argument with his corporate superiors as they wrangled over budget issues. The thing he found most surprising was not that they rejected his argument, but that they seemed mystified that he would have

introduced such a thought during a budget discussion. Stewardship was simply not relevant.

There has always needed to be a balance struck between stewardship and profitability, and by newspaper industry standards the
*Los Angeles Times* was overstaffed and had a news budget that did
not fit corporate guidelines. Carroll's position was that the *Times*
was magnificently profitable—over $200 million annually—and
that the money was not wasted, was essential for serving the community, and was the proper way to ensure that the paper would
remain essential to its readers.

His Tribune bosses sometimes spoke with ridicule of the
"priesthood" of the newsroom, meaning those zealots who resisted
cuts and changes intended to bolster advertising at the expense
of covering more serious news. Carroll came to believe that his
corporate bosses not only took little pride in the *Times*'s burgeoning reputation but viewed it as a hindrance, and the battle over
budgets and staffing became increasingly bitter. When the *Times*
won five Pulitzer Prizes in 2004—a staggering recognition of
excellence—the bosses in Chicago at the Tribune Company all
but ignored it. In June, a week after Carroll went to New York to
celebrate the Pulitzers at the award luncheon, he and his managing editor, Dean Baquet, met with Tribune's two most senior
executives to persuade them that the budget cuts they demanded
were too deep and would damage the paper's mission and blunt
the momentum the Pulitzers had created. Tribune was not persuaded, and a program of buyouts, backed by involuntary layoffs
if there were not enough volunteers, was announced. The problem was a drop in newspaper advertising revenue, according to a
Tribune announcement.

Since that June, the saga of the *Los Angeles Times* has been one
of cut after depressing cut. In 2005, Carroll resigned as editor,
in part because he did not want to preside over what he viewed
as the dismantling of a great newspaper and also because he
had come to view the Tribune's management style as absent any
coherent strategy. "With each round of cuts, the message was:

give us the money now; we'll talk later about where the paper is headed." He was succeeded by Dean Baquet, who was fired in 2006 for refusing Tribune's demand for more cuts. Baquet was followed by James O'Shea, who had been a top editor at the *Chicago Tribune* and was sent by the Tribune Company to rationalize the rebellious executive ranks at the *Times*. In January of 2008, O'Shea was also fired for resisting too much. *Los Angeles Magazine* pegged the paper's staff in 2000 at 1,200, which was the level it had had since the 1980s. The magazine estimates that when O'Shea was fired the news staff had been reduced by almost 30 percent. In 2007, Sam Zell, a billionaire with no previous newspaper experience, gained control of Tribune Company through a complicated transaction that left him with $13 billion in debt. He demanded more cuts, slashing the news hole—the space in a newspaper devoted to news rather than advertising—by 15 percent and demanding hundreds of further staffing cuts. Many of the paper's best journalists have left voluntarily, been forced out, or are looking for a new job. In one notorious incident, he visited the paper's highly regarded Washington bureau and told the assembled journalists that, as the bureau generated no revenue, he regarded them as "overhead." In 2008, Paul Steiger, the former managing editor of the *Wall Street Journal*, began hiring investigative journalists to fill 24 slots for ProPublica, a new nonprofit investigative reporting enterprise. He was pleased to get over a thousand applications from highly qualified journalists. But he was dismayed that so many came from respected colleagues at the *Los Angeles Times*. "It's tragic," said Steiger. In December 2008, Tribune Company filed for Chapter 11 bankruptcy protection, which allows its papers to keep publishing. But by the spring of 2009, half of the once-mighty *Los Angeles Times* news staff had vanished, and there was little reason to think the cuts would not continue.

Until recently, iron core reporting in all of its forms has been artificially protected and subsidized because of an American bargain in which public service was harnessed to voracious capitalism as news spawned a business. In the 18th century, newspapers tended to be subsidized political organs or promotional vehicles for businesses whose real profit came from commercial printing. The *business* of news was a product of technological advances in the 19th century that were as revolutionary in their time as digital technology has been in ours. From hand-to-mouth enterprises, newspapers—especially in cities—suddenly became businesses, and a new economic model was invented for them.

In the distant past, what little income newspapers had came from subsidies by unions, political parties, and other interested groups, as well as circulation revenue, the price readers paid for a subscription or a single copy. Since costs of production were high, newspapers charged as much as they felt they could get away with, and this relatively high purchase price tended to limit the number of copies sold. When new technology made it practical to manufacture newspapers quickly and cheaply, a new economic model was born, based on selling advertising, which in turn required attracting the largest possible audience.

The devil's bargain was struck as newspapers sought to marry commerce with the social responsibility of preserving a free press, which had been singled out for protection by the First Amendment as a mission close to sacred. They elected to fulfill that mission not by printing narrow political broadsides but by publishing *news,* which was the foundation of a modern free press and also had a far broader potential audience, a decided virtue. Newspaper owners, who were now businessmen, were interested in attracting an audience so they cut the price per copy. In 1830, the *Transcript* in Boston became the first of the penny papers. Soon, in other large cities, the penny press began to appear, so called because the publisher charged only a penny, which was far cheaper than the normal six cents. These new mass audience newspapers used news to draw a crowd. The money to pay for gathering that news was to come from advertising. The self-interest of creating high profits was accompanied by the understanding that a significant part of those profits would be used for the public purpose of providing news.

However, the bargain was neither that simple nor that pure. While serious—if still partisan—news on politics and public affairs was one of the things that owners put into the columns of their papers, it was hardly the only thing—and perhaps was never the principal appeal of the burgeoning newspaper business. Scandal, crime, and gossipy social and celebrity news were staples of most newspapers, especially in the penny press. Newspaper "crusades" for various social reforms had the added—often, primary—appeal of whipping up circulation. For instance, William Randolph Hearst's campaign to drag America into a war with Spain over Cuba was, at least in part, a gimmick to boost sales.

Soon pictures and cartoons, poetry and book serials, and sports, and all kinds of other things were poured into a newspaper's pages—anything that would lure readers into buying a paper. In 1913, Joseph Pulitzer's *New York World* came up with a new crowd-pleaser: the crossword puzzle. For advertisers, the content was only important in that it brought readers whose eyes passed over their solicitations to buy pots, pans, and patent medicines. The iron core style of news may have been the ostensible heart of newspapers, but the reality was that both advertising and lighter, racier content outpaced serious news from the start.

To the best of my knowledge, no one has ever tried to measure just how much of what has appeared in newspapers over the decades could be considered iron core news. My best guess is that the amount of serious reporting on important topics would average around 15 percent, with a somewhat higher percentage during times of national crisis and a much lower percentage in the typical fat Sunday door-stopper, which in most American towns is stuffed with ads and is otherwise filled with content that is deep as a pie pan, as we say in the South. This was true from the period in the 1800s when commercial newspapers were born, and it has remained consistent for 150 years. The total amount of this kind of news grew with the size of newspapers, but the percentage seems to have remained virtually constant. About half the space in a typical newspaper is devoted to advertising. If roughly

15 percent is core news, the other 35 percent is taken up with crowd-pleasing soft news, features, comics, gimmicks, editorials, entertainments, amusements, and such. Even in the elite newspapers, the percentages don't vary much. The *New York Times, Washington Post,* and *Los Angeles Times* all devote reams of space to sports, entertainment, and other non-core news. Even the *Wall Street Journal* has created a separate Personal Journal section, with vacation tips and book reviews.

It would be like unscrambling an egg to try to put a precise number on how many people have bought newspapers for their serious news, as opposed to the smorgasbord of entertaining fare to be found there. But it seems reasonable to think that if there had been clamor for more serious news by newspaper readers, they would have been accommodated. That there was no such clamor for a century and a half suggests that publishers got the percentage about right, for a mass audience with an interest—but a limited interest—in such news.

But it was the prospect of doing serious news that drew most of the best reporters and editors to journalism. Reporting accountability news carried the most prestige. It was the most expensive to produce, took the most time, often got the biggest play, and required the greatest expertise. Much of the other content was provided by syndicates and services or reporters lower in the pecking order. But serious news required employing an experienced news staff that expected raises and vacations, health insurance and pensions, and took themselves increasingly seriously as professionals.

It is this kind of news that is recognized in prizes and awards, which in turn validate the newspaper's inevitable claim to be fulfilling not just a commercial but a societal role. It was this kind of news that was thought important enough to be protected by the First Amendment—though what the amendment actually protected was free expression rather than high-quality news. Even so, in the 20th century, the public service of publishing iron core news was what gave newspaper owners a mantle of honor and respectability that went nicely with their growing profits.

No matter the real reason for subscribing to a newspaper, those who bought one got the news too. It came with the package. The result was a virtuous circle of profitability and public service. The greatest news expense was for serious journalism, which was not necessarily the part of the paper that prompted the most sales, but which was in the public interest. A cascade of amusing and titillating material swelled the paper's audience, which in turn brought in the bountiful ad revenues that were used to pay for the serious news that by itself would likely not have attracted an audience of sufficient size. From the 1980s until recently, the paper almost certainly made handsome profits, the public was served with both news and entertainment, and few in the newsroom spent much time thinking about the fact that their salaries were paid by people who had limited or even no interest in the journalistic work they did. Newspaper readers who didn't really want that kind of news had to buy it anyway because it came with the paper. They presumably would glance at the iron core news, or even read it carefully upon occasion, but they didn't seek it out. For this group of indeterminate size, the serious news was essentially a bonus that came with the sport section or the ads—which, in themselves, were a major attraction.

The readers who cared intensely about serious news were able to get a report far richer than what could have been supported had it depended on their readership alone. As the 20th century progressed, both radio and television adopted the same essential formula, though the time in their broadcasting day devoted to iron core news was even less than the 15 percent in newspapers. The essential point from a business perspective was that serious news almost certainly got a disproportionate share of the revenue from advertising, based on raw popularity of content. And the public benefited.

Digital technology—and especially the Internet—is rapidly blowing that long-standing economic model to smithereens. Traditional news was already in trouble, but the digital revolution has hit the news business with crushing force. And as the old mass communication model is rapidly being replaced by one of increasingly narrow specialized audiences, the department store is becoming a mall of boutiques. Serious news, which had been the sheltered child, is increasingly being cast into a cruel world to sink or swim on its own. It has gone from being protected— a bit like dairy farmers—to something more like a pure market environment. And while some view the market as the best arbiter of what lives and dies, allowing unfettered market forces to rule is increasingly seen as having a high social price. Wal-Mart, for instance, is resisted in communities where people fear their local merchants will be swept away. To its opponents, the benefits of a megastore are not worth the small businesses that would be lost, and with them a sense of community.

I grew up in the 1950s, and the plight of newspapers reminds me of the situation faced by local hardware stores when the big chain stores began to appear. On Main Street in my hometown, there were three hardware stores in the same block. They were sleepy places where everything seemed to go in slow motion, but each had its own group of loyal customers of long standing among the county's farmers. If a farmer gave his business to a particular store, it was a gesture of respect from the farmer and a source of pride for the store. On Saturday mornings in those days, the town was full and there was always a joshing community of men with sunburned faces and bib overalls in each store, which all seemed to make a living. They competed with each other, but there was enough business to sustain them. Then the world changed on them, and they did what any businessman would do. The big outfits charged less, so they tried to find new ways to make a buck and at the same time cut their expenses. Employees were let go. Extending credit became a luxury they could ill afford. They trimmed their inventory to the bone and stocked only the most popular items that they felt sure they could sell. But in doing so they lost their character and the personal connection with their customers. And, of course, they all went out of business. One of the storefronts is now a lawyer's office. The others are empty. Saturday is silent on Main Street now.

There is no evil here. The farmers embraced the lower prices they got from the big stores. They were sorry to see the old stores pass, but it seemed inevitable. The old hardware merchants did what they could to save their businesses, and their decisions to cut costs and try to lure the farmers in new ways seemed to make sense. But the market prevailed and they were swept away. I'm not sure the traditional news industry is like these hardware stores, but it is having much the same reaction to the disruptive change that is threatening its livelihood. News organizations are trying, rationally, to save their business, but that is not the same thing as saving the news. Indeed, they increasingly view their news operations—especially the part of the budget that goes for iron core news—as an expense that doesn't contribute as much as it costs. In the media world now evolving, the resources of a news operation will be whatever its audience can generate and the focus of a newsroom will likely be whatever the market prefers. In a world of virtually infinite choices, just where this new equilibrium will be struck for iron core news is uncertain at best.

While many Americans sense that something calamitous is happening with news, the air of crisis is most acute not among the public but in the nation's newsrooms. Of the problems that constitute the news crisis, the one next in importance to the eroding core of accountability news is the crisis of leadership and morale inside the world of journalism. Even at the elite news organizations, reporters and editors and news executives as a group are discouraged, not so much because they get pummeled for bias but because many of them have begun to doubt their calling. Editors who once brought galvanizing energy and a zestful moral outrage to the news and sought to inspire their newsrooms are now obliged to spend most of their time managing budgets and devising new ways to get by with less. Reporters are watching news jobs disappear all over the country as corporations that own news organizations cut costs. With jobs increasingly scarce, journalists cling to positions that are less and less focused on what made most of them yearn to be in news in the first place. Instead of a job that they regarded as valuable and exciting and serving a larger public purpose, many have come to feel they are on a treadmill of mediocrity, asked only to provide a quota of "content" that will fill the news columns at the lowest cost. And any executive running a news organization who resists the home office on budget targets is apt to have a short tenure.

*Good Work*, a groundbreaking book by Howard Gardner, Mihaly Csikszentmihalyi, and William Damon, examined the attitudes toward their jobs of two groups of modern professionals, geneticists and journalists. In both fields, information is generated and manipulated, and both depend for job satisfaction on feelings of achieving high-level performance accompanied by a sense of fulfilling a social responsibility. The book describes how geneticists nearly leap out of bed each morning, thrilled with the chance to do quality, important work. In contrast, based on scores of interviews, the authors found journalists to be "deeply disillusioned," without inspiring leadership and with a sense that their best efforts are not appreciated—or even wanted—by their bosses.

The comments from journalists in *Good Work* are heartbreaking to those who believe that a strong, independent, vigorous press is essential to democracy. Joe Birch, a Tennessee-based broadcast journalist, reflected the general angst at what many journalists see as a profession that is disappearing out from under them:

> I see the country drifting in this mindless direction and I see it has invaded television news, and it's here. And only the people with the intestinal fortitude to stand up to it and to reject it are going to save us from it. Because the temptation, see, is to get an audience by having all these lurid stories and some celebrities. And say to yourself, "Well see, look at our ratings. Isn't that wonderful?" And that is an abdication of our responsibility. While news can be entertaining, that's not our job, to be entertainers. Our job is to be informers.

In their research, the authors found that when journalists talked of what had gone wrong, they described a situation without villains, but rather a very human scramble to survive a hurricane of change. The corporate owners of the nation's news organizations want to save them at a time of great peril, but in many cases what they are trying to save is not the same as what journalists view as primary. Saving the business is not the same as preserving the public service obligation that has long been part of traditional media. They are not villains trying to damage the news organizations that they oversee, but they see their mission—and their priorities—in a way that is different from the "priesthood" in their newsrooms.

In 2006, the newspaper industry went into a collective panic about the decline in newspaper circulation and ad revenues, which was especially acute in lucrative classified advertising. The reason classified advertising is so highly profitable is that, despite the relatively low cost of each ad, the cumulative revenue from a page of classified advertising comes to more than the income from a full-page ad elsewhere in the paper. Newspaper advertising is sold on the basis of a price per column inch, and inch for inch, a page of classified advertising brings in far more cash than a single ad that covers a page and thereby merits a discounted column-inch price.

Craigslist.com, the free classified Web site, and other searchable Internet sites have played havoc with newspaper classified ads. For instance, craigslist has made itself an alternative to the sorts of ads that have traditionally appeared in the back pages of newspapers. On craigslist, you can create a listing to sell unused exercise equipment or find a rental apartment, and it costs nothing. It is simple to use, searchable, and allows you to print photographs of what you want to sell. Similar online sites for selling cars and finding jobs have proven devastatingly effective compared to the old way. For newspapers, for which classified advertising has been a crucial financial artery, the rise of such sites has been devastating, and the erosion is growing worse. While newspapers are creating online capabilities of their own for classifieds, it's hard to compete pricewise with free.

As the audience declines and advertisers experiment with new media, newspaper advertising and circulation revenues are under enormous pressure and are declining at many papers. To make things worse, the costs of labor and newsprint—a newspaper's two highest expenses—have spiraled up. Contractual agreements are making increased salaries unavoidable, and the cost of newsprint has increased dramatically in the past few years. Profit levels of over 20 percent had become commonplace at newspapers, and the squeeze between declining revenues and unavoidable cost increases has sent newspapers into a tailspin. In many cases, the newspaper companies have huge debt obligations from buying other papers in more optimistic times, only to see the revenues dwindle that are needed to pay interest and principal. The reaction at many newspapers has been to cut news staffs—including people who create the type of news that much of the audience considers boring and is expensive, requiring the best, most experienced reporters, who also command the highest salaries. Increasingly, this kind of news is viewed more as a luxury than an essential, and even a turnoff to readers who prefer to know what's up with Hollywood.

As a result, the iron core is in trouble.

A case can be made that the core will not only survive, but grow more weighty through new forms of news media, such as Web-based citizen journalism and journalistic bloggers. Traditional media are trying to find news ways to report news that will appeal to a younger, Web-savvy audience, and creating new publications and Web sites in response to reader tastes. Perhaps that is what will happen. But so far, we appear to be losing this important kind of news far faster than we are replacing it.

Even worse, the sense of social responsibility that has long existed at traditional news organizations is in retreat. This has been true for some time, but a gradual slackening in commitment to news as a social responsibility has become a headlong rout because of the panicky scramble to shore up profit margins. News and business have always been linked in the United States, and traditional news organizations have been commercial enterprises that had profit as a priority. But there was also the parallel priority of social stewardship.

This stewardship was at best uneven, especially in times of financial crunch. It would, of course, be ridiculous to idealize journalism. There was no Golden Age in which the typical publisher was a self-sacrificing paragon, eager to demonstrate his rectitude by trading profits for high ideals. There were a few of those, but they were always the exceptions. Nor was there an Arcadia when news was not sometimes compromised by laziness, human error, greed, and bias. Journalism is a human endeavor, with all the attendant weaknesses.

But it would be just as wrong to suggest that nothing has shifted in the values of the news business, and that the overwhelming power of market thinking has not had a corrosive impact on those values.

Without phony nostalgia, I know that it used to be different. In 1978, I attended my first convention of the American Society of Newspaper Editors (ASNE). I was the young managing editor of the *Daily Post-Athenian* in Athens, Tennessee, circulation 10,000, and was dazzled to be going to the ASNE's annual spring gathering in Washington, D.C. ASNE is the most prestigious newspaper editors' organization in the nation, and was the counterpart on the news side to the business-oriented American Newspaper Publishers Association. At a newspaper, the publisher is the ultimate boss, but the editor was king in the newsroom—a place that in those days most publishers treated with caution or even awe. While the publisher had the ultimate authority, to veto an important decision by the editor would have been like the president of the United States countermanding the order of a general on the field of battle. A publisher's nightmare was that the editor might quit on principle, and editors felt their strength.

That ASNE convention was almost entirely white and male, but the politics of those attending ran the gamut, often in the same town. The *Nashville Banner* was conservative; the *Tennessean*—its Nashville competitor—was a champion of civil rights. In Charleston, West Virginia, one paper was in the hands of the conservative, genteel Clay family, and the other was headed by Ned Chilton, a liberal with a taste for full-throttle political battle. The publishers' convention was always a lush affair, with extravagant parties given by newsprint companies and other vendors whose representatives courted their publisher customers with lavish attentiveness. My grandmother went to the publishers' convention, and always relished the attention of a charming Englishman who represented Bowater Paper Company and danced divinely. The *Greeneville Sun*, needless to say, bought most of its paper from Bowater.

The editors' convention had plenty of drinking and was hardly Spartan, but did not approach the publishers' in opulence. Instead, the editors prided themselves on substance and a program studded with newsmakers. The president often spoke. The meeting was always in Washington, while the publishers favored New York. And the editors had *attitude*. At my inaugural ASNE convention, I was thrilled by the blatantly adversarial tone of the editors at the lectern. Their aggressiveness was not aimed at the politicians present but at the absent publishers. It was oddly like being at a union convention, but with newspaper editors talking frankly about how to keep meddling publishers at bay and strategizing on how to preserve their newsrooms from the influence of the bean counters. There was a feeling of intimacy and kinship, of being an embattled band of brothers on a noble mission.

The president of ASNE that year was Eugene Patterson, the editor of the *St. Petersburg Times*, the Florida newspaper that— then and now—routinely appears on lists of the nation's ten best papers, unlikely as it was that such a publication would be based in a town best known for retirees. Gene had been a tank commander for General George Patton during the fabled rush to relieve Bastogne. While editor of the *Atlanta Constitution*, he had won a Pulitzer Prize for his editorials protesting the Georgia legislature's refusal to grant Julian Bond a seat because of his active opposition to the Vietnam War. Patterson then served as managing editor of the *Washington Post* under executive editor Ben Bradlee, but abandoned the job in frustration. When asked why he had decided to leave the prestigious job, he observed with the saltiness of his native Georgia, "Ben Bradlee needs a managing editor like a boar needs tits."

Though built like a fireplug, he was a towering figure to his peers and spoke at that convention with a galvanizing energy and conviction that was mesmerizing to a young editor from the sticks. He spoke of the growing confidence of the nation's newspaper editors after the convulsive switch to adversary journalism, which challenged the government as a result of the civil rights movement, Vietnam, the Pentagon Papers, and Watergate. "We remember the generally obedient press born of Depression and world war, which tended through the 1950s to respect the authority of established power," he told the assembly of the nation's newspaper editors. "Just as a major part of our adversary role is to watch those who exercise power, we carry a companion obligation to be guides to the people so that they can more clearly comprehend the issues which the wielders of power may be managing and mismanaging, and especially those vital issues they may be avoiding." I recall leaving the convention ignited with ambition and inspiration.

The ASNE is still the nation's most important journalistic organization, because newspapers are overwhelmingly dominant in the actual gathering and reporting of news. But ASNE conventions are very different now. Only one of the four newspapers in Nashville and Charleston remains family-owned. The others are closed or sold to chains. Outspoken mavericks like Ned Chilton are rare. At one time, editors who became publishers were required to resign their ASNE membership, but that rule was gradually relaxed as editors migrated to the corporate side. In the 1980s, the adversarial posture between editors and publishers began to be viewed as a relic. It wasn't long until the president of ASNE was, in fact, a publisher, and the blurring of roles has only gathered steam. Even editors now spend enormous amounts of time worrying about budgets and management. In those other times, they were more apt to be directing news coverage.

In 2006, the ASNE convention was addressed by John Carroll, who a few months earlier had left his job at the *Los Angeles Times*.

Many considered him the most respected newspaper editor in the country. He called his speech "Last Call at the ASNE Saloon," and it was an elegy to that other time, when the corridors of the convention were paced by the likes of Patterson, Bradlee, and Abe Rosenthal of the *New York Times*. "With all due respect," Carroll told the editors, "there is no such pride of lions roaming among us today. This is not entirely our fault. Our jobs are harder than theirs. Our papers are shrinking and so is our confidence." Word reached him later that some of the assembled editors had been hurt by what he said. They felt beleaguered already, and having one of their own say such things was extremely painful.

The unhappy truth is that newspapers that sought to retain readers by investing in their newsrooms have not been able to show that this strategy pays off with a surge in circulation. The argument that quality will keep readers is not one that can easily be demonstrated. It appears that newspaper readership is a habit and one that is predictably generational. The members of the World War II generation were devout newspaper readers, the Baby Boomers significantly less so, and many of today's young people think of newspapers and all traditional news as anachronisms.

Part of the news crisis is finding a solution that will pay the significant costs of generating the accountability news that is essential to our democracy and still allow an acceptable profit. This is a riddle that has yet to be solved, and so the iron cannonball of accountability news continues to grow lighter and shrink. But if within the traditional media a commitment to a social stewardship becomes mere window dressing and an empty boast, the loss will be terrible indeed.

Embedded in the flight from newspapers is the larger problem of what many see as a flight of the young from news itself, which is yet another part of the news crisis. In some surveys of young people, they say that they spend significant time on news but do so mostly online. But it isn't clear yet exactly what that means, or how young people define news. It seems unlikely that they meant accountability news. Surveys also show that there is a perhaps not so shocking lack of knowledge about government. A 2006 Zogby poll found that nearly three-quarters of Americans can correctly name the Three Stooges, but fewer than half know the three branches of government. Mocking videos of Americans looking baffled when asked to identify the vice president or to locate Iraq on a map have become a comedy staple.

Then there is the often-invoked issue of media bias. It has always been a problem. It will always *be* a problem, because journalism is performed by individuals who are better or worse at what they do. Some are lazy and some are on a crusade. Some are corrupt. I know that some journalists are biased in their reporting and that some editors are not sufficiently ruthless or motivated in seeing that their news organization tells it straight.

But these are second-tier problems. They are irritating and visible, but they are not what is at the heart of the news crisis. They are symptoms rather than the illness itself. Part of the glory of traditional objective journalism is that it can be held accountable. Ironically, when the public thought more highly of news organizations, there were probably even more errors than there are now. The Pew Research Center for People and the Press says that newspaper believability dropped to 54 percent in 2005 from 84 percent in 1984. One of the good results of the public's skepticism about the media is that news organizations are now more careful and more transparent.

But two decades ago, when the news media were not ranked so low in opinion polls, an error was viewed as a mistake. It may have been a whopper, and it may have done damage, and it may have been caused by any number of things from sloppy reporting to an honest mistake to a biased perspective. But in those days, flawed reporting was not instantly *assumed* to have been caused by bias. It was a mistake. It needed to be corrected, it was regrettable and maddening, but bias was only one of many possible explanations, and usually—I would say—not the culprit. Laziness and honest error, in my experience, are far more common in traditional news than bias.

One of the genuine problems that has sprung from the perception of media bias is that traditional news organizations have lost part of their ability to persuade people with facts. Unwelcome facts are almost as easy to dismiss these days as unwelcome opinions. But, again, this is a problem that will wax and wane. If the larger, more structural problems are not solved, the landscape will be so changed that this polarized perception of bias will likely become ingrained and it won't be possible to persuade with facts.

Indeed, the reason that losing the news—the accountability news—is so important is that a dearth of reliable information will force us to chart our national path with pseudo news and opinion that may be more appealing but will be far less reliable. The news in that pitted, old iron sphere was far from perfect, but it was—and is—essential.

# CHAPTER TWO

# MEDIA AND DEMOCRACY

*As Jefferson and Madison put it, unless all citizens have easy access to the same caliber of information as society's wealthy and privileged, self-government cannot succeed.*

—Robert W. McChesney, in a *Los Angeles Times* op-ed

THE PIVOTAL DECISION IN ESTABLISHING THE MODERN relationship between the press and the American government was made around 2 A.M. in a London hotel room in June 1971. The person making that decision—Arthur Ochs "Punch" Sulzberger, publisher of the *New York Times*—was excruciatingly uncomfortable to be faced with the dilemma his editors in New York had roused him to resolve. But the decision he made set a new standard of defiantly independent judgment that most Americans seem to value in press coverage, though not necessarily when their favored ox is being gored.

As Eugene Patterson proclaimed in his speech to the nation's newspaper editors in 1978, the most important modern development in the media's role in our democracy was the transformation from an "obedient press" to an "adversarial press." That change took place gradually, but if there was a defining moment of the new aggressive press, it was the *New York Times*'s decision to publish what came to be known as the Pentagon Papers—and then to continue to publish in defiance of the president. It is one of the most instructive examples of the way the media can serve democracy, and perhaps the *Times*'s greatest single moment.

The Pentagon Papers were in fact thousands of documents, many of them classified, that had been gathered at the order of Robert McNamara when he was secretary of defense under President Lyndon Johnson. The war in Vietnam was increasingly looking like a quagmire, and McNamara wanted to know the truth about how the nation had found itself in such a mess. Though he was considered one of the architects of the war, he didn't really know how it had come about.

This archive of documents told that story, in damning detail. The Papers recounted the consistent lies and misdirection that had been used by the government from the time of the Eisenhower administration. Daniel Ellsberg was one of the men who assembled the materials, which were never intended to be public knowledge. He was appalled at what they showed, and he painstakingly photocopied them and then leaked them to the *New York Times*. The Vietnam War was still under way and the materials prompted a stormy debate within the *Times* about what should be done. Some wanted to publish the story that the Papers told, but not quote the documents themselves because they were classified. The *Times*'s long-time lawyers refused even to look at the papers and said they would not represent the newspaper if the materials were used at all. Abe Rosenthal, the paper's executive editor, argued that it was the *Times*'s duty to its readers to tell them the truth about an issue of overwhelming importance. He believed that the classification of the documents was phony, and that there were no secrets disclosed, only embarrassment and chicanery. He said that if the *Times* did not publish them, the paper's honor would be tarnished forever.

Punch Sulzberger, the *Times*'s publisher and head of the family that had owned the *Times* since 1896, came down on Rosenthal's side of the argument. In what proved to be one of the most crucial journalistic moments in terms of the media and democracy, the *Times* began to publish the Pentagon Papers on the front page on Sunday, June 13, 1971. Ironically, President Nixon at first was not disturbed by the Papers because they were mostly damning of the Johnson administration. But on Sunday afternoon, Secretary of State Henry Kissinger whipped him into a lather by arguing that printing such confidential documents would expose Nixon as "a weakling." When the second edition appeared on Monday's front page, Nixon went into a rage. Since there had been no reaction on Sunday, Punch had left for London, greatly relieved. On Monday night, two hours before the third installment was to go to press, *Times* executives in New York received a telegram from Attorney General John Mitchell to Punch saying that publication of the Papers was a violation of the Espionage Act and that further disclosures would cause "irreparable injury to the defense interests of the U.S." and asking that Punch cease publication. Though there was no explicit legal threat, Mitchell called a *Times* lawyer, Herbert Brownell, to say that the Justice Department would bring suit if publication continued. The telegram prompted a screaming argument among the paper's editors, business executives, and lawyers about what should be done. Louis Loeb, the paper's general counsel, advised that publication stop. Rosenthal was adamant that publication continue. Only Punch could decide, and so a transatlantic call was placed to his room at London's Savoy Hotel.

Punch was a former Marine and politically rather conservative, and he had been steeped in a family tradition of *Times* stewardship since earliest childhood. In the Sulzberger family, the paper came first. As was his way, Punch asked what everyone thought. James Goodale, an in-house counsel who was present and on the side of continuing publication, recalled that Punch's voice on speakerphone made him sound like he wished he weren't the paper's publisher. With deep ambivalence, knowing he was acting against the advice of many of his top advisors, Punch nevertheless decided that the principle of not buckling under was paramount and that he would defy the attorney general and the president, even though it almost certainly meant getting into a legal battle. When Rosenthal returned to the newsroom with the decision, it erupted in cheers. The next day, Attorney General Mitchell sought and got a temporary restraining order, and the *Times* ceased publication until the Supreme Court could decide the matter.

With the *Times* enjoined, Ellsberg went searching for other powerful news organizations willing to continue publication despite the government's objections. He offered the Papers to each of the three major television networks. All three turned him down. But then something quite astounding happened. The *Washington Post* took up the baton and began to publish materials from the Papers. Then the *Boston Globe* and the *St. Louis Post-Dispatch* did the same. All were enjoined and halted publication, throwing the issue to the courts. When the Supreme Court ruled, the decision was that, because of the First Amendment, the government did not have the power to stop publication. The newspapers could be punished for endangering national security under the Espionage Act if it could be proven that they had published damaging secrets, but they could not be prevented from publishing in the first place. The Pentagon Papers were then published in full, with no apparent damage to national security, and the government did not bring other charges against the newspapers. It was a benchmark in accountability journalism and set the stage for the Watergate investigation a few years later and for the continuing national debate about when it is appropriate for news organizations to publish information against the wishes of the government.

The value of a vigorous adversarial press is hard to argue against when one sees the efforts that dictators around the globe go to in order to silence dissenting views. In Russia, the vibrant and irreverent press that emerged after the collapse of the U.S.S.R. has been throttled, and in China the Communist Party maintains a stranglehold on coverage that it views as threatening the Party's rule or counter to the Party's policies. The Bush administration was hardly comparable in its efforts to control the press, but under the proclaimed "War on Terrorism" it had systematically narrowed access to government records of all kinds and assailed news organizations that challenged its behavior as unpatriotic or worse. For instance, President Bush denounced the *Times* in December 2005 for reporting that he had, according to the front page article, "secretly authorized the National Security Agency to eavesdrop on Americans and others inside the United States to search for evidence of terrorist activity without the court-approved warrants ordinarily required for domestic spying, according to government officials." The Obama administration has promised greater openness, but press clashes with the president are almost inevitable—and healthy.

It is an article of faith among journalists that what they do is essential to democracy. Indeed, if one were to eavesdrop on a gathering of traditional journalists deploring the state of the news media, it would be easy to conclude that without high-quality journalism, American democracy would be hugely diminished. This is a view also shared by many nonjournalists of all political persuasions, even though these same people might also be very critical of the media. Despite their quarrels with the news, they recognize that reliable news is important. If news isn't credible, it loses its ability to persuade. If news institutions cease to be trusted to be honest brokers of information, then disagreeable or politically unwelcome news will be dismissed as spin and bias. In such an environment, the argument goes, a genuinely informed citizenry is replaced with an anarchy of half-truths, misinformation, and propaganda.

But before we journalists wring our hands about the state of news, we owe it to journalistic skepticism to take a clear-eyed look at ourselves. When most things taken on faith come under close scrutiny, uncomfortable facts usually emerge that can shake that faith. Most of us don't enjoy subjecting our faith to such a test, but journalism is rooted in fact, and if it cannot stand up under such scrutiny then it isn't worthy of being worried about. Journalism has a role in democracy, but defining it is not an easy task. Is it, indeed, essential? One must ask whether a genuine, vibrant democracy can thrive without the iron core of traditional, objective journalism. If that kind of journalism should largely pass into history, there would be a cost, but its exact nature is unclear. If journalism has a significant role in democracy, it should be evident in the way American society has evolved. We should be able, without straining, to see the impact of high-quality journalism on who we are as a society and in our shared values, especially as they evolve. By that standard, America since World War II can be instructive when it comes to understanding the power of news—and its limits.

In 1939, Cole Porter's new show, *Dubarry Was a Lady,* premiered on Broadway with Betty Grable, Ethel Merman, and Bert Lahr. It was a ribald musical about a hatcheck attendant who mistakenly takes a Mickey Finn and wakes up thinking he is King Louis XV of France. A spicy romp, it included double entendres and King Louis being shot in the posterior with an arrow. It ran for a year, and that success led to an MGM movie version starring Lucille Ball and Red Skelton. But before the film could be released it had to pass the censors of the Production Code, who protected American audiences from what they judged unwholesome and inappropriate material. The censors found much fault with the film and produced page after page of puritanical objections. According to William McBrien's *Cole Porter,* "not even the word 'jerk' was allowed."

There are still societies where ludicrously puritanical codes endure, but the United States is not one of them. In little more than half a century, we have moved from excising "jerk" to allowing hard-core pornography on demand as a normal video service in even the best hotels, not to mention on the Web and in the magazine racks of convenience stores in the smallest, most God-fearing towns. Words that were long forbidden are now routinely on television and even creeping into newspapers, and we have become a society that seems to tolerate vulgarity without a second thought. In 2006, my wife and I were having lunch in a self-proclaimed family restaurant in Myrtle Beach, South Carolina, and noted that the teenage busboy shuffling from table to table was wearing a T-shirt emblazoned "Fuck you." No one seemed to notice. Whether you regard our national tolerance for such things as a triumph for free speech or a victory for coarse vulgarity, it represents a sea change in our national culture.

Since 1940, America has been transformed in many respects. While "all men are created equal" and "the pursuit of happiness" are the foundation of our sense of American values, the way those values are interpreted by the broad American middle class has undergone a revolution. In our understanding of what we value, we are in profound ways a very different country. In popular culture, the restrictions of the Production Code era seem so distant as to be pre–Civil War. In areas such as racial civil rights, the role of women, the legalization of abortion, our embrace of the environment, and the acceptance of gays, the changes are staggering.

Finding the fingerprints of journalism in that torrent of change is worthy of a lifetime's study, but there is a commonsense answer. In the area of segregation and civil rights for African Americans, journalism had a crucial role in making the violent injustice of racial prejudice something that could no longer be ignored. And the press also had a strong role in reshaping our national attitude about the environment, although the passion to clean up our nation probably got its greatest initial push from a series of public service television ads that first appeared on Earth Day in 1971. They showed an aged, granite-faced Indian on horseback or paddling a canoe and surveying a landscape defaced with discarded tires and abandoned hulks of refrigerators. As the camera closed on his face, it showed a single tear falling down his weathered cheek. Suddenly, everyone was against littering. In the years to come, the environment has been a staple of iron core journalism, but the Indian's tear prepared the ground for that journalism. Iron Eyes Cody, the weeping "Indian," was actually an Italian-American, born Espera de Corti—a bit of compromising invention that was not widely known then, but that the blogo-sphere would have pounced on.

It was not journalism that prompted the Supreme Court to view abortion as it did in the mid-1950s. I do not think women owe it to journalists that they gradually earned rights and roles that had long been denied them. Similarly, the status of women in the workplace and ever more explicit language and imagery came not because of journalism—or at least not mostly. It came, first, because the courts cracked open the door. Then news and popular culture stormed through that door to turn what had become legal into something that we as a nation now mostly accept as normal.

All this change did not come without a fight, and in many ways what is viewed as the partisan divide in this country is largely about efforts to shove the genie of cultural change back into the bottle on many of these issues that have so powerfully redefined middle-class American values. There is an ongoing culture war over whether to roll back such changes, and the news media have played a powerful role in that battle, which has taken place in the realms of politics and policy—the areas where the iron core does most of its job. It is in scrutinizing the role of government and the exercise of power that the news media make their contribution to our democracy. And it is in this realm that our values are not formed, but refined and applied. When the news media are doing their job, we have enough information to make informed deci-sions, and when they do not, we are—as a nation—in jeopardy of being misled.

One of the most surprising changes in the nation's sense of itself has been the revolution in what it means to be gay in America. The censors of *Dubarry* were particularly insistent that "there must be no single 'pansy' flavor." Homosexuality was the greatest taboo; in the 1959 best seller *Advise and Consent*, the hero—a U.S. senator—committed suicide because he was about to be exposed as having had a gay episode during World War II. While his death was tragic, it was quite plausible that he would take this way out rather than endure the scalding humiliation of being publicly exposed as a homosexual.

In 1964, as my parents drove me to my freshman year in college, my father mumbled a warning that I must be wary of homosexuals. He was horribly embarrassed and I was utterly mystified, as I barely knew what homosexuality was and certainly could not imagine actually encountering such a creature. It was a taboo so extreme in my middle-class Southern family as to be unspeakable.

Not long ago, I asked my niece—a recent high school graduate—about gays at her school. She was nonchalant. She said everyone knows who at the school is gay. She doesn't think gays are harassed or persecuted. She said no one cares, or not much. No big deal. The school she was describing is not in a city or a sophisticated suburb, but in a rural Southern town of 15,000. I suspect there is more prejudice than she described, but for her to be able to say what she said demonstrates a profound change, and a stunningly fast one. The interplay of the media with the change in the perception of gays makes for an illuminating example of media's complex role in our national conversation about who we are—the essence of media and democracy.

Dudley Clendinen, coauthor of *Out for Good: The Struggle to Build a Gay Rights Movement in America,* believes that the media—in all their forms—were in what could almost be considered an elaborate political opera in which the other major figures and forces have been gay rights activists, their opponents, the courts, legislative bodies, public opinion, and large, unforeseen, transcendent events.

In the counterculture of the 1960s, gay rights and women's rights took a decided backseat to race issues and the antiwar movement. Gay activism was virtually unknown, but in cities like New York and San Francisco, a critical mass of gays had created a still-furtive community based mostly on bars that catered to homosexuals. The only time homosexuals—the word "gay" was unknown outside the homosexual world—appeared in newspapers was when the police raided a gay bar or arrested people caught in the act in a dark park. Homosexuals were considered "perverts," and depicted that way in the mainstream press. But a nascent sense of anger and resentment at this treatment was simmering.

In the early hours of June 28, 1969, the police raided a gay bar called the Stonewall Inn in Greenwich Village, which had happened before. But for some reason, this proved a spark to dry tinder, and the Village's gay population erupted in several days of riots protesting the persecution of gays and lesbians by police. Something new had been born, and within six months two gay activist organizations were organized in New York and three gay newspapers had been established. On June 28, 1970, the anniversary of Stonewall, the first Gay Pride march took place. Press coverage was generated by these developments, and it was hostile and dismissive. But the cadre of activists that Stonewall forged began to organize in major cities all over the nation to change laws they viewed as discriminatory. In most places, their quiet activism drew little media attention, but they had a big success in 1977 in Miami, where they managed to get an ordinance passed that prohibited discrimination on the basis of sexual orientation.

This drew media attention, and the news accounts prompted a backlash led by Anita Bryant, a well-known pop singer of hits like "Paper Roses" and the girl-next-door spokesman for the Florida Citrus Commission, where her wholesome image was used to promote Florida orange juice. She was also a devout Southern Baptist and Sunday School teacher who believed that homosexuality was an abomination in the eyes of God, and she agreed to become the high-profile emblem of a crusade—"Save Our Children"— to get the ordinance repealed. "If gays are granted rights," she said at one point, "next we'll have to give rights to prostitutes and to people who sleep with St. Bernards and to nail biters." The ordinance was soundly—and quickly—overturned, but a national crusade against gays had been sparked as surely as the Stonewall riots had energized gay activists.

After the ordinance repeal, Bryant had a pie thrown in her face in Des Moines by a gay activist, and her quip, "At least it was a fruit pie," got reported widely. Just before she had been "pied," she had said, "We are going to go on a crusade across this nation to try and get rid of all the homosexuals." It was a catalytic stimulus to what became the powerful religious right political movement.

Reverend Jerry Falwell came to Miami to support Bryant, and not long after founded the Moral Majority, which became one of the largest political groups for evangelical Christians and was instrumental in delivering a huge block of votes to Ronald Reagan in 1980. One of the principal targets of the Christian right has been opposition to homosexuality, and so a national battle was joined. The press thrives on conflict, and the fight over the gay rights issue began to find its way into news columns. But the stories again and again were of gay rights defeats, of equal-rights laws repealed, and were delivery systems for people asserting things damaging to gays, such as that gays were trying to recruit heterosexual children. Clendinen describes the press coverage during this time as overwhelmingly negative.

The widespread public revulsion for homosexuality was exacerbated by the coverage, but the largely negative spotlight was still illuminating something that had hitherto been hidden and unknown. The gay rights issue had become an ongoing national story, which was something that had never happened before. The issue was in play, was being debated and argued over. Attention from the media, despite its negative cast, seemed to embolden gays, and the gay rights movement grew as hitherto closeted gays were impelled to reveal their sexual orientation publicly. For some heterosexuals, it was alarming to learn that gay people were everywhere. But the coverage also had the effect of beginning to put a human face on homosexuality. Celebrities such as Barbra Streisand and Mary Tyler Moore endorsed gay rights, and a boycott of Florida orange juice was launched. Though the tide of opinion was with Bryant, she became the symbol of homophobia, and that word became an epithet. Johnny Carson began to make jokes about Bryant in his monologues on the *Tonight Show,* and the popular television program *The Golden Girls* began to include cracks mocking Bryant, usually by a character who was pronouncedly effeminate. Even so, gay rights laws were going nowhere, and mainstream political parties kept their distance.

The unforeseen event that turbocharged change began in June 1981 with a little-noticed item in a weekly bulletin from the

Centers for Disease Control in Atlanta. It said that a strange outbreak of a lethal form of pneumonia was spreading among gay men. An article appeared not long after on page 20 of the *New York Times,* but it was not until late in 1982 that AIDS, or Acquired Immune Deficiency Syndrome, was given its name; by then, it was clearly cutting a deadly path through the male homosexual community. Once again, the news was a blow to the image of gays, because the religious right depicted the AIDS epidemic as the wrath of God and proof that homosexuality was a sin. But AIDS was news. While the promiscuous gay lifestyle was vilified in the media as the reason for the spread of AIDS, a more humane reaction began to take shape as the plague devastated the gay community. It was, after a while, as though the news was like a casualty report from a war zone; almost everyone knew someone with a loved one or a neighbor's nephew who had contracted AIDS. It was a deadly disease without a cure, and the pathos in its wake roused a feeling that may not have been empathy, but was at least sympathy. For gays, the issue was no longer gay rights but survival. The government was slow to show any interest in aggressively seeking a cure, which sparked yet another furious and panicky round of activism that took the form of political action as well as books and plays, such as Larry Kramer's *The Normal Heart.* Another powerful symbol was the AIDS Memorial Quilt, with individual 3-by-6-foot panels as tributes to individuals who had died of AIDS. In 1987, when it was first displayed on the Mall in Washington, it was larger than a football field. It drew more than half a million visitors and became another big media story, though President Ronald Reagan ignored the issue. While the situation may have seemed a tragedy to most Americans, it was visited on people with whom they felt little identification.

This perspective of gays as unlike most people was one of the stubbornly enduring stereotypes for gays to overcome. My wife and I were living in Greenwich Village in 1984 and went to a gay rights parade, essentially as tourists. We took no part in the gay rights battle, but we were curious. We wandered among the outrageous drag queens and gaudy characters inspired by the gay anthem "YMCA." But by far the most arresting person we saw was someone in his 30s—about our age—who was wearing a blue cotton shirt that probably came from Brooks Brothers, khaki pants, and looked like he could have been in a fraternity at a conservative college. On his chest was a button that said, "I'm one too." I was naïve enough to be taken aback, but I got the point.

And then came one of those rare moments that seem to change things, to shift the conversation and cause people to see something differently and even to alter a long-held belief. In July 1985, the American Hospital in Paris announced that Rock Hudson was there and being treated for AIDS. News of his secret homosexual life followed, and two months later, he was dead. The revelation was a huge news story, covered by every news organization from the *Washington Post* to *People* magazine, and it seemed to throw a monkey wrench into the emotional circuitry of many people. If you loved Rock Hudson before the revelation, could you now hate him? Liberace died of AIDS two years later, prompting some of the same disconnect between love for the man and revulsion for homosexuality. I recall my 72-year-old mother's reaction to the death of Liberace, who was one of her favorites. For her, homosexuality was the darkest fate that could befall someone, and she would say that she had never encountered it—despite having dear friends whom everyone else acknowledged as clearly gay. Her method of dealing with this conflicted situation was what I came to call the "I-won't-ask-and-I-don't-want-you-to-tell-me" policy, which President Bill Clinton later adopted as the more elegant "don't ask, don't tell" approach when he was dealing with gays in the military. Many people found this a solution to embracing the gay person despite disapproving the sexual orientation. When I asked if she had accepted that Liberace was gay, she retorted, "I wasn't under the bed, so I don't know." It was a middle ground, a place that wasn't approval but was also not hate. It provided a compromise, and gradually gays began to be seen as remarkably like the rest of us, and entitled to basic rights.

Was this something that the media did? Certainly, the media—both the news media and the popular media—had a critical role in telling the stories that had shifted public opinion, just as they had had a significant role in arousing hatred of gays and spreading the view that the AIDS epidemic was God's judgment on sin. In general, the iron core news was the vanguard from which people learned the facts, and the creative entertainment sector followed suit. For instance, in May 1991, the popular CBS comedy *Northern Exposure* aired an episode called "Slow Dance" that concluded on a dance floor with two gay men dancing, their arms around each other, as the straight residents of Cicily, Alaska, joined them. The thing that was striking was that the gay men were not the effeminate stereotypes who had wisecracked about Anita Bryant on *Golden Girls* just over a decade earlier, but were very much in the spirit of the man who had worn the "I'm one too" button at the Gay Rights parade. They were portrayed as ordinary. Regular. And, as it happened, gay. It is impossible to calculate the effect of such a moment in a television show, but what seems undeniable is that such a moment would not have been on the air only a few years before. Something big had changed, and since then the presence of gays on television has become commonplace. Has that shaped opinion? What is the persuasive power on gay issues of a likeable Ellen DeGeneres or a feisty Rosie O'Donnell, who are lesbians and don't hide it? It seems intuitively sensible to assume that it mattered when a megastar like Tom Hanks portrayed a gay lawyer dying of AIDS in the 1993 movie *Philadelphia.* But quantifying such a media moment is all but impossible.

It would be ludicrous to suggest that gays are not viewed with suspicion, alarm, even revulsion by many Americans. The Episcopal Church is being split asunder over the issue of whether the church should have gay bishops. The issue of gay marriage is also a hot button for many Americans. But the reality is also that, especially for a younger generation, being gay is just something that is part of you. The media have had a big hand in that, but their role has not been advocacy so much as enabling the national conversation in which some views were hardened and some significantly changed.

The role of the press in our democracy has been under constant and generally critical scrutiny during the post–World War II period in which so much of our national character has been reshaped. In the 1930s, Henry Luce, the cofounder and editor-in-chief of *Time* magazine, denounced what he saw as a dangerous trend for news organizations to merely give people what they wanted. The result, as he saw it, was rampant vulgarity and sensationalism and the creation of "an enormous financial incentive to publish twaddle...square miles of journalistic tripe." He complained that the press was failing in its duty to provide the news that nourished democracy—a worry that isn't new.

A few years later, Luce's money paid the expenses for one of the most admired and ignored efforts to chart a course for the nation's news media—the Hutchins Commission, which was named in honor of Robert Hutchins, president of the University of Chicago, who headed it. The commission's report, issued in 1947, was intended to be a blueprint for a responsible press in a dangerous, complex world. The year before, Winston Churchill had described an "iron curtain" of Soviet tyranny that divided Europe; the prospect of nuclear holocaust was terrifyingly real. The disruptive technology of television promised to upend the old world of newspapers, magazines, and radio as the dominant purveyors of news. The intellectuals who made up the commission were idealistic and anxious, and their vision—as time has shown—was both shrewd and near delusional.

They were principally worried that serious news was going to disappear in a torrent of trivia, sensation, and greed. Ironically, they saw television as a savior from such media degradation, and envisioned a nation of households sitting raptly by their television sets, listening to debates in the United Nations General Assembly and soaking up culture and wisdom along with information. They saw clearly the problem of a commercial media that carried the added burden of delivering substantial and serious news, but what they almost absurdly underestimated was the actual power of that commercial engine and how America's news would have to struggle to find its place in our money-focused culture.

Taken whole, the American media are a colossal and confounding mess, and simply blaming "the media" for various ills has become misleading shorthand. After all, media conglomerates now typically include a range of types of media, and media companies incorporate value systems and objectives that are as widely divergent as a music company that offers classical and children's music and also the most profane hip-hop. It's all music, and it's all intended to make money, but the people who perform it are after different things and satisfy different audiences. Similarly, each form of media makes its own contribution to our democracy—including, at times, the slimiest tabloids and the most banal movies.

Political scientist Robert M. Entman has devised a way of isolating the differences in the American media that makes sense to me, and he makes distinctions that are as profound as they are surprising. According to Entman, the media can be divided into four categories: traditional journalism, tabloid journalism, advocacy journalism, and entertainment.

The first way to distinguish each from the other is on the basis of its commitment to five key journalism standards. The first four are accuracy, balance, holding government accountable, and separation of news from editorial and advertising. The fifth standard is the degree to which there is a determination to maximize profit. Bear in mind that all these forms of media are intended to make a profit, but one of Entman's key insights is that they are different in the *degree* to which maximizing profit is a motivation.

The traditional commercial media, which includes news organizations such as the *New York Times*, CBS News, *Time* magazine, and local newspapers, historically have a commitment to all five of the key journalistic standards. Their mission, as they have come to understand it, is to be accurate, meaning to report truthfully and to provide a factual basis for what appears in news columns.

This means relying on people who have some basis to be believed, and in practice often means quoting people and documents from powerful, credible institutions.

Entman defines balance as providing "roughly equivalent treatment to contending sides in disputes" and keeping personal views from coloring reporting. This is essentially an effort to be objective, which has been the American journalistic standard for over a century.

Democratic accountability means keeping government accountable, and has expanded over time to also mean keeping a watch on other aspects of power, such as business and—increasingly—the media themselves. The traditional media feel they have a watchdog mission, especially regarding public officials, and it is part of the ethos of the traditional media to give prominence to journalism that fulfills this accountability mission, such as stories on public policy issues and the actions of the president. Most investigative reporting is justified on the basis of fulfilling this accountability mission.

The fourth key standard for traditional news organizations is a wall—or, actually, two walls. The first wall is between news and editorial, meaning that the news operation does not slant the news—or what it covers—based on the opinions that appear on the editorial page. When I worked at the *New York Times,* for instance, the news department was housed on the third floor of the building on West 43rd St. and the editorial department was on the tenth. Max Frankel, a Pulitzer Prize–winning reporter for the *Times,* was chosen to be editor of the paper's editorial page and took up residence on the tenth floor. When, a number of years later, he was made executive editor of the paper's news operation, he moved to the third floor, but he had not set foot in the newsroom in all the time he had been editorial page editor. It was considered inappropriate and would have been a breach of protocol, because the editorial and news functions are considered separate. This claim does not impress many of the critics who see the *Times*'s news operation as an echo chamber of the editorial columns, but within the paper the distinction is real.

The even more strictly enforced wall at traditional news organizations has been between advertising/marketing and news. Reporters should not consider the potential damage of a story to an advertiser, and—similarly—they don't do puff pieces and flattering profiles to be helpful to the advertising and marketing departments. The standard is that news decisions are to be decided on their merits, by editors and reporters, and that the "bean counters" on the business side of the news organization have no role on the news side.

Entman's particular insight is to list among the "key journalistic standards" of traditional news organizations what he calls "checks on pure profit maximization." He defines this as using professional news judgment—and not audience or profit considerations—in deciding what stories to cover, how much prominence to give them, how to allocate time and resources to following up, and other such journalistic decisions. No traditional journalist is unaware that the news organization is a profit-making enterprise. Indeed, the financial success of the news organization is essential to the journalistic mission. But traditional news organizations have operated with the belief that seeking to maximize profit would be both bad and wrong—bad, in the long term, for business, as news was thought to be a key drawing card for their audience, and wrong, in a moral sense, because the traditional news organizations had a social role as well as a commercial one.

Traditional news organizations differ in their assessment of what a reasonable profit should be. But overall, the traditional culture of the newspaper industry has been that you have a duty to your readers before you have a duty to your shareholders, or at least an obligation to both. That has certainly been the culture of the nation's newsrooms, which has increasingly put them in conflict with the corporations for which they work.

Traditional news organizations have a commitment to all five of these key journalistic standards: accuracy, balance, accountability, independence, and checks on profit. This is the ideal, the way it *should* be at a traditional news organization. For traditional news organizations, the number one organizational value and mission is to be a democratic watchdog. Profit comes second. And third would be giving information that helps people function as citizens in coping with the world. It is traditional news organizations that have the most consistent and direct role in performing the news function and creating the iron core.

Each of the other forms of media can be analyzed on the basis of these same standards, because all serve a news function to some degree. But the differences are striking and illuminating.

"Tabloid journalism" is a category that Entman defines as one that puts profit as its top priority. The thing that separates the tabloid from the traditional is this one profound difference. Tabloid journalism varies in its commitment to the standards of accuracy, balance, accountability, and independence. But in this key respect, all tabloid news organizations are united. For them, maximizing profit is the number one consideration.

By this definition, tabloid journalism includes local television news, where decisions on content have long been almost entirely based on what will draw the biggest audience rather than on what is important news to cover. Two decades ago, there were local television stations—most of them locally owned—that were as ambitious in their watchdog role as any newspaper. They produced programming on local policy issues and tackled problems that don't lend themselves to television's inexhaustible appetite for action and pictures. But they didn't make big profits, because the audience was not as large as it could have been with a different kind of programming. When local ownership gave way to corporate ownership, the priorities changed and local television news left the ranks of traditional news organizations and became tabloid, because they put profit first.

It was simply the way the world worked. Locally owned television stations were sold for as much as they would bring, which made them very expensive. Few of us would be so selfless as to sell to less than the highest bidder. The buyers were willing to pay a premium because they knew that the previous owners had *not maximized profit!* That was the glorious point! These local television stations were potential gold mines and they had been operated by people who had been willing to leave a lot of that gold in the ground. They had derived the psychic income of being owners of a powerful and influential local institution that made them proud because of the quality of the programming, the journalism awards that boosted their prestige, and the comfortable knowledge that they were making lots of money, though not as much money as they *could* have made with a different kind of management.

But when these high-minded people decided to cash out on their prestigious investment, they almost always wanted top dollar. And that top dollar came from people who were willing to pay a premium because they intended to extract every bit of gold that was there. In such a situation, the purchased business is expected to pay for itself, and if the purchase price is high, so too is the pressure to produce the profits that will justify such a price and pay off the mortgage. So the owners got rich, the buyers got even richer, and the public lost out in the sense that costly news operations with a lot of locally produced programming were scrapped as too expensive. Even more damaging, the focus of local television news shifted away from any coverage that would have been part of the iron core. Instead, the formula became—and remains, with very few exceptions—a mixture of crime, accidents, fires, and other bits of local mayhem, followed by weather, sports, and feel-good local human interest features. In the past decade, local television has been laced with segments that purport to be about health—such as the latest way to remove cellulite—but are sometimes video productions sent out by drug manufacturers that look like news but are actually promotions.

In major cities and small markets, local television stations have all but abandoned meaningful coverage of politics and policy. When government can't be ignored, there are few specialists on politics to turn to. The news staffs aren't organized that way. Everyone on the news staff is considered on general assignment and has to do the best he or she can with the short time allotted and little or no background, and most often—with serious news—they crib what has appeared in the local newspaper. It is the same for elections. Fresh-faced, good-looking television reporters who know little about politics are assigned to cover it, and the result is usually as superficial and vapid as one would expect.

This does not mean that local television news does not aspire to be accurate and balanced. It embraces two of the standards of traditional news. But it is not focused on holding government accountable, nor does it make news decisions without considering the impact on ratings, and—most important—maximizing profit comes first. Until the recent downturn, a local television station that was showing less than a 60 percent profit margin was performing below the industry standard. This is three times the profit margin of most local newspapers.

There are other news organizations in this category. The obvious ones that come to mind are the *National Enquirer* and its brethren at the lower end of the supermarket tab food chain. Then there is *People* magazine and its pack of imitators, which are increasingly putting heat on *People* to abandon some of its standards in the service of gossip and human interest news. For instance, huge headlines on a 2006 *People* cover proclaimed "I'm in love!" next to a picture of Jessica Simpson, a tabloid favorite. But as it turned out, the quote was not from Jessica, but from an anonymous "friend," who claimed Jessica had said it. Such flimsily sourced covers were typical of *People*'s competitors, but not of *People*.

The tabloid media tend to be a lot more fun than the traditional media. They are intended to be, just as ice cream is a treat. And like ice cream, they provide some nourishment, mostly in short snippets from wire services. But when it comes to accountability news, they are leeches, saving their own resources for racy stories and sensational crowd-pleasers. When New York's governor, Eliot Spitzer, was caught with a prostitute, New York City's two tabs—the *New York Post* and the *Daily News*—joyously poured money into unearthing every juicy detail. Their interest in reporting on issues of public policy of vital concern to New Yorkers is considerably less intense.

According to Entman, tabloid news organizations put profit first and the obligation to be amusing, entertaining, and diverting second. A distant third is influencing the national agenda and having some impact on policy. Bill O'Reilly describes himself as a watchdog, and certainly he has every intention of having an impact on policy. Entman places him in the tabloid category, because he apparently views popularity—which is shorthand for ratings and profit—and entertainment as O'Reilly's primary objectives. I would be more inclined to put him in the third category of journalism, advocacy.

This category, in its purest form, is almost indifferent to profit. This kind of journalism isn't *about* profit. It is about influence. Many of the most influential advocacy news organizations are money-losing ventures, or—at best—only marginally profitable. For instance, the *Nation,* the *Weekly Standard,* the *New Republic,* the *National Review,* the *American Prospect,* and similar organs of advocacy are no one's idea of gold mines. Documentary filmmakers, with few exceptions, are lucky to make a living, much less a fortune, and they exist from project to project, hopeful always that some angel will come along and literally *give* them the money to complete their film.

In this form of news, the democratic watchdog role is the top priority, interpreted as an ongoing critique of opposing views. And second is having an effective role in setting the national agenda with an impact on public policy, which means reporting information selectively based on whether it bolsters the organization's own advocacy position. Accuracy may be observed, but not necessarily truth. In advocacy journalism, facts may be true, but the impression they create may not be accurate because other facts are ignored or distorted. Similarly, balance is not a standard of advocacy, nor is a separation of editorial and news.

Finally, there is entertainment, the fourth category of media, which still has its own role to play in journalistic terms. In its pure form, news that is in the form of entertainment could be thought of as the various infotainment programs on television, such as *The Oprah Winfrey Show* and *Today.* Television dramas on terrible diseases and movies based on fact fit here, as do novels that treat subjects that address serious themes. As with tabloid journalism, entertainment's top priority is profit, followed by a mission to be as amusing and diverting as possible. It has no meaningful commitment to accuracy, balance, holding government accountable, or separating news from editorial or advertising, except insofar as those things help garner ratings. For instance, some television dramas make a point of being faithful to the facts, for promotional reasons rather than journalistic ones. More often, the literal truth is enhanced by dramatic license that gives a point of view and hence a message. Oliver Stone's *J.F.K.* was a version of the assassination of President John Kennedy that strongly suggests a conspiracy among the Army, C.I.A., Vice President Lyndon Johnson, and others, followed by a cover-up abetted by Chief Justice Earl Warren—all with no evidence to support the charges. It is regarded by the vast majority of historians as total rubbish, but was no doubt accepted as true by many who saw it. In that same vein, Steven Spielberg's *Saving Private Ryan* is a fictional story set during the D-Day invasion. Though the story itself is made up, the harrowing depiction of the actual Normandy invasion is considered by many to be terrifyingly accurate. The invasion sequence of *Saving Private Ryan* was the most frightening 20 minutes I've ever experienced in a movie, and I think it is a prime example of truthful entertainment that had a message beyond storytelling. My father, who served in Merrill's Marauders behind Japanese lines in Burma during World War II, is now haunted by his combat memories. I advised him not to see *Saving Private Ryan* because it seemed too close to the truth.

While all four types of media perform a news function, traditional media perform this vital social service most consistently and overtly. There is also news in advocacy journalism, but without the authority of fact and balance. In tabloid journalism, the news function is rarely performed, and entertainment serves as news only indirectly. In other words, if news is important to democracy, it comes mostly from traditional journalism, and that role is performed at its best when the five standards of accuracy, balance, holding government accountable, separating news from editorial, and establishing checks on maximizing profit are observed.

The monster storm that has been advancing on traditional news over the past two decades has had the impact of pushing traditional news in the direction of tabloid news, advocacy news, and entertainment. The values of local television news are rapidly being adopted by network news and local newspapers. When watchdog news and accountability news are deemed too boring and news choices are made on the basis of attracting an audience instead of their importance as news, then the tabloid news standard is being applied. Effectively, the nation's traditional news organizations are being transformed into tabloid news organizations, and it is happening at a blisteringly rapid pace.

What happens to a nation such as ours if most of its press is either tabloid, advocacy, or entertainment? There is no doubt in my mind that the standards that have been the defining principles of traditional news are in danger of being largely swept aside to salvage the fortunes of the corporations that have owned the organs of traditional news. If the iron core shrinks, the nation will be much the worse for it, and the momentum at present is in the direction of tabloidization—meaning a news media whose sole priority is profit rather than the public good combined with profit.

The decline of traditional news raises a question about the role of news in a democracy versus the role of free speech, which is somewhat different. The First Amendment speaks of both "freedom of speech" and "of the press," and at the time that meant the ability to speak one's mind both verbally and in print. The concept of accurate information reported with the journalistic standards of accuracy and fairness was to come much later in our nation's history.

When the concepts of "free speech" and "free press" first became a clarion call, for the common man they mainly meant freedom to speak against the British king. In more intellectual

circles, the British philosopher John Locke and other Enlightenment thinkers had introduced ideas of reason and individual liberty that provided the framework for much of what later appeared
in the Constitution and Bill of Rights. Thomas Jefferson famously
said in 1787, "Were it left to me to decide whether we should
have a government without newspapers, or newspapers without a
government, I should not hesitate a moment to prefer the latter."
But this was a sentiment that sprang from resistance to the con-
trols of the press by King George III, when the struggling colonies
were enthusiastic about free speech, but only so long as it was not
speech favoring British rule. Tory free speech was often rewarded
with tar and feathers. With American victory came politics, and
a vicious power struggle was quickly under way between the Jef-
fersonians, who had a vision of an agrarian paradise of independent farmers and small government, and those, like John Adams
and Alexander Hamilton, who were fervent advocates of a strong
central government and ambitious public works. It was an environment of almost unlimited free speech, much of it venomous
attacks on the opposition, and there was little of what in the 20th
century came to be considered traditional journalism. Perhaps
not surprisingly, after Jefferson became president and endured
this bash-and-batter version of a free press for a few years, he said
something not frequently quoted by journalists: "The man who
reads nothing at all is better educated than the man who reads
nothing but newspapers."

It seems clear that free speech, even irresponsibly free speech,
is what was being protected by the framers of the First Amendment. If traditional news stops being the American journalistic
norm, free speech will survive nonetheless, presumably. The
blogosphere is filled with would-be pamphleteers like James
Callender, who first attacked John Adams and then turned on
Jefferson, exposing his relationship with his mulatto slave, Sally
Hemings. If we return to this earlier model, Americans would be
presented with competing versions of reality, as they are now in
many ways, and we humans tend to choose to believe what we
want to be true.

But what will be lost is the professional improvements in journalism that came out of the Progressive Era and found a home in the economic model of traditional journalism. It is sometimes forgotten that the evolution of a journalism with professional standards and expectations took place at the same time that professions such as medicine, law, education, and accounting were being reformed. Just as journalism was long considered a job for scoundrels, at one time many of those practicing medicine did so as a sideline of barbering and suffered a similar lack of respect. But the Progressive Era of the late 19th and early 20th centuries brought improvements that have been essential to the high quality—and high esteem—that the various professions have enjoyed, at least until the last few decades.

While journalists often claim to be professionals, in the United States they have resisted establishing the certification system of professions such as medicine and law because it was felt that any licensing of journalists would violate the free speech that the First Amendment was created to protect. But even without a true professional status, journalism in the 20th century shaped itself into a craft with standards and ideals, and with a growing body of people who were taught those standards and ideals in journalism schools and newsrooms. Though the *New York Times* and a few other elite news organizations were considered the very top of the field, organizations such as the Society of Professional Journalists were organized with chapters all over the nation for journalists who worked in the vast network of smaller, less elite news organizations, but who believed that they were bound by the same journalistic code as the most celebrated *New York Times* reporter.

The news organizations they worked for were ones which, as businesses, embraced the values of traditional news and served their communities. Some were far better than others, but the standard was the same. It was the American standard they espoused, which was not the only journalistic standard that worked well. In the rest of the world, and especially in Europe, other styles of advocacy-oriented journalism have created a different standard that has been part of a robust political debate and a successful democracy. Indeed, the various models for news raise the question of just how much information a population needs to support democracy. How informed must a nation be to be considered knowledgeable about its own best interests? These questions prompted a decades-long philosophical battle that is still under way, but could be said to have begun with Walter Lippmann and John Dewey in the 1920s.

The issue that both men pondered was the nature and survivability of democracy itself. Lippmann was only 24 when he became one of the founding editors of the *New Republic*. A few years later he was coauthor of an influential analysis of the *New York Times*'s coverage of the Bolshevik Revolution, which he found biased and inaccurate, a chronic problem for the media to his way of thinking. Lippmann, who won two Pulitzer Prizes during his long career as a newspaper columnist, viewed the role of the press as a kind of intelligence service providing information that would inform a cadre of elite experts and highly knowledgeable policy makers who actually governed. He regarded the broad public as highly subject to manipulation and viewed government by genuinely informed consent as almost impossible outside the scale of a New England town meeting. He was also skeptical of the ability of journalists to report effectively without a rigorous effort to test their findings. While some have depicted him as an antidemocratic elitist who sneered at the public, historian Michael Schudson has argued that what Lippmann actually said was that "democratic self-government has nothing to do with native gray matter, but with the insufficiencies all of us share, a limited ability to attend to matters beyond our everyday experience."

John Dewey, who was 30 years older, was an influential philosopher, psychologist, and progressive educator. Though he never actually debated Lippmann on these issues, he has long been viewed as representing the other side of the argument about how democracy should work. Dewey also saw the public as susceptible to manipulation, but he believed that a host of small publics could inform themselves sufficiently to govern effectively, and the press had an important role in that process. While this is an oversimplification of Lippmann's and Dewey's dense theories, it seems to me that Lippmann would have viewed professional journalism as key to effective self-government by elites, whereas Dewey would have wanted quality news to educate the masses. Lippmann would have viewed the Web's wide-open democratic interaction with skepticism, whereas Dewey would have hailed it. But both would have viewed the iron core as essential to self-government.

One school of thought would maintain that having an opinion is enough, regardless of whether all the facts support that opinion. This view essentially argues that democracy is sufficiently safe in a nation that has free speech, so that everyone can speak their mind. But journalism is based on the premise that it is necessary—or at least much preferable—to have informed free speech. That belief opens the door to the murky question of whether it is really necessary for more than a small minority to be well informed. But it goes against America's sense of itself to cede the country's governance to a small minority of powerful interests, activists, and political leaders, with the rest of us content to have opinions, but little real information, at our command.

In the old model of near media monopolies, the American population was privy to what was essentially the same news. In the future, high-quality news will be mostly consumed by elites, with headlines and articles tailored to the short attention spans of people who tend to get their news on the Web. In 2007, I heard a futurist at the *New York Times,* whose job is to imagine what's coming in the next few years, tell a group of journalism school deans that they should train their students to write so that they could get everything necessary for a news story into 50 words...less than the length of this sentence. He wasn't kidding.

The press supports democracy by being both the vehicle for free speech and the principal means for informing and educating through news reporting. The culture of Web journalism, which is rapidly becoming the delivery system of choice for younger audiences, generally does not support news in depth or investigative journalism. The culture of Web journalism is one of multi-platform storytelling that can be enormously compelling and fascinating. But an article on the Web of more than 150 words is generally considered too long and unlikely to be read. Do such things matter? Obviously, boring news stories that are also tediously long do little good. But we are on the brink of living in a world in which the vast majority of news is in such bite-size pieces that serious, nuanced reporting may disappear save for a small elite.

This is really happening, and it is not simply alarmist fearmongering from the dinosaurs of the traditional media, who see their rice bowl being stolen by tabloid, advocacy, and entertainment news. The evidence is readily apparent by picking up almost any newspaper aside from the handful at the top, and even those are feeling the pressure to squeeze their news budgets. At most local papers, the fashion is for hyper-local news, which often means news that looks a great deal like local television news—wrecks, fires, and features, but little on politics, policy, accountability, and watchdog journalism. It is evident when one sees how CNN and MSNBC have shifted their focus from news to opinion, in pursuit of Fox News's highly successful mix of news and advocacy. It is evident in *Time* magazine's decision to shift from an emphasis on original reporting to more analysis, which means reasoned advocacy and is a step away from traditional news. It is apparent when you pick up a thick, advertising-heavy Sunday newspaper in most American cities and can make your way through its substantive news in about five minutes.

The world that looms will be one of abundant free speech, but it may have a dearth of reliable, traditional news. And also passing may be a kind of journalistic courage at the top that is the crucial backbone of the journalistic sense of mission at even the smallest papers. My father once told me that it was all but impossible to have friends and run a newspaper. He said that if you do your job, sooner or later you will make everyone mad. He seemed at peace with that.

# CHAPTER THREE

# THE FRAGILE FIRST AMENDMENT

*Congress shall make no law respecting an establishment of religion, or prohibiting the free exercise thereof; or abridging the freedom of speech, or of the press; or the right of the people peaceably to assemble, and to petition the Government for a redress of grievances.*

—Amendment I, Constitution of the United States

TO AMERICANS, THE RIGHT TO SPEAK FREELY UNDER the protection of the First Amendment is a certainty. Or so they believe. The First Amendment has been part of our Constitution since 1791, and its explicit guarantees are as comforting as they are familiar.

The amendment is a masterful and shrewd summation of the essence of the American sense of liberty that is elegant and almost poignant in its idealism. There are three freedoms guaranteed, each separated by a semicolon. First is the freedom to worship unencumbered by government, which essentially guarantees each citizen the freedom to believe according to one's conscience. Third is the right to assemble as citizens and to petition the government for a redress of grievances, which is shorthand for a promise that we may engage in political action and protest. Second, and linking conscience to political action, is the essential assurance of free speech and free press. These guarantees are almost as old as our democracy.

But what most Americans conceive to be the First Amendment's guarantee of free speech and a free press is only about 75 years old. While there was vigorous reporting, such as that of muckrakers like Ida Tarbell, such investigative work was legally vulnerable to the caprice of the state where it appeared. As a national legal principal, a free press as it is understood today began with a Supreme Court decision in 1931 involving a rabble-rousing bigot in Minneapolis. Until that time—for nearly two-thirds of our history—the First Amendment was either ignored or overruled when it came to assuring all citizens the free speech we now take for granted. Based on the First Amendment's checkered history, especially during times of war, it is reasonable to think that freedoms most of us believe inherent in a functioning democracy may be in jeopardy, and are certainly subject to reinterpretation and restriction. The First Amendment is what the Supreme Court says it is, and that has proved to be an uncertain guarantee of the protections we assume are fixed. Is the First Amendment fragile? It is in that what it means—and what it guarantees—has waxed and waned with the political winds.

Make no mistake. American law provides far more protection for free speech than that accorded anywhere else in the world. We have a near total ban on prior restraint, which would prevent news from being reported. The Pentagon Papers ruling, in all likelihood, would have been decided differently in every other democratic nation in the world. We significantly limit the government's power to punish speech. And we may well be the most open nation that has ever existed anywhere, by virtue of the First Amendment and the Freedom of Information Act. It would be incorrect to suggest that these freedoms are teetering on the abyss. But it would be naïve at a time of potentially catastrophic mass terror and a history of tailoring free speech to the political environment to view the First Amendment with complacency.

From the start, politics shaped the idea of what a free press should be. At the time of the Revolution, a free press in the rebelling colonies meant freedom to denounce King George III. The Founding Fathers recognized that a free press and the freedom to speak freely were crucial to holding government accountable, and at the time "government" meant the arbitrary power of Britain. Guarantees of free speech were in the constitutions of almost all of the original 13 colonies. When it came to writing the first national constitution, the objective was to persuade 13 independent colonies to give up some of their autonomy in order to forge a single nation with a powerful central government. It was difficult enough to reach agreement as to what the powers of the new United States government would be, and histories of the forging of that original Constitution are filled with intrigue and paranoia among the colonies. Those gathered at Philadelphia in 1789 to create the new nation decided that defining the rights of citizens was a contentious distraction that could be left for later. Indeed, many thought that a constitution that included a Bill of Rights would have gone down to defeat because, though there was general agreement on such rights as free expression and open trial, every state defined those rights its own way.

But once the Constitution was ratified, the Congress turned immediately to creating a Bill of Rights, which was the name given the first ten amendments to the Constitution. Once the Bill of Rights was approved in Philadelphia, the challenge was to persuade two-thirds of the state legislatures to ratify the amendments so that they would become the law of the land, which happened in 1791. Lost in the mists of history is the fact that three states did not ratify the Bill of Rights until 1939, in anticipation of its sesquicentennial: Georgia, Massachusetts, and Connecticut.

When the First Amendment became part of our body of law, the United States took a step that very few nations have taken. Britain, for instance, is considered one of the world's great democracies, but there is no written constitution and no specific statement of individual rights. The freedoms enjoyed by British citizens are determined by Parliament, and may be limited as Parliament sees fit. The impact of this today can be seen in such things at Britain's Official Secrets Act, which allows the government to put severe limits on what British subjects may be told by the media. The existence of a First Amendment in the United States can sometimes make Britain's lack of one almost bizarre to American eyes.

One strange case of Britain's brand of press constraints that took place in 1987 is recounted in *The First Amendment Book,* a summary of the amendment's history by Robert J. Wagman. The book includes an account by Andrew Neil, editor of the *Sunday Times* of London, of flying to New York to purchase *Spycatcher,* a nonfiction exposé of bad behavior by the British intelligence services that was a best seller in the United States but had been suppressed by the British government for revealing vital intelligence. The editor smuggled the book back into Britain and published an account of its contents. "I considered it absurd that such serious allegations could be published and debated in the United States, but not in Britain," wrote Neil. He and the paper were charged with criminal—not civil—contempt and an injunction was granted against publishing any more excerpts from the book. After 15 months and more than $5 million in legal costs, the *Sunday Times* won, but not because the court agreed that it was wrong to keep such information from the British public. Rather, the judges viewed the issue as moot because there were no more secrets to be kept. The newspaper's argument that a public interest had been served by disclosing public wrongdoing was largely ignored.

"Watergate could never have happened in Britain," wrote Wagman, meaning that the press coverage that brought down a president would have been all but impossible in the United Kingdom. The same could be said of the Pentagon Papers case, in which the Supreme Court ruled that the press could be punished for publishing, but—barring extreme circumstances—could not be *prevented* from publishing. But neither Watergate nor the Pentagon Papers could have happened in the United States during much of its history. The story of free speech and free press in America has inspiring moments, but much of the saga is riddled with political expediency, judicial double-talk, and bald repression.

The first press freedom case in America to draw broad attention came in 1734. John Peter Zenger was a printer who was also publisher of the *New York Weekly Journal*, which is considered the first political party newspaper in the nation. He was charged with seditious libel for articles assailing the governor of the New York colony, William Cosby.

Sedition and libel have frequently been invoked as the basis for silencing speech. *Webster's New World Dictionary* defines sedition as "the stirring up of discontent, resistance or rebellion against the government in power" and libel as "any false and malicious written or printed statement, or any sign, picture, or effigy, tending to expose a person to public ridicule, hatred or contempt or to injure his reputation in any way." At issue from the dawn of our country's history has been just how much "stirring up" is within the bounds of permissible free speech.

Under the 18th-century British law that was applied to Zenger, truth was no defense. Indeed, publishing defamation that was true was considered even more damaging by the courts of the day. Andrew Hamilton, a prominent lawyer in Philadelphia who thought differently, agreed to come to New York to defend Zenger. He argued that the jurors were not bound by the law of Britain and that in America, truth *should* be a complete defense when criticizing government. Despite being instructed by the judge to the contrary, the jury found Zenger not guilty because what he had published was based on fact. The decision was so popular that Hamilton, who had taken no fee, was given lavish honors by the city. While the law did not change because of the Zenger trial, the case struck a deep chord and was very much on the minds of the men who framed the First Amendment more than half a century later. One of the charges Zenger had leveled against Cosby was that he had vengefully fired an ancestor of Gouverneur Morris, one of the Constitution's principal authors. The younger Morris called the Zenger trial "the germ of American freedom."

But within only a few years of the First Amendment's ratification, vicious political infighting would make its guarantees virtually meaningless. President John Adams, who had succeeded Washington in 1797 and was head of the Federalist Party, was in a bitter struggle with the Democratic-Republicans, led by Thomas Jefferson. The Federalists were pushing for an ever-stronger central government, while the Democratic-Republicans wanted power vested in the states. Newspapers on both sides were rabid in their attacks. Making the atmosphere more explosive was the prospect of a war with France. The end of fighting in the United States had not meant the end of hostilities between Britain and France, which had only gotten worse, and the Federalists—who were sympathetic to the British—viewed the Democratic-Republican advocacy of France to be treasonous. As the election of 1800 approached, the journalistic atmosphere grew ugly and—to Adams—highly threatening to his ambitions for reelection.

The Federalist-controlled Congress solved its newspaper problem by passing the Alien and Sedition Acts of 1798. The laws threatened up to five years in jail and a $5,000 fine—a stupendous sum at the time—to anyone who "should conspire to oppose any measure of the government... by writing, printing or speaking" in a way considered damaging. The arrests began immediately, and most of those taken into custody were Democratic-Republicans. According to Federalist judges, the law forbade publicly stating specific reasons why President Adams should not be reelected. In one instance, a man was jailed for printing "peace and retirement to the president."

The Democratic-Republicans' efforts to fight the laws on First Amendment grounds went nowhere. Nonetheless, Jefferson won the election and control of Congress shifted to the Democratic-Republicans. The Alien and Sedition Acts had expired at the end of Adams' presidency, and the Democratic-Republicans did not seek to extend them. Jefferson then pardoned those who had been convicted under the Acts. Even so, that victory for a free press did not mean that the First Amendment was a guarantee with any teeth. For the rest of the 19th century, and well into the

20th, the concept of a free press and free speech as we understand them today were hardly the law of the land.

At that time, the U.S. Supreme Court viewed the First Amendment, as intended by the framers, as applying to action by Congress, not the states, in what was the "dual sovereignty" theory of federalism. The effect was that free speech and free press, because of state laws sometimes setting stringent limits, was not a guarantee to all citizens. By the 1830s, slavery had become a highly divisive issue and abolitionist newspapers began to spring up. Many legislatures in southern states passed laws against fomenting slave rebellion, and any advocacy of abolition was regarded as tantamount to encouraging a bloody uprising. Being caught in the south with an abolitionist newspaper, much less publishing one, was a crime punishable the first time by imprisonment or the lash. A second offense usually meant death. In 1837, a mob in Alton, Illinois—just across the river from St. Louis—murdered the editor of the *St. Louis Observer*, an abolitionist newspaper. That such a thing could happen in a free state made it even more shocking, but there were no successful arguments that the First Amendment applied.

At the start of the Civil War, a drumbeat of pro-Confederate opinion continued to be published in the North here and there, but at the publishers' peril. The book *Lincoln's Wrath* tells the story of the *Jeffersonian*, a small pro-Southern Democratic newspaper in West Chester, Pennsylvania. The paper was stridently anti-Lincoln, opposed the war, and supported the right to secede. In August 1861, a mob destroyed the presses and subscription lists. Soon after, federal marshals came to complete the job, citing the Confiscation Act, which made it possible for federal authorities to seize the property of any citizen who supported the Confederacy. But silencing the press is a tricky proposition, and Lincoln generally tried to avoid such fights when the cost of doing so outweighed the gain. When one of his generals shut down the *Chicago Times* for its disloyalty to the Northern cause, Lincoln revoked the order, but not because of any reverence for free speech. Ever the pragmatist, he wrote that the irritation of such acts are "likely to do more harm than the publication would do." In Massachusetts, a similar newspaper was silenced when a mob tarred and feathered the editor—a response Lincoln did not condemn. In the South, after the war began, a pro-Union newspaper was unthinkable.

At the end of the Civil War, Congress passed the 13th Amendment, ending slavery. Accompanying that change was the assumption that former slaves would automatically assume all the rights of white citizens. This proved not to be the case, especially in the Reconstruction South, where new laws aimed at blacks made such things as voting difficult if not impossible. To remedy this, Congress passed the 14th Amendment, which stated that a state could not pass laws that had the effect of abridging rights guaranteed by the Constitution. In theory, this should have ended the doctrine that the First Amendment's guarantees of freedom of speech and of the press could be countermanded by state laws. But it didn't work out that way. Despite the 14th Amendment's presumed power, the courts—after the withdrawal of Union troops from Southern states—effectively ignored the abridgement of constitutional rights for blacks—and for free speech. Southern legislatures used an array of Jim Crow laws to create a segregated society that was not ended until the second half of the twentieth century. For many years, the 14th Amendment was similarly ineffective when it came to fighting state laws that were aimed at silencing the press.

It is typical of the history of the media that there were surprisingly contradictory things taking place simultaneously. Despite the fact that there were no effective First Amendment guarantees for the press during the 19th century, it was a period in which newspapers were known for savage political attacks in the most vitriolic language. When the sensational journalism of the yellow press emerged later in the century, it thrived on exposés and scandal. At the start of the 20th century, a group of determined investigative reporters who turned up dirt on the nation's most powerful institutions were denounced for "raking muck." In 1904, Lincoln Steffens published *The Shame of the Cities,* exposing widespread municipal corruption, and Ida Tarbell came out with her magisterial *History of the Standard Oil Company*, which was a detailed chronicle of bullying and business malfeasance. Two years later, Upton Sinclair's *The Jungle* appeared, with its sickening account of the meatpacking industry. Despite such an apparently robust and free journalistic environment, the reality was that journalists were at the mercy of capricious and often vengeful state governments that could shut down newspapers and silence criticism by passing a law. While there was often language guaranteeing free speech in state constitutions, state judges tended to side with the politicians.

The Supreme Court began to view press freedom differently in the wake of the excesses in muzzling free speech that came during World War I. In *Gitlow vs. New York* in 1925, the court upheld Gitlow's conviction for writing and distributing a manifesto advocating the overthrow of the government. Justice William Sanford, a conservative Tennessean, wrote that the case had been accepted for review because the First Amendment applies to state law and action. It was a reversal of the court's opinion only two years earlier. Then in 1927, in a due process case, Sanford again asserted that the Fourteenth Amendment meant that the protections of the Bill of Rights applied to the states.

But the most definitive case began that same year in Minneapolis with a most unlikely champion. He was Jay M. Near, a man with a catalog of prejudices and a vile disposition in print. His newspaper, the *Saturday Press*, sneered at Catholics, ridiculed Jews, insulted blacks, and disparaged unions, and his partner in the newspaper was a failed mayoral candidate who had already been convicted of criminal libel. But Near also had a hatred of municipal corruption, though he assailed it in his own bigoted way. For instance, he charged that Jewish gangsters were "practically ruling" the city when he accused the chief of police of graft—a charge that, though laced with anti-Semitism, was likely the truth. Other favored targets of his broadsides were the city's mayor, the county attorney, and members of the county's grand jury, who he said were either incompetent or willfully derelict in doing their duty.

Minnesota had already passed a Public Nuisance Law, known as the "Minnesota Gag Law" because it could permanently silence those who created a public nuisance by publishing a "malicious, scandalous and defamatory newspaper." The county attorney— who later became governor of Minnesota—filed a complaint against Near, claiming that allegations against him and other public officials and the paper's anti-Semitism violated the Nuisance Law. A cooperative judge issued an injunction that barred Near from editing, publishing, or circulating his paper or any other publication that contained similar material. The injunction was granted without Near even being notified and was upheld by the Minnesota Supreme Court, which compared the *Saturday Journal* to other nuisances such as houses of prostitution. While there was a free press guarantee in the state's constitution, the court ruled that it was not to protect scandalous material but only to be "a shield for the honest, careful and conscientious press."

Near was effectively out of business and frantically sought help from the larger fraternity of newspapers, though he was hardly a member in good standing. His rescuer proved to be the owner of the *Chicago Tribune,* Robert R. McCormick, who had decided prejudices of his own but a lot more money, as well as an awareness that he too could be silenced the way Near had been. With McCormick's financial backing, the case eventually made its way to the United States Supreme Court as *Near v. Minnesota,* which proved to be a landmark. Lawyers for Near argued early in 1931 that the articles in the *Saturday Journal* were indeed defamatory, but, as in the John Peter Zenger case, they were also true. On June 1, 1931, the Supreme Court ruled 5–4 in favor of Near. The court held that the Fourteenth Amendment meant that the protections of the First Amendment applied to all the states and made censorship unconstitutional except in rare cases.

The core press freedom issue in this case was that of prior restraint. The Court found that the government could not prevent publication of Near's paper, though he could be punished after the fact. If he published libel, for instance, he could be held accountable, but the government could not create a prior restraint to publication save in extreme circumstances. The concept of no prior restraint by the government was the heart of what many of the Founding Fathers meant by press freedom when the First Amendment was adopted.

The court had previously ruled that a free press and free speech were not absolute rights and could, under certain circumstances, be restricted. But this was not one of them. The Public Nuisance Law's provisions against the press were deemed unconstitutional, even if what had appeared in the *Saturday Press* had proved *not* to be true. The most important point, the court ruled, was that the Minnesota law posed an "unconstitutional restraint upon publication." The ruling made clear for the first time that under the due process clause of the 14th Amendment, Minnesota had been wrong to pass a state law that abridged the constitutional guarantee of a free press. It had taken 140 years for this provision of the First Amendment to genuinely become the law of the land.

The *Near v. Minnesota* decision gave judicial muscle to the First Amendment's protections, but that strength has remained conditional, based on the limits set by the U.S. Supreme Court. Up until the *Gitlow* and *Near* decisions, the Court had virtually ignored the First Amendment, but after *Near* the justices have repeatedly had to define what the First Amendment means. The notion that the First Amendment's guarantees and limits are fixed is a misconception.

It has long been recognized that there were limits to free speech. Justice Oliver Wendell Holmes famously wrote in a unanimous 1919 decision, "The most stringent protection of free speech would not protect a man in falsely shouting fire in a theater and causing a panic." And he had added, "The question in every case is whether the words used are used in such circumstances and are of such nature as to create a clear and present danger that they will bring about the substantive evils that Congress has a right to prevent." Few would argue with such reasonable and sensible words. But they actually appeared at one of the most notorious moments in the First Amendment's convoluted history, and were the justification to silence speech at a time not unlike our own. The words themselves may have sounded comforting, but the application of them was chilling.

Scholars have noted a pattern of American debate during times of war. The period before fighting begins is generally one of intense debate and a free-for-all of passionate argument. It is what has come to be known as a "secular" period, in which it is accepted that there will be expressions of near-violent disagreement. But when the decision to go to war is made and American soldiers take the field, the "secular" gives way to the "sacred," and argument ceases. In the South before the Civil War, pockets of Union loyalists loudly campaigned against secession. An ancestor of mine was a two-term congressman from Tennessee in the 1830s and '40s. Though an old man in 1861, he tried desperately to keep Tennessee from seceding, and his agitation was tolerated until war came. He was then silenced and would likely have been put in prison had all his sons and sons-in-law not been in the Confederate Army. The time for argument had ended in the South, and, with few exceptions, in the North as well.

Similarly, when World War I broke out in Europe in 1914, a blistering debate began in America, and there was furious opposition to the war in some quarters. When President Woodrow Wilson finally declared war, he quickly forced through Congress the Espionage Act of 1917, which called for long imprisonment and heavy fines for objectionable publications that conveyed "false information" that hindered the war effort. The law allowed the government great leeway in defining "false information." The same year, Wilson pushed through the Trading with the Enemy Act, which was aimed at censoring all communications going abroad and was especially targeted at foreign-language newspapers, which could be barred from the mails under the law.

The nation was seized by patriotic zeal and fury at those who criticized the war. One such unlucky naysayer was a Montana rancher named Ves Hall, who apparently had one too many in a bar and began to declare his objection to the war, his hope that Germany would win, and his highly profane thoughts on President

Wilson. A fight broke out and the luckless Hall was arrested and prosecuted under the Espionage Act. The judge hearing the case had the remarkable brass to order acquittal. He ruled that while Hall's intent was to cause insubordination and obstruct the draft, his "unspeakable" statements were made in places like a hotel kitchen and in "a hot and furious saloon argument" and presented no threat to general order or to the draft. He compared it to bringing a charge of attempted murder against a man who had fired a .22 caliber pistol at someone three miles distant. The citizens of Montana were outraged and local politicians apoplectic, and the state legislature quickly passed a law outlawing any speech calculated to incite or inflame resistance to the war. Montana's two U.S. senators proposed a national version of the law to Congress, and the result was the Sedition Act of 1918.

The Sedition Act created a category termed "unpatriotic or disloyal language," and gave the government almost unlimited power to censor or punish it. The law also made into crimes anything that might obstruct the sale of war bonds or bring discredit or scorn on the government. Certainly the vocal and printed opposition to the war in Iraq would have been punishable by a stiff prison term. During World War I, almost 2,000 prosecutions involving things written and spoken were mounted under the provisions of these laws, and more than a hundred publications were harassed or stopped.

One of the cases, *Schenck v. U.S.*, involved two New York socialists who printed and distributed handbills denouncing the military draft as despotism arranged in the interest of Wall Street and urging violation of the law. Unlike the *Gitlow* and *Near* cases, which addressed the power of states to limit speech, the *Schenck* cased focused on the power of Congress. The two men were arrested and convicted under the Espionage Act, and their case did not come before the Supreme Court until 1919, after the war had ended. Their lawyers argued that the First Amendment guaranteed "absolutely unlimited discussion" of public matters. The government's response was to assert a right to self-preservation that trumped the First Amendment, and it claimed that the government alone had the right to determine when self-preservation was at stake. This led to the unanimous decision in which Justice Holmes laid out the "clear and present danger" standard. While the court agreed that the First Amendment had limits, it declined to allow the government to be the arbiter of those limits. It reserved that job for itself, but favored the government's argument. The conviction of Schenck was upheld, and he was packed off to jail.

The "clear and present danger" standard supplanted the less demanding standard that the speech might have a "reasonable tendency" to do damage, and in that sense it was a movement in the direction of greater press freedom. But the definition has been weakened and strengthened several times in the ensuing years. The current definition for when incitement of illegality or violence justifies curtailing First Amendment guarantees was set in 1969 in *Brandenburg v. Ohio,* which had at its center a bigot very much like Jay Near.

Clarence Brandenburg was an ardent member of the Ku Klux Klan, and at a rally on a farm near Cincinnati he thundered that if changes weren't made in American society, violence might well be the next step. He was arrested and convicted, but the U.S. Supreme Court reversed his conviction and in so doing set the standard for seditious speech that guides courts today. The Court ruled that such speech must not only be directed at inciting imminent unlawful action, but must also be *likely* to produce that action *immediately.* The Court ruled that "freedoms of speech and press do not permit a state to forbid advocacy of the use of force or of law violation except where such advocacy is directed to inciting or producing imminent lawless action" and is likely to succeed. This was language is far more protective than was the "clear and present danger" test, and went beyond anything that exists anywhere in the world, according to Floyd Abrams, one of the nation's preeminent First Amendment lawyers. "Brandenburg may well be the single most protective First Amendment ruling of all," he said.

In broad strokes, it could be argued that the battle over interpreting the First Amendment has been a long struggle by the government to keep objectionable or damaging information from being published. While this was usually framed as an effort to serve the broad public interest, it frequently took on the appearance of a determination to avoid political embarrassment or to undercut political opposition. For most of our history, the weapon was sedition laws, but that path of attack has largely been blunted. It is unthinkable today that a full-throated opposition to war would be punished by a jail term on the basis that it was "unpatriotic speech."

But the battlefield merely shifted. There is a legitimate public interest in striking the proper balance between a press that is free to be a watchdog on government and unlimited press freedom, which would be anarchy. While I can offer no statistics, I would bet heavily that a vast majority of people—including journalists—do not believe that press freedom is or should be absolute. For instance, absolute freedom would mean a license to publish military secrets, to libel anyone, or to invade anyone's privacy. But I also think that most people consider some press protections essential. The Supreme Court has blown hot and cold regarding such protections, and two cases have special pertinence today as they help make clear where the ongoing struggle between the press and the government is being waged.

The first case established the principle that the media should be allowed to be wrong when it comes to political speech and public affairs. From the days of the Zenger trial in the 18th century, the accuracy of what was said of public officials was the argument that was used in libel actions as a defense. But in what may at first seem a strange decision by the court, that standard was shown to be insufficient through a landmark case rooted in the civil rights struggle.

In 1960, the South was teeming with civil rights protest and civil disobedience. The general response by authorities—especially the police—ranged from willful refusal to protect black demonstrators to active complicity in attacks made on them. The Rev. Martin Luther King Jr. had become a particular target. In March, a group calling itself the Committee to Defend Martin

Luther King bought a fundraising ad in the *New York Times* head-lined "Heed Their Rising Voices." The ad, which had several typographical errors, described a series of acts against Southern Negro students that constituted an "unprecedented wave of ter-ror" in the South. It spoke of Orangeburg, South Carolina, where 400 students at a lunch counter sit-in had been sprayed with fire hoses and arrested en masse. And then it described an incident in Montgomery, Alabama, where students sang "My Country 'Tis of Thee" on the Capitol steps, whereupon their leaders were expelled. The ad asserted that truckloads of police ringed the campus of Alabama State College and the entire student body protested by refusing to reregister, at which point "their dining hall was padlocked in an attempted [*sic*] to starve them into sub-mission." In fact, the students had sung "The Star Spangled Ban-ner," their leaders were expelled for a different demonstration on another day, police didn't actually "ring" the campus, and the dining room lockout apparently did not happen.

About 650,000 copies of the paper were printed, and 394 were sent to dealers in Alabama, where 35 found their way to Montgomery. The state of Alabama rose in fury, and, though no one was named in the ad, several officials filed libel suits against the *Times* and the committee, which consisted of 64 prominent Americans, both black and white. Among those who filed the suit was L.B. Sullivan, one of three Montgomery city commissioners, who demanded $500,000 from the *Times* and also sued four black Alabama ministers who had helped place the ad.

The case came to trial in Montgomery before Judge Walter B. Jones, who, according to *The First Amendment Book*, "treated the Civil War as if it had ended only the week before and with a tragically wrong result." He spurned arguments rooted in the First Amendment and instructed the jury in ways that made the outcome inevitable. Sullivan won on all counts, and after the Ala-bama Supreme Court upheld the judgment, it went to the U.S. Supreme Court.

The benchmark ruling came almost exactly four years after the ad first appeared. For the *Times* and other serious news

organizations, the implications of such a libel case were tantamount to life and death. If a state court with a stacked jury could
make extravagant damage awards stick, it would be open season
on a newspaper such as the *Times,* which circulated nationally and
frequently published the kind of articles and political ads that
included criticism of local officials—some of them with factual
errors like those that existed in the paid ad. Even small local newspapers that had a subscriber in another state could be victim of a
vengeful jury thousands of miles away that wished to punish it.

The U.S. Supreme Court's unanimous decision was written by
Justice William J. Brennan Jr., the son of uneducated Irish immigrants who had married his high school sweetheart, gone to Harvard Law School, and been appointed to the court by President
Dwight D. Eisenhower. Brennan was wary of laws that would create a "chilling effect" on the press, a phrase he coined in a later
decision, and his ruling in *Times v. Sullivan* gave an invaluable tool
to news organizations in their coverage of politics.

The ruling first dismissed with a tone of contempt the Alabama
Supreme Court's argument that the 14th Amendment's due process clause did not pertain to state libel actions. The Alabama law
and action were compared to the Sedition Act of 1798, and were
therefore unconstitutional.

But the core of the ruling was that political speech was entitled
to special protection. The court ruled that the First Amendment's
guarantee of free speech and press requires that public officials
should not be able to successfully sue for libel using the accuracy
standard that applied to ordinary citizens. Brennan's opinion
said that, in the rough and tumble of politics, a news organization could report something defamatory and false about a public
official, provided it is related to official conduct and provided the
falsity was not intentional. He stated that there was a "profound
national commitment to the principle that debate on public
issues should be uninhibited, robust and wide open." But the ruling was intended to protect mistakes, not calculated lies or wan-
ton indifference to the truth. The court said that such a public
official could recover damages if the false statement was made

with "actual malice," which was defined as publishing something defamatory with the knowledge that it was false, or with "reckless disregard of whether it was false or not," which the court made clear a few years later required actual suspicion of falsity.

The ruling then examined the *Times* ad based on this standard and found that, while the paper may have been slightly negligent in accepting a political ad with some errors it could have found out were inaccurate, its conduct did not rise to the standard of actual malice. The Court had already thrown out sedition laws and viewed libel actions as just another way to silence press criticism. *Times v. Sullivan* closed libel as a substitute for sedition laws and gave the press the ability to be wrong, but not intentionally or recklessly wrong. Though Brennan was criticized by some for breaking stunning new ground protecting inaccurate political speech, Justice Hugo Black in a concurring decision argued that Brennan had not gone far enough. He felt the First Amendment provides absolute protection of criticism of the government, including speech published with actual malice. Black, who was then 78 years old, had been the youngest of eight children born on a hardscrabble Alabama farm and in his youth was briefly a member of the Ku Klux Klan. Appointed by FDR to the court, he had evolved into a champion of what he perceived to be the guarantees of the Bill of Rights, but his views on an absolute press freedom were never embraced by a majority of the court.

The power of the *Times v. Sullivan* decision was in creating a legal bastion for free speech that, inevitably, is laced with exaggerations, mistakes, distortions, and factual errors. Those things were part of the unfettered political argument that the press facilitated. If news organizations could be severely punished for being wrong, the inevitable effect would be to publish only what was safely within a buffer zone of certainty and perfect accuracy. Anything else would risk catastrophic libel judgments, and such an economic threat would undermine what the First Amendment was created to foster. The Supreme Court later said this protection applied to public figures—such as business and labor leaders, movie stars, and baseball players—as well as to public officials.

Was this too much freedom? There are those who argue that the *Times v. Sullivan* case has done great damage to our political environment by making it all but impossible for those in politics to defend themselves and their reputations through libel actions. Movie stars have successfully sued some of the racier tabloids over such things as allegations of drunk driving or drug use that proved false. But for political figures, the ability to punish lies in the press is scant, and there is no question that the *Times v. Sullivan* protections have created a media environment that can be brutal. Undoubtedly, some excellent people shrink from political life from fear of the harsh press scrutiny that often accompanies political power. But the positive side of the argument is also compelling. Americans have astonishing protection for speaking their minds about their government—even if they are wrong on the facts. It is a balance that the Supreme Court felt should be weighted in favor of vigorous free speech. It should be noted that the rest of the open, liberal democratic world has not been willing to go nearly this far, and have still maintained robust political debate.

The court tilted the other way—and effectively put a curb on the freedoms of *Times v. Sullivan*—in a case decided in 1972 that has had great ramifications in our current climate of bitter battles between the press and the government. The case was *Branzburg v. Hayes*, and in it the Court seemed to be saying that *Times v. Sullivan* should be the limit when it came to protecting journalists. More would be too much.

The focus of *Branzburg v. Hayes* was whether there was a First Amendment right for journalists not to have to testify about the stories they write, and especially about confidential sources who had been promised they would not be exposed. Paul Branzburg was a reporter at the Louisville *Courier-Journal* who covered the youth culture that was flowering all over the nation. Part of his reporting was on the local drug scene, where he wrote about such things as manufacturing hashish. He was subpoenaed by two grand juries to reveal what he knew about these illegal activities, but he refused to testify on the basis that he had a First Amendment right to protect the identity of his news sources. In two similar cases, reporters had refused to testify about the Black Panthers after doing articles that had involved spending time with the black separatist organization known for violence and crime. They too had cited the First Amendment as providing immunity from having to testify about news coverage. The three cases were combined into *Branzburg v. Hayes,* and the result was a 5–4 decision by the Supreme Court ruling that there was no First Amendment protection for reporters called before a grand jury to testify about potentially serious crimes.

That same majority seemed also to be seeking a balance that would not turn reporters into policemen or informers and thus greatly hamper their ability to report. The majority 5–4 opinion was written by Justice Byron White. He had been one of two dissenting votes opposing the *Roe v. Wade* decision recognizing the privacy right to abortion, and he was legendary for his gruff prickliness. Yet he was also a strong proponent of affirmative action and of treating gender as a suspect classification. In this case, he came down decidedly against the press, and his opinion was cold and dismissive. He said that the court declined "to grant newsmen a testimonial privilege that other citizens do not enjoy." Essentially, the court said that journalists were citizens and had the duty to testify when called upon. The First Amendment was no shield when it came in conflict with the Sixth Amendment, which guaranteed "the right to a speedy and public trial" and the right to be confronted with witnesses against you and to compel witnesses for you to appear and testify.

But while the White opinion declared there was no First Amendment right for journalists not to testify, it was two other opinions— one concurring and one in dissent—that defined the way the nation's lower courts actually behaved when it came to journalists being called to testify—at least until the Lewis "Scooter" Libby trial in 2007. The concurring opinion was by Justice Lewis Powell, a Virginian who had been a close friend of Edward R. Murrow, the nation's pioneering television journalist. Powell had joined the majority opinion, but he also wrote a separate concurrence that emphasized the "limited nature" of the decision, as if to say that there were times when journalists should not be compelled to testify, though he did not specify when those times might be.

Justice Potter Stewart's dissenting opinion set forth a precise framework for when journalists should be forced to testify. Stewart, somewhat to his chagrin, had become best known for his comment in an earlier pornography case that defining hard-core pornography was difficult, but "I know it when I see it." In his dissent, he laid out a three-part test that should be met before reporters were compelled to testify. The information the reporter had should be clearly relevant to the case, it should not be obtainable through any alternative means, and there must be a compelling and overriding need to get the information.

For over 30 years, the Potter Stewart "rules" were generally observed, and reporters were rarely brought before grand juries. It was a practical "don't ask, don't tell" solution to the problem, in that the reporters didn't actually have the right to refuse to testify, but the government didn't want to force the issue for political reasons because doing so always caused a ruckus. Prosecutors were reluctant to pursue reporters if it was avoidable, and when they did seek information, reporters were generally able to strike some compromise that avoided a confrontation. When a confrontation was unavoidable, some reporters went to jail rather than betray the identity of confidential sources. Indeed, in the journalistic scheme of values, it was considered more honorable to disobey a judicial order and go to jail than to break a promise to keep silent.

The compromise was blown to pieces by U.S. Attorney and Special Counsel Patrick Fitzgerald in his pursuit of Scooter Libby, the senior White House official accused of lying to a grand jury about his conversations with reporters. Libby, who was a top aide to Vice President Dick Cheney, had systematically leaked information to reporters on a confidential basis that was intended to discredit a C.I.A. report that was judged harmful to the administration's case that Iraq was seeking nuclear weapons. Fitzgerald subpoenaed Judith Miller, a *New York Times* reporter, to testify to a grand jury about her conversations with Libby, and when she refused, he had her jailed for contempt of court. He wanted the information that Miller had, and he based his demand for that information on his belief that the *Branzburg* decision flatly barred any consideration of First Amendment interests at all so long as a grand jury was acting in good faith. This was, in fact, not an unreasonable way to interpret *Branzburg*, though First Amendment lawyers for years had been trying to avoid such a clear and unambiguous interpretation of it. Fitzgerald prevailed, and eventually all the reporters testified.

The conviction of Scooter Libby was embarrassing for the Bush administration, but the case's real importance is that Fitzgerald may well have delivered a devastating blow to serious investigative reporting. No sane journalist wants to go to jail for a story. A legal environment in which journalists are sent to jail for contempt because they won't divulge confidential sources is one that is bound to cause far fewer journalists to write stories that might invite a grand jury inquiry. Similarly, journalists who divulge the identities of confidential sources in court would seem certain to make anyone with sensitive information wary of trusting a journalist's word. Not everyone believes that the absence of journalistic privilege to protect sources would make a significant difference in what was published, but for journalists it is an article of faith that failing to protect sources would be disastrous.

While the anti-sedition laws have been laid to rest, a widespread practice of subpoenaing journalists would have much the same result as sedition laws: less reporting. Much of the most important journalism regarding the government is based on confidential sources. But no news organizations want to incur the cost of defending journalists who won't identify sources except when it is unavoidable. It seems certain that in the future, journalists—and their employers—will be more reluctant to guarantee confidentiality, and sources will be less sure that they can be protected. Of course, much of what is protected—as in the case of Scooter Libby—was not whistle-blowing but political spin. Even so,

I believe that on balance the public benefits when journalists can report what they are told in confidence, even when it is leaked for odious reasons. Most confidential sources are acting not in the public interest but in their own. To my mind, chilling this commerce in confidential information would be bad for the robust conversation the First Amendment is supposed to foster.

Similarly, while libel suits brought by public officials or powerful interests may be more difficult to win because of *Times v. Sullivan*, the cost of defending them can be crippling, especially to news organizations in the midst of a financial crunch. Citizen journalists and other untraditional news organizations and freelancers are even more vulnerable to threats of libel or other litigation, because defending the cases, even if they win in the end, can be ruinous.

The Bush administration used its power after September 11 to weaken the Freedom of Information Act by restricting access to hitherto public documents on national security grounds. The Reporters Committee for Freedom of the Press has documented repeated efforts by government in recent years to prevent or punish reporting that the government did not want done. For instance, when the *New York Times* published its scoop on the president's authorizing domestic eavesdropping without warrants, the Justice Department opened a criminal investigation to try to find out the sources for the story. The president had also pushed passage of the Patriot Act in the wake of 9/11, which greatly broadens the government's power to dig into hitherto private telephone, e-mail, medical, financial, and other records, making confidentiality even more difficult to assure.

The war on terror has raised legitimate questions about the limits of free speech and how those limits are to be balanced against the reasonable concerns of a government that important secrets be kept. Similarly, as citizens we all are protected by both the First and Sixth amendments, and a journalist also has a responsibility as a citizen. But how will that responsibility be interpreted should the nation be plunged into another paroxysm of reaction by terrorist attacks? Would the First Amendment's guarantees, which have ebbed and flowed for our entire history, be able to stand up to the fear that would be sure to come? Or will they prove to be a fragile bulwark, a guarantee that for much of its history has been more uncertain than sure? I wish I felt more confidence that freedom would prevail.

# CHAPTER FOUR

# OBJECTIVITY'S
# LAST STAND

*"I don't think objectivity was ever attainable."—Jeff Jarvis, Buzzmachine.com "When advocacy is defined as journalism, then we get into a problem."—Callie Crossley, Nieman Foundation*
—Exchange on *The News Hour with Jim Lehrer*, June 18, 2007

BAD JOURNALISM HAS THE WORLD'S ATTENTION, AND endless hours are spent by those who care about news dissecting what is bad and why. "Bias" is a word that gets used a lot. "Unfair" and "unbalanced" are also familiar epithets, as are "shallow" and "lazy." "Inaccurate" is usually part of the rap.

But what is good journalism? What *makes* journalism good? Everyone would agree on accuracy. For most consumers of news, the next requirement would be lack of bias: journalism should be fair and balanced. More than two-thirds of us say we preferred getting news from sources without "a particular point of view," according to a 2007 poll by the Project for Excellence in Journalism. In the United States, this neutrality has long been described as journalistic objectivity, a term that came into popular use early in the 20th century and has been claimed as the standard ever since by most of the news media. Much of journalism's decline in public esteem is due to the public's perception that journalists don't live up to this objectivity standard. True, there are other causes, such as sensationalism, overaggressiveness, and outright fraud. But the heart of the problem when it comes to credibility is that much of the public doesn't believe that the press is objective in its coverage.

But even as the public is complaining of the lack of journalistic objectivity, the concept that news should be objective is increasingly treated within the profession as old-fashioned and outdated. When I tell colleagues that I still believe in journalistic objectivity, I tend to get looks of embarrassed perplexity that are not unlike what I used to see at New York dinner parties when I said I was from Tennessee. In that situation, my dinner companions knew that there *were* people from Tennessee, but they had never actually come face-to-face with one. So it is these days with those who still espouse the old-time religion of journalistic objectivity. In many sophisticated journalism circles, if you still subscribe to that standard, you are viewed as naïve, dishonest, or—at the very least—behind the times.

To my mind, a great deal of what makes journalism good is entwined with what I would term authentic journalistic objectivity, as opposed to the various flavors of phony or faux objectivity. I believe it is essential that genuine objectivity should remain the American journalistic standard, but we may be living through what could be considered objectivity's last stand.

I define journalistic objectivity as a genuine effort to be an honest broker when it comes to news. That means playing it straight without favoring one side when the facts are in dispute, regardless of your own views and preferences. It means doing stories that will make your friends mad when appropriate and *not* doing stories that are actually hit jobs or propaganda masquerading as journalism. It sometimes means doing something that probably is not done nearly enough—betraying your sources! A journalist uses charm and guile to help extract information that can benefit the public, and then spills the beans to the public. And sometimes the source of the information feels betrayed. Objectivity also means not trying to create the illusion of fairness by letting advocates pretend in your journalism that there is a debate about the facts when the weight of truth is clear. He-said/she-said reporting, which just pits one voice against another, has become the discredited face of objectivity. But that is *not* authentic objectivity.

The critics of objectivity begin by declaring that it is impossible to *be* objective. They say that even if there were a pure truth, journalists are incapable of reporting it. We journalists are humans with prejudices that inevitably creep into our work, even if we are trying to keep them out. "We were never in the job of delivering the truth; we've always been in the job of helping the public decide what is true," said Jeff Jarvis, one-time reporter and editor at the *Chicago Tribune* and founder of the blog BuzzMachine (www.buzzmachine.com). He was taught objectivity at journalism school, but now believes it is "a false high standard that we could not help but fail."

In addition, critics rightly point out that there are certain beliefs that are unstated in American traditional journalism, but that skew the framing of stories even before the first word is written. For instance, the articles that appear in mainstream newspapers are written with the undeclared assumptions that capitalism isn't inherently evil and that freedom of speech is a virtue. Critics argue that such cultural and political assumptions are inescapable, and bring with them inevitable bias. For instance, an Islamic journalist, who believes as a matter of faith that free speech is the handmaiden of blasphemy, would almost certainly report the furor over the Danish cartoons depicting Mohammad in a different way than would a Western journalist. Those critical of objectivity argue that prewired beliefs make genuine objectivity impossible, even if the effort is made to overcome the prewiring.

The critics also argue that the pretense of offering objective journalism is inherently dishonest and misleading. If journalists offer their work as the objective truth when it is not, they have betrayed and misled their readers. Would it not be less deceitful to stop pretending to do something that is impossible under the best of circumstances? In fact, they say, what claims to be objective news often isn't even a sincere effort, but is frequently skewed by prejudice, deadline pressure, or simple laziness.

Critics point to the phony objectivity in which the reporter quotes advocates of both sides of a controversy without any independent probing to discover the facts. They point to the shabby practice of pandering to vocal political interests by giving equal weight to all views, no matter how unsubstantiated by evidence. Global warming is considered a fact by the vast majority of climate experts, yet many news stories "balance" their coverage by giving significant weight to the views of a small minority of skeptics who are sometimes industry shills.

The more penetrating critics also point out that the journalistic convention that news should be objectively reported creates an especially fertile opportunity to spin the truth. The public relations industry was born and has boomed in a world of ostensibly objective journalism. The main purpose of PR is to place information favorable to a client in a context of news so that it has more credibility with the public than the same message might have if it were presented in the form of a paid advertisement or from a clearly self-interested source. In a sense, the public's assumption that a news organization is at least trying to present its journalism objectively gives heightened veracity to whatever appears in news columns and programming, which is why standard PR tools such as video news releases are produced to look as much like objectively reported news as possible. The critics maintain that news organizations that claim to report objectively provide the cover that makes spin persuasive. If the same spin appeared in a frankly conservative or liberal publication, or as the work of a reporter with a clear agenda, or in a publication that was candidly the voice of an industry such as Big Pharma, the bias of the message could better be taken into account.

And finally, there is the argument that people—especially young people—don't *want* objective news anymore. They want to hear a *voice*.

The reason that so many in the journalistic world are giving up on objectivity is that these criticisms—all of them—are legitimate. But, to my mind, giving up on objectivity will create worse problems than it will solve.

A source of enduring argument among journalists is over what objectivity actually means and how it came to be the American news standard. There is one school of thought that objectivity sprang mostly from the commercial interests of newspaper moguls in the 19th century, who wanted to sell papers to as many people as possible. Republicans, Democrats, anarchists, socialists, and Know-Nothings all needed to buy dishes and thread, girdles and cigarettes, medicine to treat piles and ease bunions. A newspaper that could reach all of them was the kind of newspaper that advertisers would support, and one way to accomplish this was to strip the political point of view out of news reporting. In other words, objectivity was a commercial necessity that was turned into a virtue by its advocates, who saw news without political bias as a desirable side effect of what was essentially a matter of self-interest.

Given human nature, it would be easy to believe that making a buck was the compelling reason for objectivity's rise, and that our commercial culture was the determinant. Where the economic model was different, so was the journalism. In Europe, the media were less commercial, and the notion that news should be objective did not find traction. The European style of journalism was far more subjective and politically driven. You got news from the conservative French papers that had a conservative set of givens reflected in the way news was reported. If you read the newspapers published by the Communists or royalists or socialists or anarchists or fascists, you got a journalism that was selective in its facts and was framed to advance a political agenda.

Some news historians, such as Michael Schudson, have argued that the adoption of objectivity in the United States was in a significant way a reaction to just this kind of ideologically driven news, which was the norm in this country through much of the 19th century. Progressives and reformers viewed the highly partisan American press as more the captives of special interests than as the voices of political philosophy. Labor unions, political parties, and other interest groups were viewed as corrupt, using their newspapers like sledgehammers to push self-interest rather than the broad public interest.

Objectivity became the journalistic norm at a time when journalists were taking themselves more seriously professionally, creating codes of conduct and ethical standards, and trying to elevate what had been viewed as a rather shabby, even odious, calling. The basis for much of that ill repute was the public's belief that journalists would do anything and say anything. They would twist the facts and distort the "objective" truth. They would sneak into a house of a family mourning the loss of a child and steal a picture of the child off the wall. They would lie and connive. In the financial press, it was thought almost normal for journalists to be slipped money for publishing favorable stories, and even more for withholding damaging information.

In politics, the reporting could be venomous or slavish, depending on the reporter's convictions or susceptibility to corruption. The Progressive Era was born out of public outrage and revulsion at all kinds of corruption—financial, commercial, political, and journalistic—at the end of the 19th century. By this reckoning, objectivity was born, in part, as an antidote to press corruption, as a new best practice that would set clear standards and allow news organizations to be held accountable.

But what, exactly, *was* objective journalism? Were all-too-human journalists supposed to stop being humans and somehow expunge all the prejudices that they carried inside them? Were they to *be* objective, meaning that they would approach each new subject like a blank slate without opinions? Enemies of objectivity argue that because journalists must be free of bias to be objective, and because this is impossible, it follows that objectivity is a false ideal. As a group, journalists probably have more opinions than most, and it is very rare that a reporter starts working on a story without having some notion as to what happened—in other words, a point of view. But objectivity does not require that journalists be blank slates free of bias. In fact, objectivity is necessary precisely because they *are* biased.

In their book *The Elements of Journalism: What Newspeople Should Know and the Public Should Expect,* Bill Kovach and Tom Rosenstiel describe what they call "the lost meaning of objectivity." As journalism was reforming itself late in the 19th century, the initial goal was to substitute a reliable accuracy for the partisan assertion that dominated journalism. The buzz word of that time was "realism," and the concept was that the publishing of facts would naturally lead to revealing truth. But there were shortcomings to this concept. Facts can be chosen selectively, and while what is presented may be factually accurate, it may create an impression that is far from the truth. Selecting certain facts and ignoring others is the basis of advocacy, which may range from political punditry and public relations to the gross distortions of propaganda.

Journalism is something different, or it should be. In 1920, when Walter Lippmann was the rising champion of political punditry, he coauthored an influential analysis which concluded that the *New York Times*'s coverage of the Russian Revolution had been twisted by cultural blinders or willful distortion by reporters and editors. "In the large," he wrote, "the news about Russia is a case of seeing not what was, but what men wished to see." Lippmann's solution was a journalism in "the scientific spirit," because even "honest efforts" by journalists were not enough. He called for a method of verification and gathering journalistic evidence that would allow a reporter to "remain clear and free of his irrational, his unexamined, his unacknowledged prejudgments in observing, understanding and presenting the news." His focus was on finding ways to help journalists defeat the distortions of their own inevitable bias.

As Kovach and Rosenstiel point out, "In the original concept, in other words, the *method* is objective, not the *journalist.*" It was *because* journalists inevitably arrived with bias that they needed objectivity as a discipline to test that bias against the evidence so as to produce journalism that would be closer to truth.

They argue that the quickening of objectivity as the American journalistic standard was born of a desire to have a more scientific way of approaching news. The nation's faith in science was surging, and the scientific method seemed suited to journalism. Scientists begin their research with assumptions. They have expectations of what will happen, but they don't *know* what will happen. They have, in other words, their own opinions and beliefs—their point of view or even bias—about what is likely the truth, and they do their research to *test* those assumptions. Their objective, scientific inquiry is not one that is without bias, but one in which bias has to stand up to evidence and results.

This is the sensible and realistic approach to objectivity that might be termed *genuine objectivity*. It begins with the assumption that journalists have bias, and that their bias has to be tested and challenged by gathering facts and information that will either support it or knock it down. Often, there is information that does both, and that ambiguity needs to be reported with the same dispassion with which a scientist would report variations in findings that were inconclusive. If the evidence *is* conclusive, then that is—by scientific standards—the truth.

But journalistic objectivity is an effort to discern a practical truth, not an abstract, perfect truth. Reporters seeking genuine objectivity search out the best truth possible from the evidence that the reporter, in good faith, can find. To discredit objectivity because it is impossible to arrive at perfect truth is akin to dismissing trial by jury because it isn't perfect in its judgments.

One of the bludgeons for pummeling objectivity is to cite cases in which "objective" journalism failed. Perhaps the example most often cited is press coverage of Senator Joseph McCarthy in the early 1950s. This was indeed a journalistic failure, and the blame has generally been put on journalists for covering McCarthy using the principles of objectivity.

In 1950, McCarthy made a notorious Lincoln Day speech to the Republican Women's Club of Wheeling, West Virginia, entitled "Communism in the State Department." While delivering the speech, he waved a piece of paper and, according to most accounts, declared, "I have here in my hand a list of 205—a list of names that were made known to the Secretary of State as being members of the Communist Party and who nevertheless are still working and shaping policy in the State Department." The Cold War was at its height, and a U.S. senator making such an assertion was big news. Not surprisingly, it captured headlines all over the nation. The story that first day was that Senator McCarthy had made sensational charges. To my mind, it made sense to cover the story simply because he said what he said. If a U.S. senator were to assert today that the State Department was harboring 205 terrorists, it would receive broad coverage just for the fact that someone of that stature and rank had made such an explosive allegation.

The glory of objective news reporting is that you go back and seek evidence. But this did not happen in the case of McCarthy, and that was a journalistic failure, not the failure of objectivity. McCarthy was not challenged to produce the names by the press, and a few days later he said in Salt Lake City that there were 57 Communists in the State Department. Later that month, he said in the Senate that the number was 81. Democrats in the Senate demanded the names, but McCarthy refused to provide them. In fact, he had no names.

Over the next several years, the country was wracked by what became known as "McCarthyism," a term popularized by the editorial cartoonist Herblock and meaning a particularly nasty form of destructive demagoguery. Through much of this period, the press simply reported what McCarthy said rather than explain that his numbers had changed repeatedly, his allegations were unproven, and that he had repeatedly made claims he could not support. This was sometimes framed as objective journalism because the "fact" of what he said was being reported factually. But this was moral cowardice, not objectivity. Any authentic application of the standards of objectivity would have painted a truly objective picture—which at the time was a politically dangerous thing for news organizations to do.

Indeed, it is important to bear in mind that objective journalism is not just a matter of how reporting is conducted and articles are written. It is also embedded in the decisions editors make about what news will get covered. Not assigning a story about the inconsistencies in McCarthy's allegations was a failure to apply the principles of objectivity—and of journalistic ethics. It was failed objectivity because the country clearly needed to know, and it was a failure of ethics because the decision not to do the story was made from fear rather than journalistic judgment. Though the McCarthy coverage has been used to blacken the name of objectivity, it was the decision not to be genuinely objective that was the problem. Objectivity is not dictation.

But neither is objectivity—in the ultimate sense—done with a completely open mind. This is something that I have found peace with, and it gets to the issue of cultural bias and framing. For instance, as a news consumer I accept that the reporters who are trying to ascertain truth are doing so with a cultural bias. I hope they are doing their best to be mindful of cultural hard wiring that will skew their reporting, but they are not trying to pretend that they do not have a national heritage or a set of beliefs. Does this make objective journalism inherently dishonest? Not to my mind. It is a skewing that allows a practical truth that is useful to me. I expect reporters covering the war in Iraq for the *New York Times* to be mindful of the other value systems to be found in Iraq. Indeed, I expect them to explain those perspectives to me, objectively. But I do not ask them to forget or suspend the beliefs that are American. Rather, I want them to view the world with the objectivity that comes from intelligence and observation and makes note of the misinterpretations of others that may spring from projecting one's own cultural perspective onto very different cultures. Do I think, for instance, that an American journalist could report objectively on the practice in some parts of Africa of genital mutilation of women? I want to know what the African cultural perspective is, but I feel that an American journalist is capable of presenting that without distortion caused by prejudice. A heated denunciation of genital mutilation is much less useful to me than a nuanced explanation of why it happens, where it came from, and why it persists. The point is that being a part of one culture should not keep you from being, in practice, objective in your journalism.

Perhaps no issue illustrates the importance—and difficulty—of objective reporting more than the political and moral debate over abortion. Reporters as a group tend to be pro-choice, and pro-life advocates have long complained that these biases have skewed the way the story is reported. This was very much the case when, in 1995, a bill was passed in Congress that would ban an abortion procedure called intact dilation and extraction, which became better known as partial birth abortion. Those opposed to abortion, who had sought to frame the issue as protecting the fetus, felt that this procedure was so grisly that they could score a victory over the pro-choice perspective, which had framed the issue as one of women's rights. In partial birth abortion, the fetus is dragged by the feet through the birth canal and the head of the living fetus is punctured so that it can be removed.

The key questions quickly emerged: How many such abortions were performed each year? At what point in the pregnancy? And was it essentially an emergency procedure?

Organizations supporting abortion rights issued a torrent of statements and statistics asserting that only a few hundred partial birth abortions took place each year, and that most of them happened in the third trimester when there was severe fetal deformity or to protect the life or health of the mother. The pro-life side countered with statistics of its own, claiming that the procedure was performed thousands of times each year, often in the second trimester, and usually on healthy fetuses and healthy mothers.

In the mainstream media, the pro-choice "facts" won the argument hands down. Peter Jennings of ABC News described it as a "very rare procedure," a claim echoed in the *Washington Post* and other major news organizations. The *Los Angeles Times,* citing unnamed research groups, put the total number of partial birth abortions performed in the United States each year after 20 weeks at about 500, which meant it was relatively rare. On *60 Minutes,* five women told the harrowing story of their pain and grief after deciding to have a partial birth abortion, which in every case was justified by some medical tragedy and took place in the third trimester. One woman described how she learned late in her pregnancy that her baby's brain was growing outside its body. The other side of the argument got only a faint nod. The message of most mainstream coverage was that the procedure was a tragic necessity for emergencies, and President Clinton vetoed the bill.

The reporting throughout was one in which one set of statistics and claims was pitted against another, which is the kind of phony balance that gives objectivity a bad name. This kind of he-said/she-said reporting is not objectivity but laziness. And the pro-choice statistics were generally treated as more credible, which made the coverage not merely unenterprising but tilted.

Then, 14 months after the bill to ban partial birth abortion had been introduced, a reporter at the *Record* in Bergen County, New Jersey, was assigned to take a look at the issue. Ruth Padawer reached out to both pro-choice and pro-life organizations and had them send her their materials. What she discovered was two very different versions of reality. She then called two New Jersey abortion doctors and an abortion clinic administrator, and—as sometimes happens when reporters ask questions—she got answers. She was told that, in New Jersey alone, there were at least 1,500 partial birth abortions each year, mainly in the second trimester and mainly on healthy women and fetuses. When she wrote her story, headlined "The Facts on Partial Birth Abortion," it was the first independently reported article on the subject to appear in a mainstream news organization, though the issue had been in the news for more than a year.

David Brown, a medical doctor who is also a reporter for the *Washington Post,* then did his own independent investigation and found essentially the same reality, but on a national scale. Shockingly—and disappointingly—the other great news organizations generally ignored what Padawer and Brown had found.

To my mind, this situation gets to the heart of the objectivity problem. The reporting of Brown and Padawer is a tribute to *genuine* objectivity, which does not depend on the political views of the journalists who are doing the reporting. Both Brown and Padawer are, personally, pro-choice, and they were well aware that their reporting would be damaging to that side of the argument. But they did their job anyway, objectively and based on the best factual information they could find.

The failure of many of the nation's premier news organizations to report with the same objectivity is the kind of skewed journalism I fear will become acceptable if genuine objectivity is abandoned as the iron core dwindles. It is important to keep that standard if only to be able to complain when the standard is not met. If the standard is subjective truth and personal voice, then ignoring the other side of the argument is justified. Just as bad, to my mind, is the practice too often used of disguising this kind of subjectivity with a token paragraph given to the other side of the argument. This weak tea of faux objectivity with its pseudo balance has damaged the concept of objectivity by being clearly not the real thing. It is exactly this kind of slippery self-justification that makes me cling to genuine objectivity—objectivity based on intellectual honesty, facts, and reporting, not the bogus he-said/ she-said junk. Real objectivity is content to let the chips fall where they may, even if it means goring one's own ox.

I became aware of the partial birth abortion story as executive editor of *Media Matters*, a PBS program of media criticism. When I and others were discussing whether we should do a segment that highlighted this as a case of journalistic failure, I remember being quite aware that we were creating something that would be used by pro-life advocates as a weapon to discredit the pro-choice side of the argument. In fact, we learned later that the 20-minute video segment was shown repeatedly to pro-life groups as proof positive that the press was biased and to discredit claims made by pro-choice advocates. Our purpose had been to provide a case study that would spur greater adherence to genuine objectivity and hence enhance journalistic credibility. That purpose was subverted, and it was used to undermine press credibility instead. I had no illusions about this. Like myself, the producers of *Media Matters* were pro-choice. The segment we were considering putting on television was going to be used by people with whom we had strong disagreement. But we agreed that this was an important story and that it should be aired, regardless of how it might be used. In the piece, we quoted Diane Gianelli of American Medical News, who said, "You have to be not pro-life, not pro-choice, but pro-truth...You have to go to both sides, the primary sources, and then sit down and write it straight."

I offer my minor role in this controversy not as a paragon of objectivity but to stress the point that it is not only how news is reported, but whether it is reported, that is at issue. Objectivity is a state of mind that begins with the belief that a journalist's obligation is to the truth, and often the most critical objective decision is the one to report on a subject at all. The spirit of objectivity, when it works, is embedded in every decision in a newsroom, and its principle at every level is that the news should be delivered straight, whatever that might mean under the circumstances.

There is much irony involved with embracing the standard of journalistic objectivity. Measuring journalistic performance on the basis of objectivity provides a needed way for journalists to be held accountable. But much of the criticism of perceived failings in objective reporting is far from objective itself, and the cumulative impact of this constant bashing has been to undermine press credibility. One of the good things for journalism that has come from the Web is a relentless scrutiny of coverage by bloggers. This generally takes the form of press bashing from the left or the right, depending on the blog, and any journalist doing serious work knows now to expect to be savaged online. Even so, the perception that one's work is going to be put under a microscope is a spur to check facts and go the extra mile in getting the story right, which is an antidote to the sloppiness and even carelessness that are the constant scourge of journalism.

Similarly ironic is the persuasive power of objective journalism, which can be far more apt to change minds than journalism that is from a subjective point of view. In these highly polarized times, it would seem that advocacy journalism is where the power to persuade would lie, but advocates tend to attract those who already agree with them. It is eminently human to discount information that contradicts our existing beliefs, and both the right and the left have been very successful in turning that instinctive rejection of unwelcome facts into perceptions of bias. This has fueled the trend toward choosing a news source that in effect gives you news that bolsters rather than challenges. Would abandoning objectivity lift this environment of knee-jerk criticism? In a sense, a frankly liberal or conservative news report cannot be criticized effectively for not being fair to the other side of the argument. That is not the standard. Being released from the rigor and accountability that expectations of objectivity demand would be a welcome relief to many journalists who get clobbered from all sides by charges that they are not sufficiently "objective." It is tempting, certainly, to cede the objective standard as impossible simply because there is no way to satisfy a shared perception of what *is* objective, given so relentless a partisan divide.

In their political views, Americans run the gamut from far right to far left, but most of us are bunched at the center. It is with this group, which might be considered the persuadable middle, that objectivity is meaningful. Even bunched at the center, Americans tend to the right or the left, but they are not rigidly fixed in their views. This is the center that made Bill Clinton president twice, and then did the same for George W. Bush, because they were persuaded and then changed their minds and elected Barack Obama.

The power of objectivity is that, for this group, a change in reality can prompt a change in opinion. The war in Iraq was passionately supported and opposed by groups of people whose views never changed. But many Americans supported the war and then came to doubt it based not on advocacy but on what they perceived was a changed reality. Despite their suspicions of the press, they came to believe that the portrait of reality that was being painted by the nation's news media was closer to the truth than the one offered by the war's advocates. They were persuaded of something, not by arguments but by gritty reporting and facts that they decided to trust, which were put before them by news organizations that were rooted in the standard of objectivity. Critics from the right denounced the press for failing to report all the good and positive things that were happening in Iraq, and those on the left scathingly attacked the media for not being tough enough. Ultimately, public opinion about the war shifted because of the dangerous and expensive process of reporting, gathering facts, and presenting an account of what was happening that may not have been perfect truth, but was a practical, objective truth.

The public relations industry, which is booming, is built on this power to persuade using the news. Those who disparage objectivity, in a form of rhetorical jujitsu, denounce it for being so persuasive—but *misleadingly*. There are plenty of egregious examples of lazy and corrupt journalists who are manipulated by public relations people. But if journalists do their jobs, PR can function as a useful tool rather than a fifth column. As a reporter for the *New York Times*, I had frequent dealings with public relations professionals, and they were usually invaluable to me. Journalists tend to disparage PR people and sneer at them as "flacks," but that is disingenuous. Good and honorable public relations people facilitate good reporting, and the best ones know that their client's best interest lies in adherence to the truth. But one must never forget that public relations professionals have *clients*. Their job is to promote the interests and objectives of those clients. Like lawyers, they are advocates. Journalists have a different agenda—the best truth they can discover.

But the public relations industry does bear responsibility for a shameful practice that has become a standard of the industry. This is the VNR, or video news release, which is a stealth bomb of journalistic dishonesty. Not that the information in such VNRs isn't true; it is just not the whole truth. And they are usually crafted—at great expense—to look *just* like objective journalism. These are the video segments that are most frequently seen on local television news programs, often with an earnest, but unidentified, "doctor," stethoscope around his neck, speaking about a new drug of some kind. One of the staples each year around March, as the spring break swimsuit season draws near, seems to be a new pill or cream or treatment that the "doctor" says will eliminate cellulite. The last one I saw was introduced with the usual teaser by the familiar anchorman, saying something like,

"Spring break's coming, and doctors say there is a new way to get rid of that cellulite, quickly and easily." Then the VNR appeared, as though the hard-hitting news team had been out doing cellulite research and returned with this objective report.

VNRs got a particular black eye in 2004 when one was produced by the Bush administration to promote the new Medicare prescription drug benefit. The VNR was produced to look like objective reporting, complete with a closing line saying, "In Washington, I'm Karen Ryan reporting." The problem was that Karen Ryan was a PR rep, and she was reading a script provided by the U.S. Department of Health and Human Services. The "report" included President Bush receiving a standing ovation from a crowd on the day he signed the benefit into law, but there was no mention of the controversy swirling around it, and there were no critical voices. VNRs are constantly arriving at local television stations, and they are oh-so-tempting to use at a time when budgets are tight. They *look* like news, but they cost nothing. Local news professionals defend the use of them by saying that they are no more misleading than printed press releases, which is true.

Press releases, of whatever kind, are a legitimate way to advise the media of some development, but they are intended as a catalyst for further reporting, not as a substitute for it. PR professionals I know have told me how amazed they are at the frequency with which their press releases—printed or VNR—make it into the news barely changed. This *is* a subversion of objective journalism, but the answer is not to throw out objectivity. Rather the solution is to *insist* on genuine objectivity.

Of course, while Republicans and Democrats, blacks and whites, men and women, gays and straights, Christians and agnostics *say* they want objective news, they *perceive* objectivity in news very differently. This comes as no surprise in a country that is now sharply divided between red and blue, and where "media bias" is the clarion call of every identifiable group. The *objective* truth is that there *is* media bias of every sort. But I would argue that media bias is like the germs in one's body. They are always there, and they can be dangerous if they gain critical mass. But becoming germ-phobic can be paralyzing—suddenly, the inexorable presence of germs can overwhelm one's fundamental sense of safety and health. The distinction is between hypochondria and sensible monitoring of one's health. I believe that Americans are collectively suffering from a severe case of media-bias hypochondria, and are in danger of becoming like Howard Hughes, an intelligent and accomplished man whose germ-phobia made it impossible for him to shake hands and who lived the final years of his life in crippling isolation to avoid germ contamination.

The credibility of the traditional media has steadily declined in recent years, in part because of their own failings but even more so, to my mind because media bias has become the default response to any news that delivers an unwelcome message. The words "liberal media" have been invoked so often that for many the two words have become fused. And some on the liberal side of the political argument have learned to be similarly strident, using the anything-goes environment of the blogosphere to scorch those whose journalism displeases them. The reality for journalists now is that any article that stakes out the objective truth in a way that is perceived to favor one side over the other will prompt a reaction of abusive outrage. In my own experience, appearing on *The O'Reilly Factor* has always triggered an angry outpouring from some of his viewers. I once went on the show to argue that news organizations should cover terrorists' views so that we could better understand the people trying to kill us. I immediately got an e-mail from someone identified only as spookyooo1 which began, "You are just a piece of worthless primordial ooze slowly decaying in the light of reason," and went downhill from there into a page of apoplectic rage, climaxed with an imaginative spew of threats and curses. When I showed it to one of my university colleagues, he asked if I had contacted the police. I was shocked at his reaction, because for journalists this was par for the course.

If there is to be a final nail in the coffin of the objective news standard, it will most likely be something that journalists can do little about: passion sells. Opinionated journalism draws a crowd.

The fortunes of Lou Dobbs on cable news spiked after he began to infuse his newscasts with strident advocacy opposing amnesty for, as he always puts it, "illegal aliens." Dobbs's newscast is a mixture of ostensibly objective reporting and his own passionate opinions, which he maintains people have no difficulty separating. The thing that has attracted CNN's notice is the spike in ratings. In the world of commercial news, the form of news that draws the biggest audience is almost certain to carry the day. Opinion sells. And opinion is, relatively speaking, cheaper than news. Ranting makes entertaining TV, so expect a lot more of it.

Young news consumers seem to greatly prefer news in a format that is anything but objective. Indeed, they seem to find objectivity not only dull, but less credible than someone who is apparently speaking his or her own mind. It does not seem to matter that such opinionated pronouncements may be claptrap and based on nothing but shallow knowledge. The culture of the Web is one of individual voices, and a chorus of independent voices is regarded as the best way of, as buzzmachine's Jeff Jarvis said, "helping the public decide what is true." But I am not convinced. Ultimately, this may be because I know that opinion is a cheap way to create content, and reported news is costly. I have always believed that, for the most part, you get what you pay for.

So, where does this leave us on the subject of good journalism? There is a place for advocacy. It is important. But advocacy and journalism are different things, to my mind, and should be kept separate as a matter of professionalism. I want my news to be delivered by someone acting as an honest broker whose goal is the best possible truth. I accept that this is not ever going to be perfect, and that I may perceive bias at times. I welcome the fact that separate reporters, both seeking to be objective, can report the same story in somewhat different ways, albeit based on the same set of data and similar observations. There may be differences in what is observed, but what is reported should nonetheless reflect the discipline of verification. I want my news—my iron core news—to be reported with the intent of objectivity, and I want the story told as straight as editors and reporters can make it.

My sense is that most Americans want the same thing—that their news should be rooted in a verifiable reality that can be confirmed and that faithfully represents the ambiguity that reality usually includes. The national conversation is the means we have for interpreting and analyzing that core of objective news, and it is inherently subjective and opinionated. But if a fundamental confidence in the iron core disappears, if it is viewed as just another collection of facts assembled by someone with a political agenda, then one of the most important supports for our democracy will weaken, and the conversation may well become more of a cacophonous Tower of Babel.

# CHAPTER FIVE

# MEDIA ETHICS—THE PAINFUL BALANCE

*Draconian cutbacks in newsrooms and the speed of a multimedia news clock prompt the question: How can one "do ethics" in journalism while the world goes to hell in a handbasket?*
—Stephen Ward, James E. Burgess Professor of Journalism
Ethics, University of Wisconsin–Madison

IN THE SPRING OF 2003, THE MOST SPECTACULAR ethical scandal in the modern history of the *New York Times* virtually paralyzed American journalism. If any news organization is looked to as the standard, it is the *Times,* and for those of us who love the paper—as I do—this was a horrible failure in several respects. Jayson Blair, a 27-year-old reporter on the make, had managed to find a crease in the paper's editorial oversight and hidden out in it like a lizard in a crack. In four years at the *Times,* he had repeatedly had to publish corrections, which should have been a red flag. Sloppiness was only one of his professional crimes. In April, he got caught plagiarizing an article from the *San Antonio Express-News,* which finally triggered a thorough review of his work. It turned out he was a complete fraud as a reporter, lurking in his Brooklyn apartment instead of going on assignments and making up quotes and descriptions that were published as fact. The scandal was a punch in the eye to the *Times*'s reputation, which certainly got its attention. It is probably a good thing for an institution with the power of the *Times* to be publicly humbled from time to time, and the reforms that followed in the scandal's wake make it less likely to happen again. The *Times* did the right thing. It launched an exhaustive examination of Blair's work, conducting more than 150 interviews to try to set the record straight, and then published a warts-and-all account of how such a thing could have happened. This transparency restored the paper's honor, though the lapses in editorial oversight it revealed were mind-boggling.

But the mea culpa revealed something far more shocking to me than Jayson Blair's perfidy. There will always be charlatans and con men like Jayson Blair, though I think there aren't many in the top ranks of journalism. What appalled me far more was the small item buried deep in the narrative of Blair's crimes that described how he had made up colorful details to add spice to his article about the family of PFC Jessica Lynch, who had been captured in combat in Iraq and then rescued, turning her into a reluctant heroine. In an article that carried a dateline of Palestine, West Virginia—meaning that the reporter had been there—Blair wrote about how Private Lynch's father "choked up as he stood on his porch here overlooking the tobacco fields and cattle pastures." There was no tobacco field or cow pasture. He wrote that the Lynch family had a long history of military service, which was another fabrication. He wrote that they lived on a hilltop. They live in a valley. There were other blatant falsehoods. Blair, of course, had never been to Palestine at all. He just made it up.

Bad as that was, even worse to me was the family's statement that when they saw the article, they "were joking" about the obvious fabrications. They weren't really angry. They didn't even bother to call the *Times* and complain or ask how a reporter could make such things up. Later, when they were asked why they hadn't done anything, they said they assumed that was just how journalism worked these days—including at the *New York Times*. That is what a lot of people seem to think.

The irony is that journalism is an exercise in applied morality. Ethics is at the heart of virtually every journalistic decision, or should be. No profession does more to own up publicly to its ethical lapses than the battered corps of traditional journalists, especially newspaper journalists. Traditional journalism in the past several decades has followed the bruising code that errors should be corrected publicly and that readers and viewers are owed an explanation of what happened and why. It is a moral stance that has won them the trust of some, but has also cost them deeply in public esteem and confidence, reinforcing the image of the press as error-riddled. In a further irony, because newspapers do so much more reporting on more difficult subjects than television, they also do more correcting and may be perceived as less reliable. It is newspapers that are most apt to offer a humiliating public account of their sins when they are detected.

This kind of rigorous journalism ethics is very much at risk as news organizations move rapidly toward the more elastic standards of tabloid journalism and nonobjective news coverage.

The notion that the Web's millions of readers make it self-correcting is, to my mind, a very uncertain premise, in that most of what appears on the Web is framed as opinion. Even when factual errors are revised by the Web's self-correction mechanism, the error continues to exist right along with the correction. Anyone doubting the persistence of a damaging inaccuracy need only have the experience of trying to set the online record straight. The very notion that there is an objective truth seems to be losing traction along with accountability news itself.

Further complicating the ethical challenge to news is the culture of speed that the Web imposes on news gathering. When I was a reporter at the *Times* in the 1980s, I needed to provide a summary of my story for the next day's paper at 2 P.M., but nothing was published until the paper's first edition went to press at 10 P.M. More often than not, the afternoon "summary" was off the mark, both as to what happened and why. It was a placeholder, not considered to be *Times*-quality reporting. That came after hours of checking and talking and checking again. In today's environment, *Times* reporters are expected to file articles and updates to the www.nytimes.com Web site several times a day. And some thing go out that shouldn't. This is true at even the best news organizations, and it is not unethical reporting but unverified reporting. The result, however, is the same lack of accuracy and truth that journalism ethics is intended to prevent. To understand the impact on ethics of losing the news, it is important to have a grasp of what journalists consider ethics to be, and how they deal with the often confounding dilemmas their ethics code forces upon them. It is important that they continue to wrestle with these problems, but engagement with ethics is in jeopardy along with traditional news.

There is a painful wisdom about ethics in the exchange in *My Fair Lady* among Henry Higgins, Colonel Pickering, and Alfie Doolittle, a Cockney dustman. Doolittle has come to wheedle some money out of Professor Higgins, who is an expert linguist and has taken Doolittle's daughter Eliza into his home to teach her proper English. Also present is Colonel Pickering, Higgins's friend and fellow linguist. As Doolittle sees it, if Eliza is of interest to Higgins and Pickering, then Doolittle should make a few pounds out of it. His shamelessness fascinates them.

"Have you no morals, man?" says Pickering.

Doolittle shakes his head self-pityingly and replies, "Can't afford them, governor. Neither could you if you was as poor as me."

The uncomfortable message here for journalism ethics is that economic prosperity and commercial strength are the bulwarks that make it possible for news organizations to "afford" strong ethical standards. As a news organization, it is easier to withstand the temptation not to publish something that will offend an advertiser if there are plenty of other advertisers. If you have watched your advertising fall off a cliff, the ethical equation may look different. A strongly profitable enterprise can afford to be bolder in its coverage than a news organization that could be put out of business by an expensive libel suit or a boycott. In an atmosphere of intense competition, the niceties of moral rectitude tend to get brushed aside—something that applies equally to political campaigns and to the media environment. Similarly, a journalist who is fearful that he can't get another job is in a weaker position to refuse to do something ethically questionable than one who can quit on principle and be reasonably sure of being hired by someone else.

In a sense, we are returning to the pre–ethics code days of American journalism. Ethics codes began when commercial success made them, as Doolittle would say, affordable. In the 19th and early 20th centuries, journalists typically took money to write favorable stories, and the concept of a conflict of interest was laughable. Reporters were usually paid badly, had little education, and were looked on as a raffish and unscrupulous brotherhood. Journalists worked in an atmosphere of dog-eat-dog competition, and bribing sources to get the jump on sensational scoops was a part of the game.

But as newspapers became more prosperous, they also became more respectable. Objective news needed to be reliable and accurate if it was to be a commodity that would sustain an enduring business. Journalists began to crave professional respect as well. Colleges were beginning to offer courses in journalism, and in the idealism of the academy, journalism began to be taken as something serious. In 1909, Sigma Delta Chi, a journalism fraternity intended for students and professionals, was organized at DePauw University in Greencastle, Indiana, and began to spread to universities all over the nation, changing its name to the Society of Professional Journalists in 1973; it is the nation's largest and broadest journalistic organization. Ethics is a staple of the Society's sense of mission, and its ethics code is generally regarded as the mainstream journalistic standard. Some bloggers who aspire to be viewed as journalists have publicly embraced the code. Last revised in 1996, the Society's Code of Ethics begins with the brilliantly succinct definition of the journalistic mission, "Seek truth and report it." The Society's Code then goes on to describe a list of things ethical journalists should and should not do: they should "test the accuracy of information," "identify sources whenever feasible," and "distinguish between advocacy and news reporting." On the Society's Web site (www.spj.org) the code is available in a dozen languages, and other journalistic codes of ethics are also linked.

A slightly different way of framing journalism's ethical demands was distilled in *The Elements of Journalism*. After conducting interviews with scores of respected journalists, the coauthors created a list of principles that they found were widely shared. What separates these principles from an ethics code is that I consider them to be universal rather than a matter of national custom, or type of media. They are the principles embraced by journalists I respect, even if they are unable to put them fully into practice. Some journalists must do their work in nations that restrict a free press, and this standard may not be achievable in certain cultures or societies. But journalism that does not aspire to these standards is, to my mind, not really journalism, but more a tool for powerful forces or a vehicle for propaganda. As such, they may be said to represent the ethical core.

The principles are premised on the belief that, as Kovach and Rosenstiel put it, "the purpose of journalism is to provide people with the information they need to be free and self-governing." To fulfill this task, they list ten beliefs that journalists share. I shall only list the first three:

1. Journalism's first obligation is to the truth.
2. Its first loyalty is to citizens.
3. Its essence is a discipline of verification.

They go on with others, such as that journalists must be independent from those they cover, but they do not include concepts such as "fairness" and "balance" that are part of many codes of ethics. Such codes reflect the values and varying standards of the news organization and the nation where the organization operates. But what Kovach and Rosenstiel are trying to show is something that goes deeper and should ideally apply to all who consider themselves to be journalists.

The first *obligation* is to truth. Finding truth is a universal journalistic responsibility. It is not a goal, but a duty.

A journalist's *first loyalty* is to citizens. This means that the first loyalty is not to the boss or the owner or to the government, but to the citizens who are the consumers of that journalism.

And journalism's *essence* is a *discipline* of verification. To consider your work to be journalism, it must be subjected to the *discipline of verification.*

It would not be an overstatement to say that the concept of a first loyalty to citizens and a discipline of verification are the two core concepts that are most in jeopardy as the nation's news industry faces tumultuous change. The wide-open mindset of the Web makes its news culture one that resembles the supermarket tabloids more than the *New York Times.* And a frenzied, competitive environment makes a first loyalty to citizens something that is eroding before our eyes as the first loyalty increasingly becomes one devoted to anything that will bring readers or viewers or hits on the Web site.

The principles described by Kovach and Rosenstiel inspire journalists throughout the world. This is especially true in developing nations, where pursuing such standards takes not only a commitment to ethics but real courage. In these dangerous places, the best journalists are sometimes willing to risk their lives for principles that American journalism seems to find increasingly unaffordable. I believe that these standards are America's greatest contribution to journalism, and losing them would be our greatest failure.

I once pressed Bob Woodward and Carl Bernstein, who kept secret the identity of Deep Throat for over 30 years, on whether either would ever give up a source promised anonymity. We were on a panel marking the anniversary of President Nixon's resignation in the wake of Watergate. They said absolutely not. If ordered to do so by the court, they would choose to go to jail. Journalists consider this defiance of the law to be honorable, and so do I.

But, I asked, what if you knew that because you would not betray that pledge of confidentiality, an innocent person would go to jail? Or even be executed? They said they would do everything in their power to persuade the source to release them. "I would get down on my knees and beg him," said Woodward, which is an arresting notion. But I pressed them. Would they, if begging didn't help, at the end of the day break their promise? They declined to say. Finding the correct answer to such dilemmas is what makes journalism so ethically fraught and sometimes confounding.

There is virtually no journalistic decision in which ethics are not embedded. Everything from what quote to use to whether to go to jail to protect a source is rooted in judgments that are inherently ethical ones. Authentic objectivity depends on an ethical application of judgments about where the truth lies. It is ethics that keep at bay the rationalizations that tempt one to leave out inconvenient facts or dissenting voices. It is an ethical decision when one is choosing how to begin a story, what to emphasize, and what quote to put first. While the craft of journalism commands that a story be structured to attract and hold attention, it is an ethical decision whether or not to include a particularly tasty tidbit of juicy gossip for the sake of "edginess."

Or, for instance, what if a zealous judge imposed crippling fines for contempt because you would not divulge the identity of a source, and you or your news organization were threatened with bankruptcy? Does that change things? Would the ethical—and correct—choice be to let your news organization take a devastating financial hit or even die, or to break your word and comply with the court's order? This is an increasingly prevalent choice, given the enthusiasm of prosecutors for subpoenaing journalists and forcing them to choose between jail and breaking confidences.

More is at stake than honor. A willingness to talk to journalists in confidence depends on a faith that the journalist will keep that confidence. And many of the most critically important pieces of watchdog journalism depend on such anonymous sources. Without Deep Throat, could there have been the *Washington Post*'s Watergate stories? He was not the source, but he did provide the confirmation that gave the newspaper a strong sense that it had the story right. Similarly, the Pentagon Papers came from a source who demanded confidentiality. While anonymous sources may be overused, they are absolutely essential in certain circumstances, and failing to honor the promise to protect a source is a betrayal. Widespread breach of those promises would be crippling journalistically, as sources would no longer trust reporters.

I have long been struck by the peculiar morality of the journalistic position on divulging sources that have been promised anonymity. One of the other tenets of journalism is that you don't break the law to do your job. You don't break into an office and rifle a filing cabinet for incriminating papers, although it is ethically permissible for journalists to accept papers that someone else has broken into a filing cabinet to get. This may seem not very convincing ethically, but the point is that the journalist is not breaking the law. If someone else does so, that is a matter for their conscience.

But journalists treat as heroes those who break the law by defying judges who command them to divulge sources. Lawyers have the privilege of having their communications with their clients kept secret, but when upon occasion they are ordered by a judge to divulge such secret information, they never announce that their personal honor will not permit such a betrayal. That is, essentially, the posture of journalists—that it would be a personal betrayal, a breach of the journalist's honor, to betray the confidence. When people sneer that journalists have no morals, I think of all those journalists who have elected to go to jail for their principles and shake my head.

But it is also true that under certain extraordinary circumstances, such as the one put to Woodward and Bernstein, a promise of confidentiality may have to be breached as the lesser evil.

This dilemma of conflicting claims on honor lies at the heart of the worst ethical problems in journalism. Usually, when something goes wrong in journalism it is not because the moral path is unclear, but because of the temptation to yield to self-interest or laziness or prejudice or corruption. In the case of Jayson Blair, the ethical breach was sharp and obvious. That was an easy one. Similarly, a reporter at a news organization that claims objectivity who intentionally writes slanted stories should be fired.

But far more difficult are situations in which there are two conflicting value systems, each with a valid claim to being the ethical choice. I was editor of the *Greeneville Sun* when I ran head-on into a situation in which my principles were at best an uncertain guide to proper behavior. It was one of the worst experiences of my life.

There is a federal court in Greenville, and one day I learned from our court reporter that he had been tipped off by a confidential source that the grand jury was considering bringing charges of cocaine trafficking against an assistant district attorney who was a well-known local man. This was sensational news, but I was troubled. Grand jury proceedings are intended to be secret because they investigate many possible crimes but don't actually charge people a good proportion of the time. If someone is identified in a newspaper as being the target of a grand jury investigation, his reputation is forever tainted, whether or not he is ever charged. This was the essential plot line of a movie, *Absence of Malice,* in which an unscrupulous government official leaked the name of a liquor wholesaler whose father was a gangster as being the possible target of a government probe into racketeering. The manipulated reporter, played by Sally Field, triumphantly wrote an article based on anonymous sources, and the liquor wholesaler — Paul Newman—was duly, and unfairly, humiliated in the paper. The film's point of view painted the government official as the villain and the reporter as ambitious and indifferent to the potential damage that might be done. Her editor, who pushed publishing the story, came off as callous and interested only in the splash it would make. Paul Newman was the good guy, victimized by the press. The moral point was that the newspaper should have waited until there was something official, a delay that would have spared an innocent man, but sacrificed the journalistic coup. If the investigation had gone forward, there would still have been the opportunity to report it—but not as an exclusive scoop. It is worth mentioning that the screenplay was written by an experienced journalist who knew how treacherous this terrain can be.

I felt that I was in that same situation. In my case, I knew that my reporter's sources were good, and I believed the information accurate. But did I want to take the step, before the grand jury acted, of taking away this man's reputation by publishing a story? I had no reason to believe that the grand jury was corrupt or that it would not do its job properly. I believed that, in due course, the man would be indicted—which would be a front-page story—or he would not be indicted, in which case there would be no story at all. And so I ruled that we would not report what we knew through the anonymous source and would wait for the grand jury to act.

The newspaper in a neighboring town, whose reporter had also been leaked the information, decided differently. It trumpeted the grand jury's inquiry with screaming headlines. That put the ball back in our court. Would we now make a different decision because a rival newspaper had broken the story? Did the principle on which I had decided not to publish no longer apply? I decided that we would stick to our guns on principle. We would not publish the story and would wait on the grand jury to act.

The rival paper viewed this behavior on our part as a golden opportunity to discredit us and add to its circulation at our expense. It began publishing stories day after day about what the grand jury was doing. We still didn't abandon our stand. Then it started sending boys to hawk its paper on the streets of our town, something no one had seen in many years. I wrote a front-page editorial explaining why we were not telling what we knew about the grand jury, and what we were waiting for. But the grand jury proceedings dragged on, and soon my town seemed to lose its mind.

The *Greeneville Sun* is in many ways the kind of hometown paper that exists mainly as a nostalgic fantasy. My father, the publisher, has his name in the phone book, and our family had owned the paper since early in the century. We prided ourselves on having the highest "penetration" of any newspaper in the state, which meant that more households in our town subscribed to their local paper on a percentage basis than in any other community in Tennessee. Our citizens showed their approval and their need for us by subscribing, and we felt a bond of trust existed between the town and its newspaper.

But in this situation, with a rival trumpeting sensational drug crime news and the hometown paper silent, that trust began to crack. The issue started to be not so much what the grand jury was doing, but why won't the *Sun* tell us what's going on? The word "cover-up" began to be noised about. *Sun* employees would come to me with stories about being accosted by friends and accused of hiding the truth. There was a kind of madness afoot, fanned into near hysteria by radio ads paid for by the rival paper that effectively called the *Sun* derelict in its duty to report the news.

As our town went crazy with suspicion and paranoia, I had to decide whether we should now tell what we knew. We knew all of it, as our reporter was getting the same leaks as the opposition. Again, with the town in an uproar, I decided not to print the story on the premise that we were so far out on a principled limb that it was all we had to support us. If we sawed off our principle, we would have nothing.

It got even worse. At one point the rival paper sent us a letter to the editor from one of its readers asserting that the *Sun's* silence was because my father was himself behind cocaine trafficking in our county. We were given 24 hours to respond. In a sense it is unfortunate that the letter did not get published, because our libel suit would have most likely made us owners of the other paper, but it decided not to print the letter when the writer's sister pleaded that he had just been released from a mental institution.

While all this was happening, we were not paralyzed. We were reporting based on our own on-the-record inquiry about local drug trafficking, and we unearthed some interesting material. The sheriff talked to us, and I deputized a local woman from Colombia as a reporter to help us find out from that end about the local cocaine trade. She made calls from my office and relayed my questions in Spanish. But what we continued not to do was name a local assistant district attorney who was under investigation, by now a name that everyone knew.

Finally, mercifully, the grand jury did act, indicting the man. The news broke at midmorning. We are an afternoon paper with a 1 P.M. deadline, but that day we held the presses until nearly 4 P.M. to be first with an exhaustive account that went for pages.

Our rival, as a morning paper, got scooped this time. As suddenly as the tornado had touched down, it seemed to disappear, and the paper seemed to be restored to its place of trust. The rival made no enduring incursions into our readership, and it was as though it had all been a bad dream. A very bad dream.

A few readers wrote saluting us for keeping our heads in such a maelstrom and said that they were proud of our principled stance. But after seeing what can happen to a town, I am not at all certain that I did the right thing. I think, perhaps, that I should have recognized that you are not actually protecting a reputation if the name is being blasted in headlines by a rival newspaper. I did not want to be first, but once the story was out, I think probably we should have told what we knew.

This is not a perfect solution, in that it puts another news organization with different principles in a position to decide what we would publish. With the Web, this demon has escaped from the box in ways that make not publishing something on principle largely a futile exercise. The most disturbing lesson for me in this experience was to see what happens in a news vacuum. The paranoia and suspicion that are born when people feel they are being denied information is frightening to watch. Trust vanishes quickly, and is replaced by anger and fear and suspicion. Our reason for not publishing was too abstract to be meaningful to people who saw the story somewhere else.

In an environment of blogging and cable news and tabloid journalism of all kinds, competitive pressure and public expectation make it extremely difficult not to publish when a competitor has taken the first step. Such is the power of Matt Drudge, who started the Monica Lewinsky scandal before the reporters at *Newsweek* had decided to publish. When Drudge acted, *Newsweek* could not wait. And no matter how much tut-tutting was done about the propriety or importance of the story, news organizations all over the world reported it endlessly.

So how should journalists approach ethical issues? You begin by recognizing that virtually every journalistic decision has an ethical component. Even the most seemingly banal article can be a minefield of ethical choices if you are willing to recognize them. As a young reporter, I spent a lot of my time attending meetings of the local county council, which was the governing body. The council was fraught with politics and personal rivalry. One group of councilmen—and they were all men—came from "across the creek," meaning that they represented an area that included the smaller of the county's two communities, which were bitter rivals. In some cases, the individual councilmen were just ornery by nature and loved putting a thumb in one another's eye. They mainly had power to decide how money should be spent, which was always in dispute. One especially contentious issue was the battle over what roads would be fixed and in what priority, with outraged delegations regularly appearing to denounce the whole bunch as unfairly discriminating against one part of the county or the other.

In that little world, my articles about those meetings were important. I liked some of the councilmen better than others, and I had my own views on what was wise and what was foolish. Usually, I felt I knew more about what was afoot than had been revealed in open session at the meeting. My conscious goal was to tell it straight, to be fair, and to also be revealing. And so I came up with a method of reporting these meetings that my editor didn't like, but which I thought accomplished that mission better than simply picking one of the many subjects raised at the meeting and leading with that, with everything else buried far down the column of news.

I would, instead, pick four or five of the most important things that had happened and summarize them in boldface bullets at the top of the article. I thought I was telling readers that if any one of these was of concern, just look below. Then, in an order of importance that I subjectively determined, I wrote about each topic. I never lost awareness that the choice of a quote or of a characterization or of emphasis was a judgment that I was making. My ethical stance was that I was making these choices not to push an agenda but to tell as much of the truth as I could. That is all an objective journalist can do—make decisions on the basis of an honest judgment scoured as much as possible of prejudice.

Inevitably, there are choices—ethical choices—that are also news decisions. Do you highlight a sensational incident, such as a councilman publicly insulting one of his fellow councilmen, or do you highlight something of more importance, but with far less sex appeal as a news item? If you lead with the insult, you have a good chance of grabbing the attention of more readers, who may stick around for the more important stuff. If you go with the important stuff and minimize the insult, are you being a responsible journalist or sweeping under the rug the internal tension on the council that perhaps is as important as anything else? These are decisions that can be defended either way, and honorable journalists can decide them differently. But in the current era of hyperpartisanship, this kind of decision making by journalists is automatically assumed to be infused with political bias rather than simply taken as a news judgment with which you may or may not agree.

I worked for nine years at the *New York Times,* and I get a lot of bashing from people who view the *Times* as an organ of the devil. A Republican friend of mine once called me to deliver a scorching denunciation of the *Times* for putting pictures on the front page of President George W. Bush trying to open the wrong door after a press conference on a visit to China. The president strode to what was apparently a faux door, pulled a couple of times on the handle, made a goofy grimace when it didn't open, and exited another way. "It was pure bias," my friend declared, "to put that picture on the front page, and it proves—as if it needed proving—that the *Times* is biased in its coverage of Bush."

There is no question that the *Times* was critical of President Bush on its editorial pages and published stories that have angered and embarrassed the Bush administration. But was this an example of *Times* bias? It could have been. It could be that the editors laughed at the president's hapless moment and thought that this would be a chance to show him in a bad light. That's certainly what my friend thinks. But I think that the decision was not driven by bias, or at least not political bias. First of all, presidential trips to China are scripted to the second and utterly without spontaneity. This was the only unscripted moment in the trip, and as such gave a breath of reality that two heads of state standing solemnly at lecterns does not deliver.

But there is an even more compelling argument that this was not anti-Bush bias. Would the *Times* have published the same pictures if the president had been Clinton? Or Gore? Or Obama? Without question! I have absolutely no doubt that the bias, if there is any, is not against a Republican, but against any president in such a situation. A humorous, human, and—yes—somewhat embarrassing moment is a slam dunk, not because of the party but because of the presidency. This may be a bad thing, but it is at least fair in that it applies to both parties. And that isn't bias. Questionable news judgment? Perhaps. But not political bias.

The default priority for journalists is to make known as much truth as they can learn. Tell the people what you know. So, under the ethical guidance of journalistic professionalism, the honorable decision is usually to put it out there, whatever it is, if it has news value.

But journalists are also citizens, with obligations under the law and loyalties to the country that come with citizenship. And, in a third role, journalists are human beings, which carries an ethical stance distinct from that of the professional or the citizen. The point is that journalists must juggle all three roles: professional, citizen, and human being, with professional getting the nod under most circumstances. This is the same for lawyers, soldiers, and—in many ways—for everyone. There is a professional code, and it is usually within that set of ethical principles that proper decisions can be made. But it doesn't always work that way. The most difficult newsroom ethical decisions come when these three roles are in conflict with each other, with each making its separate demands. The key decision is often a matter of deciding which of the three roles takes precedence—which can sometimes be easy, and sometimes horribly difficult.

For instance, imagine a reporter out covering a fire who is suddenly confronted with a person whose clothes are burning. Does he observe and take notes on efforts to rescue the person?

The journalistic professional code dictates that journalists should report the news objectively and dispassionately, and not get personally involved. But in such a situation, the call of a fellow human being in great jeopardy would clearly prevail. Who could doubt that the journalist should throw down his pad and grab a blanket to help put out the burning clothes? This is a case in which the decision clearly belongs in the domain of the human, and the journalistic code is trumped.

One of the most observed conventions in American journalism is the practice by most news organizations of not identifying those who accuse someone of rape. The thinking, as I have understood it, is that the crime is so personally terrible that to publish the rape victim's name would be a further brutalization on an innocent party. In most states, there is no law against publishing the name. The name is part of police records that are open to the public. But very seldom is the name published, out of human considerations. There is a counterargument, however, that says that this is a violation of the principle of treating everyone alike. The name of the accused is routinely published, and there are plenty of instances when someone has been wrongfully accused, but damaged nonetheless by public disgrace in a newspaper.

One of the clearest examples of this tension between journalistic professionalism and human empathy came to my attention through the anguish of one of my former students. Hadley Pawlak was one of my very best students and had been a reporter for a midsized newspaper for only a short time when she called me in great distress. She had been sent by her editor to do a feature on a teenaged girl who had rescued herself from a troubled adolescence by becoming a boxer. It was a real-life version of the Oscar-winning film *Million Dollar Baby*. Hadley was only a few years older than the young boxer, and the girl, who had no experience with the press, immediately began to confide as though speaking to a trusted older sister. She told not only about her efforts to escape from a dysfunctional family by boxing, but also about various crimes and acts of vandalism that she had not been caught committing. There was no reportorial subterfuge. The young woman knew she was being interviewed for a news story and spoke into a tape recorder while Hadley took notes. But her vulnerability and ignorance of journalism were apparent as she spoke.

Hadley called me to talk about what she should do. She knew that the sensational information that had been freely offered would make the story more powerful. She thought that her editor, whom she had not told, would probably want to include it, as there had been no effort to deceive or trick. If the journalistic standard was to "seek truth and report it," then the information should be reported. Yet Hadley felt strongly that the other standard—the human standard—was in play and, in this case, it should prevail. The incidents of lawbreaking were not key to understanding this girl. That she had been arrested for other such things was in the piece. But publishing the new revelations would almost certainly get the young girl in fresh trouble with the police and tarnish, if not destroy, the fragile esteem that boxing had won her. Hadley's decision was that the human trumped the professional in this case. She left it out, and didn't tell her editor. I was very proud of her. This same reporter later did some tough and enterprising reporting for the Associated Press, and I would trust her ethical standards at any time.

One of the biggest talents a journalist can have is the ability to coax sources to reveal themselves. I came to know Carol Bradley when she had just graduated from the journalism program at the University of Tennessee. She was pretty and polite, looked younger than her years, and was one of the best reporters I've ever known, in part because the state legislators and other powerful figures she covered thought that being pretty and sweet was all there was to her. She was also tough and relentless, and could extract the most astonishing information from officials who later could not believe that this nice young woman would be so mean as to report what they said and did. She went on to become a Nieman Fellow at Harvard. The ability to get people to open up is one of a good reporter's greatest skills, and if used responsibly it can open doors to truth as journalism is supposed to do. But it is ethics that keep that ability from being a shabby trick.

Perhaps the most potent lambasting of the whole concept of an ethical journalist came from one of our most esteemed journalists, Janet Malcolm of the *New Yorker*. I was sitting at my desk in the newsroom of the *Times* in March 1989 when someone asked if I had seen Malcolm's article in that week's *New Yorker* about Joe McGinniss and Jeffrey MacDonald. The article was called "The Journalist and the Murderer," and it examined in close detail the relationship between McGinniss, a well-known journalist, and MacDonald, an accused murderer who had agreed to allow McGinniss intimate access to him and his defense team during his trial. McGinniss had decided midway through the trial that MacDonald was guilty, but had not let MacDonald know. The article by Malcolm, who was and remains one of the journalists whose work I always read because of its intelligence, elegance, and ruthless detachment, was an evisceration of McGinniss on ethical grounds for misleading MacDonald in order to preserve the access essential to his book.

The bombshell in her article was the first paragraph, which I wish to quote because it needs to be swallowed whole. She began her article:

> Every journalist who is not too stupid or too full of himself to notice what is going on knows that what he does is morally indefensible. He is a kind of confidence man, preying on people's vanity, ignorance, or loneliness, gaining their trust and betraying them without remorse. Like the credulous widow who wakes up one day to find the charming young man and all her savings gone, so the consenting subject of a piece of nonfiction writing learns—when the article or book appears—*his* hard lesson. Journalists justify their treachery in various ways according to their temperaments. The more pompous talk about freedom of speech and "the public's right to know"; the least talented talk about Art; the seemliest murmur about earning a living.

I felt like I'd been morally mugged and I was instantly livid. *"Bullshit!"* I remember bellowing. *"What arrogance! What condescension! What absolute bullshit!"* I stormed and raged and kicked the trashcan across the newsroom. But as I stormed and thundered, it was impossible to avoid the unhappy thought that I was protesting too much, that I too was a hypocrite. It was impossible to escape the cold awareness that there was some uncomfortable truth in what Malcolm had said. I had sat in Barry Bingham Sr.'s office in Louisville and encouraged him to open his heart to me so that I could lay his family's story before the readers of the *Times*. When he had spoken about the culture of silence and avoidance in the family, I recognized it as a revelation of something intensely private. And I had also seen it as a nugget of journalist gold, a piece of rare, illuminating candor. I did pride myself on an ability to get people to "open up." Journalists do not declare their intentions to sources, nor do they interrupt an interview to tell a source that he has just said something incredibly incriminating or revealing. Despite the smile on a reporter's face, the skill of interviewing is to gather evidence like a canny district attorney. It is undeniable that between honorable and dishonorable journalism is a murky no-man's-land of moral ambiguity.

That day back in 1989, I felt that Janet Malcolm had robbed me of an unquestioning moral assurance that I had not even realized was inside me. I realized that I equated journalism, done properly, with acting on behalf of the people's right to know, the attitude singled out for ridicule by Malcolm. Thanks to her, I began to grasp that my idealized journalism is actually something far more complex. Journalism is essential to our democracy, but can also do great damage. It can be inspiring and it can be corrupt or, more often, shallow. I came to see that there are many flavors of journalism, practiced by journalists who are inevitably human. Journalism is not morally indefensible. But it is always morally vulnerable, which is why standards are essential.

I find the most difficult of all ethical dilemmas to be when the journalistic ethic comes in conflict with the demands of citizenship, and none are thornier than those involving genuine secrets and other sensitive information that might do great damage if published. Contrary to what some may believe, such information is routinely *not* reported by the news media because, though under the journalist's code the information cries out to be published, the obligations of citizenship are judged more important. Traditional news organizations have long histories of keeping this balance and honoring a responsibility to consult the proper authorities before publishing. In any serious case, it would be unthinkable for the government not to be notified before something potentially sensitive is published, and frequently there are requests to postpone the article or to kill it. It is in this situation that the issue becomes a dicey one in ethical terms.

If the information is a damaging secret, it is legitimate for the government to ask that it not be published. But if the information is also very important for the public to know, there is a compelling reason to publish. So which gets priority? The *New York Times* decision to publish its article on domestic eavesdropping is a case in point. The administration felt so strongly that the *Times* should not publish that the publisher and top editor were summoned to the White House, where the president made a personal appeal. But the decision by the *Times* was that the government's engaging in domestic phone tapping without warrants could—and should—be reported without betraying vital secrets. In that case, the *Times* compromised, which is often what happens. Some information was not reported, out of deference to citizenship obligations. But the existence of the spying program was recognized properly as extremely important news and given page one treatment.

Would my friend who sees much bias against Bush in the *Times* agree with the decision to publish it? And if he did not agree that the *Times* was correct, would he view the decision as a mistaken news judgment or a calculated effort to damage Bush? Almost certainly the latter. Much was made of the fact that the *Times* published the story at the same time as the Iraq elections, and the presumption on Republican blogs was that it was done to diminish a Bush triumph.

Ethics has become part of the battle about media bias, with accusations of bias floated immediately when something appears that seems to favor the opposition. Sometimes the complainers are correct that the news story or the headline were unfair or in some other way flawed, and sometimes there is an honest difference about how a story should have been presented. But many people these days automatically assume that the reason for anything they don't like or agree with is bias. The prospect of human error and simple flawed judgment is no longer entertained as a plausible explanation; instead, everything is assumed to be calculated and therefore an expression of bias. The flawed but honest broker of news has disappeared in the minds of many, replaced by a conviction that any unwelcome media decision is rooted in prejudice.

When politics is being covered, accusations of bias fly like bullets. This was on bitter display when the *Los Angeles Times* published a report about Arnold Schwarzenegger's history of groping women five days before the election that made him governor of California. The paper was accused of bias, of course. But John Carroll, the editor, defended the story as both thoroughly reported and important. Bill O'Reilly denounced the paper as a liberal tool and returned again and again to attack Carroll personally as a radical leftist. Carroll, in fact, is the kind of editor who once sent a memo to his staff cautioning them to be fair and balanced in their coverage of the abortion issue.

Ultimately, a journalist must bring both judgment and integrity to ethical decision making and, indeed, all journalistic decisions. And both must be present to work properly. A severe tilt toward principle without good judgment can lead to a decision such as I made about the assistant district attorney after the other paper identified him. That was made on the basis of integrity, but the judgment on display was questionable. Indeed, a perceived integrity without good judgment can even lead a journalist to do something genuinely corrupt and illegal. An example of this was Michael Gallagher, a respected investigative reporter at the *Cincinnati Enquirer,* who with a colleague spent a year probing the practices of Chiquita Brands International. He found plenty of examples of corporate abuse of workers and other unsavory things. But in the course of his investigation he got access to the codes that would allow him to tap into the company's voice mail system. He could not resist prying open that tempting door and, sure enough, he found all kinds of incriminating things. But he was also breaking the law. He persuaded himself he was in pursuit of a bad guy, and he invaded the voice mail scores of times.

When the investigative series appeared, the meat and potatoes consisted of material unearthed by hard-nosed, shoe-leather reporting. But the most sensational and titillating bits were verbatim quotes from company officials that could have come only from voice mails. The truth quickly came out, and under pressure from Chiquita, the Gannett Company, owner of the *Enquirer*, renounced the entire series, removing it from the paper's Web site. They also paid a multimillion-dollar settlement and issued an abject apology. The reporter was charged with a crime, and his career was over. He had, in a sense, integrity. He told himself that he had done it to expose what he thought was an abusive company. But his judgment was so horribly flawed that he destroyed not only himself but all the legitimate work that he and others had done.

Similarly, an extreme of shrewd, self-interested judgment without integrity can lead to what we see more and more of in tabloid news. If the only consideration is profit or advancement or drawing a crowd, decisions can be made that are as wrong as the ones the *Enquirer* reporter made. If news organizations tilt to expediency for the sake of profits, the result will be a corruption of traditional news values that could be as damaging as an overtly criminal act like breaking into voice mails. As traditional news organizations edge away from their social obligation to do "accountability" news toward something that is decidedly more tabloid, they are, of course, also adopting the priorities and standards of tabloid journalism.

At the heart of the future of journalism ethics will be the people who own and control the nation's news organizations, and their ethical standards can be as courageous as those of the bravest war correspondent. One of my favorite stories, one that is emblematic of the difference a principled publisher can make, was told to me by the late David Halberstam, one of the nation's most admired journalists, who was among the reporters who first began reporting the real situation in Vietnam, much to the fury of then President Kennedy.

In 1963, Arthur Ochs "Punch" Sulzberger had just become publisher of the *Times* when he was summoned to the White House by President Kennedy. Nervous and untested, Punch didn't know what to expect and was rocked back on his heels when Kennedy immediately began to pressure him to remove Halberstam from his post in Vietnam. Punch's instinctive reaction was not only to keep Halberstam in place, but to cancel the reporter's scheduled vacation lest the president think he had caved in to pressure. Covering the story in those days wasn't easy. "The war didn't work," Halberstam said. "The evidence of that was all around us, but the hard part was not being a reporter. The hard part was being the publisher of people like me." Punch's support for his reporters inspired other publishers to do the same.

Some 30 years after the 1963 incident, the *New Yorker* gathered the reporters who had been based in Saigon during that earlier time to celebrate their journalistic guts. Five of them went out to dinner at Elio's, an Italian restaurant on the Upper East Side of Manhattan that is a favorite of journalists. Along with Halberstam were Neil Sheehan, also of the *Times*, and Mal Browne, Peter Arnett, and Horst Faas of the Associated Press. All had won Pulitzers for their coverage of Vietnam. As they settled in to tell war stories, someone noticed that sitting across the room with a group of people was Punch. "Because we couldn't have done it without him, we did what reporters have always wanted to do for publishers," recalled Halberstam. "We sent him and his table a bottle of Dom Perignon."

# CHAPTER SIX

# THE CURIOUS STORY OF NEWS

*For centuries, the idea of free and open public communication about matters of political importance did not appeal to the great and powerful. Francis Bacon's equation, "Knowledge is power," may be read not simply as an endorsement of knowledge, but also as a warning about its perils.*

—Paul Starr, *The Creation of the Media*

THE HISTORY OF NEWS IS STUDDED WITH UNLIKELY moments that proved pivotal and outlandish characters who changed everything. There was no stranger moment in the saga of news than October 11, 1898, when Adolph Ochs, the out-of-money publisher of the failing *New York Times,* rescued his paper from a lethal enemy and changed the course of American journalism at the same time. It was a mess he had gotten himself into because of his own vanity and frenzied ambition, and one he escaped by inspired and desperate guile. This was the same man—the grandfather of Punch Sulzberger—who later became an icon of journalistic probity and a model for all publishers. But that October, he was a man who was cornered.

Two years earlier, Ochs had come to New York from Chattanooga, Tennessee, and used his mesmerizing salesmanship to talk the owners of the *New-York Times,* as it was then known, into—effectively—giving him the paper. He was publisher of the *Chattanooga Times,* but had arrived in New York so broke that he had had to get a Chattanooga bank to deposit money into a phony account so he would look solvent. The *New-York Times* was also on the verge of bankruptcy, and Ochs promised the investors—who included J.P. Morgan—to restore it to prosperity in exchange for a controlling interest.

His main competition was the other "qualities," meaning those of the city's newspapers more highbrow than the Hearst and Pulitzer penny papers. The "qualities" sold for several cents more, and the dominant one was the *Herald,* with the *New York Tribune* and the *Sun* not far behind. The *Times* was far down in that second tier. Ochs came in like a whirlwind, upgrading the news and promoting his paper as the one with "All the news that's fit to print," a slogan he came up with himself. Business advertising was the paper's staple, complemented by advertising from the department stores, whose owners extended support to a fellow Jew. The paper's fortunes started to improve, but competition was fierce and it was still not profitable. Then the United States declared war against Spain in April 1898, Wall Street froze, and the financial advertising virtually stopped.

Without advertising from Wall Streeet, the only thing keeping the *Times* in operation was the revenue from department store advertising. The paper was in a circulation war with the other "qualities" for this advertising, and Ochs rashly suggested to stores such as Wanamaker's and Bloomingdale's that the *Times*'s circulation was 25,000. In fact, although it was printing about that number, it was selling fewer than 10,000 copies in Manhattan, but this was a heavily guarded secret. In an effort to cut costs, Ochs had fired a circulation department bookkeeper named W. L. Woolnough, who knew the truth and consciously set out to destroy Ochs. Motivated by spite laced with anti-Semitism, Woolnough sent an anonymous whistle-blowing circular to department stores and dry goods merchants charging fraud. "You have been fleeced by the *New-York Times* long enough," he wrote one large advertiser.

Ochs was beside himself. He hired Pinkerton detectives to try to intimidate Woolnough, and when that didn't work he invited him to a meeting to try to charm him. Woolnough responded with an anti-Semitic tirade. "We have got you where we want you," he wrote Ochs afterward. "You have no circulation and never will." When Ochs threatened to bring a suit against him, Woolnough mockingly dared him to do so. By October, Woolnough was on the verge of bringing the paper down.

With his back to the wall, Ochs made one of the riskiest and most brilliant business decisions in the history of news. Without consulting his board, which he was obliged to do, he announced that the *Times* was cutting its price from three cents to a penny! He wrapped this desperate gambit in a righteous pretense that he had done it so that the working man could afford a quality newspaper instead of the Hearst and Pulitzer yellow press. The bold move came down in *Times* official histories as one rooted in idealism. Regardless, it was a stunning success. There is little evidence that Hearst and Pulitzer readers switched to the *Times,* but hundreds of readers of the other "qualities" opted for the cheaper product. Ochs's old circulation claims were moot as *Times* sales soared, and a surge in advertising followed, bringing—finally—profitability. Even more important, the *Herald, Tribune,* and *Sun* did not follow Ochs's example and lower their price to a penny. As the low price choice, the *Times* built a circulation advantage that it never lost, and this provided the economic strength to prevail when all of the other papers ultimately failed. Ochs reinvested the profits and made the *Times* into the most respected news organization in the nation. And he forever after steered clear of circulation claims of any kind.

Such quirky turns are laced throughout the curious story of news, which includes times as transformative as the Internet is today, and to understand what is happening now requires some context. The evolution of news can be divided into three epochs, each defined by technology that was not merely significant, but revolutionary. We are now on the threshold of Epoch IV. There is an ongoing debate among people who fight over such things as to whether technological advance itself is the vehicle of transformation or whether the adapted technology is the servant of politics, commerce, and the impact of individuals like Ochs. Regardless, the journey from Stone Age grunts of warning to instantaneous news via satellite has been far from orderly.

Epoch I began at a time some scholars estimate to be 50,000 years ago and some much further into the past. It was heralded by the invention of language—systematically applying meaning to sounds. It was the greatest innovation in human history. Knowledge beyond an alarmed squawk could now be passed from person to person. Tens of thousands of years passed until the further technological advance of written language, which is thought to be a mere 5,000 years old. Written language allowed knowledge to be preserved intact and passed on to a person in another place or to succeeding generations. Knowledge represented great power and was therefore reserved for the powerful—royalty, the upper classes, and the priesthood. Reading and writing were too dangerous to allow outside the elite. In a sense, knowledge *was* news, and great efforts were made to keep the uninitiated from having it.

Inventions such as paper facilitated the accumulation of knowledge into libraries of handwritten scrolls. During the Dark Ages after the fall of Rome, Western culture was preserved by monks who devoted their lives to the tedious labor of copying books by hand. But that knowledge was only for the initiated and the powerful.

In about 1450, another transformative technological advance propelled the world into what could be considered Epoch II, the era of broadcasting to a mass audience. It was then that movable type and the first modern printing press came to Europe, and the world was rocked. Johannes Gutenberg invented neither the press nor movable type, a form of printing that had been used in China for centuries. Gutenberg's great revolution was in transforming this relatively crude printing method into something vastly better.

Until Gutenberg, printing had consisted of placing a coating of ink on raised figures hand-carved into wood, placing a piece of paper over the ink, and rubbing the paper to form an impression. The wooden figures could withstand only a limited number of impressions, and the process was time-consuming and inefficient.

Gutenberg was from a rich German family and loved working in metal. His specialty was creating the metal seals that were pushed into molten wax to seal letters. He became interested in printing and recognized that hand-carving letters into wood was time-consuming, there was little uniformity in the letters, and they quickly chipped and crumbled under the pressure of making an impression. But if the letters were cast in metal, like seals, each one could be manufactured again and again from the same mold, making them faster to create and more uniform. Furthermore, metal letters would be far more resilient and could be used to make multiple copies of the same document. His genius was in finding an alloy that would keep its shape. After trying pewter, he discovered that the optimal metallic formula for metal type was a blend of tin, antimony, and lead.

The Catholic Church had a monopoly on the printed word at the time, and Gutenberg's work was first denounced as sacrilegious. But as a businessman, he discovered that he could win the church's blessing by leaving the first letter or first few lines of a page blank so as to provide employment to monks who were still creating elaborately designed decorations for church documents by hand. With this ploy, he won the contract for printing indulgences, which were printed documents promising forgiveness in advance for a fee and were a source of enormous income for the church. It was the trade in indulgences that prompted Martin Luther to start what became the Reformation, a movement that spread thanks in part to the printed word. Gutenberg is best known for his Bibles, which had 42 lines on each page, requiring thousands of individually cast letters. It took him three years to produce fewer than 200 Bibles, but they became the wonder of the age, and were the first steps in opening a new era in communication.

The eminent historian of the press, Michael Schudson, estimates that the occupation of people being paid to write true accounts of current events that are then published on a regular basis—in other words, journalism—is about 250 years old. Our concept of journalism is, then, just about contemporaneous with the first stirrings of rebellion within the British colonies in North America that would eventually replace royal rule with representative democracy—a revolutionary concept that then swept the world. A concept of "news" had been born 150 years earlier in the form of printed renderings of what was happening in Parliament and popular journals of opinion, made possible by the spread of printing technology.

One of the enduring myths of American journalism is the fantasy of a vibrant free press at the time of the Revolution, which inspired the protections of the First Amendment's guarantee of free speech and free press. The truth is less glorious. Newspapers in most of colonial America were a side business of print shops, where the money was made from selling stationery, printing circulars, and sometimes running the local post office. The newspaper generally had four pages and contained promotions for the print shop, a smattering of local tittle-tattle, and small ads. Most of the space was devoted to dense columns of European news lifted directly from the London papers that had arrived in the colonies by ship weeks or even months after they were published.

The principal reason for such exhaustive—if out-of-date—coverage of Europe was the very pragmatic realization that the printer could not get in trouble with such news. Local political news or political news from other colonies rarely appeared because there were stringent laws against "seditious libel," meaning anything that attacked the royal governor or colonial legislature. European news was safer and less likely to antagonize anyone, which would be bad for business. Rather than an aggressive press, the colonies had newspapers that were complacent and avoided politics out of fear of causing offense. It is the model that is largely followed today by local television news, and for the same reasons.

Political bloggers like to compare themselves to the Revolution's vaunted "pamphleteers," who issued broadsides denouncing the British and had a significant role in inciting the passion for revolution. Foremost of these was Thomas Paine, whose incendiary pamphlet *Common Sense* was a best seller in 1776, attracting a readership that was comparable in relative terms to the audience for a Super Bowl broadcast today. Paine was born in England and, after repeated false starts at careers, came to Philadelphia in 1774 with the help of Benjamin Franklin and found his true calling as a propagandist. Until Paine and others of his type, pamphleteers had addressed an elite audience of political big shots in language studded with classical references. Paine used common language and addressed a broad audience, and his references were mainly from the Bible, which was known to all. "These are the times that try men's souls," he famously wrote in *The Crisis*.

With the stirrings of rebellion, newspapers became more political, but once again, the concept was not free speech in a sense of open debate. Any pro-British newspapers found themselves under attack—sometimes literally. As revolutionary fever mounted, in sections of the 13 colonies, an anti-British cast to the news became the only one tolerated. However, it was framed as freedom of speech because it was in defiance of the laws prohibiting seditious libel against the Crown. When the colonies became states, one of the first actions of many new state legislatures was to pass new sedition laws making it a crime for newspapers to criticize the state government. Schudson notes that some of the voices that had been most supportive of anti-British free speech abruptly changed their view of press freedom when the new American government came to power. According to this line of thinking, the press was not to be restrained in a society in which people were powerless because it was a vehicle for them to achieve power. But, as one of those opposing press freedom put it at the time, "to mislead the judgment of the people where they have *all* power, must produce the greatest possible mischief." It was this spirit that inspired President John Adams to pass the Sedition Act of 1798, which forbade criticism of the government.

At the beginning of the 19th century, it could be said that news was more of a function of politics than a business. What began with the bitter political struggle between John Adams and Thomas Jefferson became, as the century unfolded, a no-holds-barred battle waged in a press that was highly partisan, recklessly inaccurate, and gleefully vicious in its attacks.

But politicians on both sides of the political argument saw that the value in having newspapers was not so much to gather and report news as to lampoon the opposition and beat the drum for a favored political perspective. As a result, they sought to facilitate newspaper circulation with the Postal Act of 1792, which gave newspapers preferential mailing rates. Indeed, the first great public works project of the new nation was the creation of a postal service that would reach every hamlet, to instill a sense of connectedness and citizenship. Newspapers largely depended on political parties, churches, or other sponsoring groups for the financial support that paid the printing bills. Advertising was modest, and by 1830, the largest paper in the country had a circulation of only about 4,500, which was double the reach of a typical city newspaper.

But then things started to change. Newspapers in cities began to actually pay people to go ask questions and report what they had learned. Until then, the "correspondents" whose writing appeared in newspapers were literally that—people who wrote letters about events they had seen, but were not professionals. In 1833, the *New York Sun* declared itself a new breed of newspaper, filling its pages with news of local happenings and competing to be first with the news from Europe by sending reporters out to greet the incoming ships. The *Sun* was the first newspaper that envisioned itself as a *business* rather than a political organ and sought to make money by attracting a mass audience, distinguishing itself from the other newspapers that charged much more per copy and were aimed at a particular group of sympathetic kindred spirits.

These first "penny papers" began to appear in the cities, and they hired cadres of reporters who went looking for information that would lure a crowd. Crime stories were a hit from the start, as were stories that gave a glimpse into high society, a forbidden region for most penny press readers. Instead of subscriptions purchased by the party faithful, penny papers were hawked on the street by newsboys, and the selling point began to be who had the latest, hottest news. The problem was that printing technology was not much improved from the days of Gutenberg. Presses were slow, and setting type was a tedious, time-consuming chore in which each letter and each space had to be assembled piece by piece. Because paper was expensive and printing slow, each page was crammed with type that, by today's standards, looks minuscule. Typographers, as typesetters were called, usually had to do their eye-straining work in dimly lit cellars reeking with ink fumes. Making the work even harder was the fact that each letter in type was backward so that it would come out properly when printed. It is hardly surprising that typographers came to be considered both the most highly skilled men in the printing trade and the ones most apt to be drunkards.

With the exception of the fledgling penny press, newspapers in the United States and Europe were alike in representing a journalism of ideas more than of facts. They had small circulations, elite audiences, and little news, but plenty of opinion. The American version was more raucous, but the essential model was the same. The penny press demonstrated the potential of mass circulation built on the freshest news, but it took one of a series of stunning technological developments to move news into Epoch III, leading to the adoption of the American economic and journalistic model that has endured until the present. The most transformative of those technologies was the telegraph.

While Samuel F.B. Morse did not invent telegraph technology, he—like Gutenberg before him—was an innovator. A bevy of scientists before him had created an increasingly effective way to send pulses of electrical current over distance through a wire. Morse was a professor at New York University and his brilliant stroke was to realize that those electrical pulses could be turned into words using a system of dots and dashes—the Morse code.

In 1843, Congress grudgingly agreed to provide Morse $30,000 to construct an experimental telegraph line over the 40 miles between Baltimore and Washington. On May 1, 1844, the Whig Party nominated Henry Clay at its Baltimore convention, and the news had to be carried by hand to Annapolis Junction, which was as far as Morse's wire had reached. But then the news was sent by telegraph the rest of the way to the Capitol, virtually instantaneously by the standards of the day. A few weeks later, with the Baltimore-Washington link completed, the line was officially opened with transmission of what proved to be a prophetic verse from the Bible: "What hath God wrought?"

The impact of the telegraph as a disruptive technology is hard to overstate. For the first time in history, the barriers of time and distance had collapsed in a heap of irrelevance. For people who had grown up in a pre-telegraph world, the concept was akin to magic. Electrical current racing along copper wires was scientific voodoo to most, but the practical outcome was the meat-and-potatoes reality of being able to know what was happening far, far away without waiting for someone to make the journey to tell you. Suddenly, a core element of news was timeliness, which had not been so important in a slower world of horseback or railroad transportation. By this time, railroad lines were beginning to lace through the nation, and railroad rights-of-way made perfect paths for telegraph lines. Western Union had already been operating a transcontinental telegraph service for eight years when the Golden Spike creating the first transcontinental railroad was driven in 1869.

The telegraph alone did not turn news into a real business, but it was essential to creating wide public demand to know what was happening in other places. The technology of printing was advanced by steam presses, which allowed newspapers to be printed more rapidly than with the old hand-powered method. At midcentury, the speed was further increased by the introduction of rotary presses capable of cranking out—by hand and then powered by steam—thousands of copies, making big circulations practical. The paper for newspapers was made from cotton fiber and was expensive. New machines that made newsprint from wood pulp made paper cheap and plentiful. Late in the century, another technological advance allowed lines of type to be set by machine instead of by hand, vastly speeding the process. Linotype machines were standard equipment in newspapers across America until the 1960s, when computer technology began to replace them.

But technology had its limits, and the spread of technology outside the major cities was slow. Stories still had to be sent letter by letter over the telegraph, good telegraph operators could only transmit about 40 words per minute, and high-speed presses were a luxury of the major metropolitan dailies. In smaller towns, the news business was usually a mom-and-pop affair providing little more than a living for the owners, and the technology was often well behind the times. Most small towns had multiple weeklies, and there was great diversity in that every political ideology and notion had to have its newspaper to express those views.

The idea that a newspaper's main purpose was to actually gather news had begun to germinate before the Civil War. In 1846, only two papers had their own correspondents covering Congress, but rising sectional strife in the 1850s created great interest in politics, and soon scores of papers were demanding Washington coverage—often from the same correspondents, who frequently worked for multiple papers. For much of the century, most papers remained firmly political and were supported by political parties. The penny press was creating a different, more independent model, but even they had a political identity, and the most influential newspapers were voices of one camp or another.

What had clearly emerged by the end of the century was the realization that newspapers could be very profitable. Cities like New York had more than a dozen newspapers, and competition for readers was fierce. The penny papers, led by Pulitzer's *World* and Hearst's *Journal*, used illustrations, big headlines, and simple language to attract immigrants struggling to learn English. The "qualities" sought a demographic with more buying power.

But the economic model had been well established by the end of the century. The United States is a commercial culture, and has been from the time that the "pursuit of happiness" was enshrined as part of our national purpose. The stultifying European class structure had put rigid limits on how far one could rise in the Old World. But the New World offered unlimited opportunity, and that meant business opportunity. The First Amendment guarantee that government would not interfere with freedom of the press meant that there was no regulatory limit on how the business could be structured.

The model that emerged was new in one essential way. In the past, most newspaper revenue had been from subscriptions and circulation or outright subsidy by political parties or other interest groups. Advertising had provided only marginal additional money. In the new model, advertising was the main source of revenue, and the potential for a bounty from advertising was expanding along with the American economy. The business rationale was that you should charge less for the paper itself so as to maximize the size of the audience, and then use that audience to sell advertising. The more circulation, the higher the ad rates and the more desirable the audience to advertisers.

The thing that has always made the American newspaper business unusual compared to other commercial enterprises is that it is a business that has had a genuine social contract with the American public. Newspapers would thrive on the basis of advertising that was attracted by readers who were, in turn, attracted by the paper's news coverage. Gathering and presenting the news was viewed as a form of stewardship, a responsibility that made the newspaper business special and privileged in that it was protected in certain ways by the First Amendment. The priorities of a newspaper included making a profit, but that was not the only priority, and there was a constant balancing act within the paper between the business side and the news side. At the best papers, the business side took pride in the news side's achievements. The prestige of a newspaper was usually a reflection of its reputation as a news operation, and the families that owned them derived both a social status and genuine power from proprietorship of a newspaper.

As newspapers became highly profitable, editorial independence began to displace party affiliation and objective news began replacing the highly partisan news reporting of earlier years. But as has been noted, the decline of the partisan press was also spurred by the reforms of the Progressive Era at the end of the 19th century, which began as a Republican-led effort to weaken the big-city Democratic machines and evolved into a general disenchantment with party politics that questioned the value of party loyalty. The rhetoric stressed the candidate over the party affiliation, and newspapers in this environment made the shift toward political independence—or at least the claim of independence. Most papers were known to be either Republican or Democratic on their editorial pages, but the news was supposed to be written neutrally. Journalists began to think of themselves as professionals, and organized themselves into clubs and professional associations. Objective reporting had the effect of freeing reporters from the strictures of a political orthodoxy, and part of the result was an explosion of sensationalism, often masked as crusading for the common man. Journalists simultaneously had the images of being raffishly unscrupulous and dashingly brave. Newspapers cultivated the image of being watchdogs defiant of power, but they were also businesses deeply invested in preserving the status quo. In an institutional sense, newspapers took on a fatherly role for their readers. They assumed a position of superior knowledge and gave direction as to what one should think. They scolded and complimented, they represented power and held themselves up as strong, wise, and decent. They had dignity—and wealth.

Adding to their journalistic stature was the invention of the interview, which became a mainstay of American journalism but was all but unknown before the end of the Civil War. Until then the "correspondents" had essentially been either stenographers or commentators who created sketches or based articles on observations. By 1900, the interview was the fundamental tool of what had come to be called "reporters," and worked well with the fact-centered and news-centered content that had hitherto been mostly political commentary or florid literary writing.

The number of daily newspapers in America peaked in 1910 at about 2,200, and most towns of any size had two or more competing papers, virtually all of them making a profit. New York City at one time had 20 daily papers, and other major cities were similarly awash with newspapers. In small towns, there were apt to be multiple weekly newspapers, each a family enterprise. Like other family businesses, newspapers had changed hands in the normal course of things, and the buyer was usually another family. In the case of my small town in Tennessee, the Lyon family dominated the newspaper landscape for decades before my family succeeded them.

In the fall of 1916, my grandmother—Edith O'Keefe Susong—led our family into journalism by taking over the smallest and weakest of three weekly newspapers in our country village. She had been a schoolteacher, but had abandoned that when she had married a promising local lawyer and had two children—my uncle and my mother. Married women were considered unsuitable as teachers because they might become pregnant, and besides they should be home taking care of their families. She was, in many ways, a high Victorian and submitted to these judgments without questioning them.

But one October morning in 1916, fate put her in the unlikely position of having no choice but to take the helm of the *Greeneville Democrat,* a weekly newspaper teetering on bankruptcy in competition with two better-run weeklies. As a child I had heard this story countless times, but she was always ready to tell it again. On that October morning—as she told the story—she put on her hat and went down to the newspaper, knowing absolutely nothing about journalism or newspapers.

The town's leading newspaper was run by a man who did not admire women, and viewed my grandmother as a presumptuous upstart. "A *woman* has become proprietor of *The Greeneville Demo-crat*," he wrote with a palpable sneer in his paper that week. "This paper will not be alive when the roses bloom."

At this point in telling the tale, my grandmother would take a deep, satisfied breath and say, "Four years later, I owned *both* the other papers. And do you know *why?*" It was always my part to pretend I had never heard her tell this tale. She would fix me with her most piercing look and declare, "Because they were *drunk*, and I was *sober.*"

There was a lot of truth in that, but of course it wasn't the whole story. Finding the answer to the "why" of things is the core mission of journalism, and it almost always requires painstakingly untwisting many tangled threads. As I have already said, my family still owns and operates that newspaper in Greeneville. It is a leg-acy that our whole family cherishes. Why, we ask ourselves, have we been able to preserve a family newspaper and keep a shared sense of purpose that is essential if it is to pass to another gen-eration? As the number of such papers has dwindled, we puzzle over why we have clung to the one that my grandmother fought so hard to keep alive. It is a complex riddle, and its answer— for me—begins with the truth about how my grandmother came to be a newspaperwoman. When she passed her 80th birthday, I persuaded her to sit down with me so I could record some of the wonderful stories she had told again and again. To my sur-prise, some 60 years after she began her adventure in the news-paper business, she decided to tell the unvarnished story of what had happened.

She had been 21 when she married my grandfather, Dave Susong, who was the adored son of a Greene County clan of long standing. My grandmother told me that Dave had caught her eye because he rode on horseback so elegantly. His father wanted him to be a lawyer, and he went to the University of Virginia School of Law, where—according to family legend—he first started drink-ing. He was also a star baseball pitcher and wanted to try it as a professional, but his father would not allow it. He returned to

Greeneville, married my grandmother, and began to practice law unhappily. Eventually, he also began to drink heavily.

My grandmother had only one year of college and was deeply in love when they married, but naïve. Her father had had the occasional toddy to treat a cold, but she had never tasted alcohol and had no experience with what it could do. So she was confused to find that Dave's personality could change, after as little as one glass of wine, from being affable and agreeable to extremely unpleasant. She also found she was "not at all patient" with a drunken husband, and by the time their second child—my mother—was born in 1915, Dave's law practice and marriage were a shambles and the unpaid bills were mounting.

It was then that the owner of the *Democrat* "caught him drunk and unloaded this small newspaper on him," she told me. Dave, who was all but broke, had to get the note cosigned by his older sister, Emma. "I fought it bitterly and tried to get his sister not to sign the note," my grandmother said, "I didn't realize that I was flying in the face of Providence and trying to prevent myself having a means of a livelihood." Dave's sister, ever hopeful that her brother could turn his life around, signed the note.

The paper seemed almost certainly doomed. It was a Democratic paper in a heavily Republican county, going against two better-equipped Republican papers, the *Greeneville Searchlight* and the *Greeneville Sun,* which was the largest of the three. The *Democrat* was, as she recalled, "utterly and absolutely antediluvian," with a few cases of worn type, two ancient job presses, and a crude, hand-operated two-page Country Campbell press. To print the 600 copies every week, each letter of each word had to be assembled by hand, and then a single sheet would be fed into the press to print first one side, then the other. This large sheet would be folded to produce a four-page paper, hand-addressed, and taken to the post office for mailing. The two employees, Mr. Kennon and Mr. Nelson—as she always respectfully referred to them—tried to keep the machinery running.

As she had feared, Dave took little interest in the paper, but she tried to help out, writing short items and social news. Mr. Kennon, who saw the end near, began urging her to take over, and she demurred that she knew nothing whatever about newspapers. But as bad came to worse financially, she began to see the *Democrat* as her only hope. Dave had paid nothing on the note, so she went to Emma, his sister, and said that if the note were assigned to her, she would assume the principal and unpaid interest.

As she wrote on the 50th anniversary of her first full day on the job, October 1, 1916, "I tripped down the two blocks to the location of my 'plant' with wings on my feet. I had a mortgage for $4,000 in my hand, but I also had a means of livelihood for my two children, and I was ready to go to work with a will...Had I realized how utterly impossible the task was I was undertaking, I'd have turned at the door and fled...but since I had no slightest comprehension of what I was trying to do, I breezed gaily in, greeted the two employees, and prepared to take over."

She learned quickly that her competitor's snide prediction that the paper would not be around when the roses bloomed heralded an enduring problem about her gender. A year's subscription to the *Democrat* cost one dollar, and the custom was to pay during the tobacco market in late fall. Many times, farmers would walk into the office to buy a subscription and say to her, "Sister, where's your Pap?" They would not entrust their dollar to a woman, and, if one of her male employees was not there to accept the money, they would often walk out the door. She also found that predatory suppliers and others would try to take advantage of her on the basis of her sex, which was apparent from her name, Edith O'Keefe Susong. Her solution was to become E. O. Susong, to suggest the publisher was a man, the standard by which she wished to be professionally treated.

She reported and wrote the stories, kept the books, designed and sold the ads, folded and addressed each week's papers, and took them to the post office. To build circulation, she enlisted her small children, who accompanied her as she crisscrossed the county seeking business almost door-to-door. To her everlasting gratitude, Republicans as well as Democrats would buy a subscription or take out an ad because they felt sorry for her. "They knew the whole story, and they wanted to help," she said. After four years of constant, unrelenting work, she had managed to pay down her debt and stay in business, but little more. Throughout that time, she had continued to live with Dave in the hope he would change, but the marriage deteriorated even further and she moved with her children into her parents' white frame house, where she had grown up.

Then, one day in 1920, Mr. Kennon, her most able and valued employee, came to her and said, "Mrs. Susong, I hate to tell you this, but Nelson and I have decided to buy the *Searchlight*." She was devastated. The two men were all but irreplaceable, and what's more, they were going into business against her. "I didn't sleep for two days or three nights, wondering... What would I do?" she said. As she told me this new version of the familiar story, I realized I had never heard this before, and, unprompted, I said to her, "What *could* you do?" She looked at me with exasperation and said, "If a rabbit has to climb a tree, it climbs a tree." She acted, as had Adolph Ochs before her, with a ruthless cunning born of desperation. "I did them a favor by convincing them they could not do it. I said, 'Who is going to write your advertising? Who is going to write your news? Who is going to handle your books? You boys are preparing to lose every penny you put into this investment.'"

She told them that they must tell the owner that they had changed their minds, which they did. "As soon as they told him," my grandmother said, "I bought it." If they were angry, it didn't show, and Mr. Kennon worked as her production chief until he died, decades later.

She used similar guile to buy the *Sun*, which was owned by W. R. Lyon, who was both a rabid Republican and the heavy drinker who had foretold her failure in 1916. As his fortunes ebbed, he began borrowing paper from Miss Edith, as most people in the town called her. In October 1920, Lyon ceased publication, and my grandmother, knowing full well that he would not sell to her under any circumstances, arranged for a lawyer friend to offer to buy his paper on behalf of some out-of-town business interests. The purchase of the *Searchlight* had wiped out both her cash and her credit, so she turned to her parents, who agreed to become partners and helped to put up the $16,500 to buy the *Sun*. Her father, who had a low opinion of newspapers and newspapermen, reluctantly agreed to become business manager. And her mother Quincy, a fiery and brilliant woman of definite views, took over the editorial page, with the title "editor." Miss Edith merged the papers into a daily called the *Greeneville Democrat-Sun*, built a small brick building on the narrow strip of land next to her parents' house, and was truly launched.

I was born in 1946, 30 years after that October morning when my grandmother first set out for the *Democrat*, and even as a small boy I began to be aware that something was different about my family. My father, for reasons that were obscure to me, almost never got through supper without being called to the telephone, usually by someone outraged either because of something in the paper or because it had not yet been delivered. My world had two basic anchors: the house I lived in with my parents and four siblings and "the office," as the *Sun* was called, which included the house next to the paper across a narrow alley where Miss Edith and my great-grandmother Quincy still lived. In that house, the center of the action was the kitchen and the small study behind it where my grandmother would hammer out her endless flow of columns and articles and what she called "personals," which were tidbits of benign gossip about who had company and who had gone on a trip. They were the most popular items in the paper, next to her weekly column, "Cheerful Chatter."

The acquisition of the other two newspapers had not ended my grandmother's problems by any means. Mr. Lyon, the former owner of the *Sun*, waited three years until she had paid off the note, and on the very next day went into competition against her, which lasted for years. But my grandmother had a gift for small-town newspapering. She was politically nonpartisan by instinct and had never viewed her newspaper as a party organ, despite the name. She intended to offer a paper that would appeal to all Greene Countians, so, after a few years, the *Greeneville Democrat-Sun* became the *Greeneville Sun*. As a team, Edith and Quincy embodied the good cop/bad cop persona that a good local newspaper should have. My grandmother believed that a newspaper was the beating heart of a town and needed to be used to make the community a better place. She was a booster, but also in many ways a progressive. Quincy was the truth-telling scold who wrote scorching editorials and infuriated local politicians of both parties, whom my grandmother then was obliged to soothe. Both their portraits hang in the Tennessee Newspaper Hall of Fame, together with that of Adolph Ochs.

The newspaper world I knew in the 1950s was one filled with other families like my own whom we would see at the summer convention of the Tennessee Press Association. But it was changing. As it became evident that you could make substantial profit with newspapers, the family-to-family sale became a rarity. When all but the smallest newspapers were sold, they were almost always acquired by chains, which were corporations that saw the business potential. Families may have bought newspapers for a variety of reasons, including wanting to be a local power. In some cases, chains of papers were created to forge political muscle, which seemed to be William Randolph Hearst's primary motive. But with few exceptions, chains of newspapers were assembled to make money, and they proved to be excellent investments. As the money rolled in, the terms of the bargain between the news side and the business side meant that news gathering flourished and grew as well.

Michael Schudson estimates that by the early 1930s, the six largest chains already controlled a significant percentage of daily newspaper circulation, but many cities had competing newspapers. Then came commercial radio and television, which changed the business landscape. Guglielmo Marconi invented his primitive radio in Italy in 1894, but it was not until after World War I that commercial radio appeared, in a move many regarded as illegal.

The issue from the start was who would control the new medium that used the public airwaves and whether it would be used strictly for educational and public purposes or for commerce. As usual in America, commerce won. In 1919, General Electric, at the urging of the U.S. Navy, purchased the American operations of the Marconi company, ostensibly to prevent foreign ownership. Then, together with AT&T, United Fruit, and Westinghouse, the company pooled all American radio patents and created a new entity called Radio Corporation of America, or RCA. The consolidation, which seemed to be an obvious violation of antitrust law, helped guarantee that radio would be a business rather than a public service.

In 1920, a Detroit radio station covered a primary election. Later that year, KDKA in Pittsburgh broadcast returns of the presidential race between Warren G. Harding and James M. Cox., both without commercial sponsorship. Then in 1922, a real estate brokerage in Queens paid WEAF in New York $50 to deliver five 10-minute pitches hawking a new apartment complex, and the "commercial" was born. With radio, news quickly became second to entertainment but was nevertheless important. However, the economic model was established: advertising supported news gathering.

As it became clear that radio was going to be a national obsession, newspapers were suddenly cast as yesterday's medium and waves of doomsaying swept the industry. Radio was immediate and live, entertaining and vivid. Radio could report news before it could be printed, and would make newspapers obsolete. While the predictions were wrong, there was certainly an impact on newspapers because of competition for advertising dollars. The weaker newspapers in a town were hardest hit and began to falter. Some cities that had been able to support competing papers were reduced to one newspaper but had multiple radio stations. By the eve of World War II, 25 of the nation's large cities had only one daily paper, and the survivor was very likely to be chain-owned. It was during World War II that radio demonstrated its news power with Edward R. Murrow's broadcasts from London during the Blitz. While newspaper journalism was still vastly dominant, radio had a glamour and a personality that was undeniable. It turned out that the human voice, albeit disembodied and out of a speaker, could communicate in ways that words on paper rarely did, which is one of the reasons radio remains a powerful medium today.

With the end of World War II came an even bigger economic blow when television became a national phenomenon. Through the 1950s, news was not something that television took seriously. In 1948, NBC hired a would-be actor named John Cameron Swayze to do voice-overs for *Camel Newsreel Theater*, an early effort at TV news. It showed newsreels and was sponsored by Camel cigarettes. A year later, he was named to host NBC's first TV newscast, *Camel News Caravan*, a 15-minute program that usually included Swayze plugging Camels between reading items taken from the news wires and interviews with newsmakers. "Let's go hopscotching around the world for headlines," Swayze would tell his listeners. Douglas Edwards at CBS had a more sober style and his newscast became number one, prompting NBC to replace Swayze in 1956 with Chet Huntley and David Brinkley, whose *Huntley-Brinkley Report* retook first place. CBS answered in 1962 by putting Walter Cronkite at the helm of its nightly news. But the programs were still only 15 minutes long, and the networks viewed them mainly as a way to satisfy the FCC's requirement that broadcasters provide public service in exchange for their licenses. It was not surprising that in 1961 Newton N. Minow, the chairman of the FCC, described television as "a vast wasteland."

But wasteland or not, TV was a cultural tidal wave. Everyone watched television, especially the baby boomer generation growing up in America. In 1963, NBC and CBS expanded their nightly news shows to 30 minutes, and ABC followed suit. That was also the year that a majority of Americans for the first time said that they relied on TV over newspapers as their primary news source. Even more important, the networks and owners of local television stations had discovered that you could make money from news.

When *60 Minutes* premiered in 1968, it became the most highly rated program on TV.

Newspapers were traumatized by the cultural juggernaut of television and began to change their content in the 1970s in response. The *New York Times,* which was considered the most serious bastion of accountability news, found itself on the verge of operating in the red, which could have been terminal. The *Times*'s solution was to create a series of special sections on entertainment, food, and the pleasures of the home. Its *Living* section was lampooned by skeptics as the *Having* section for its glorification of the material good life, but the success of the sections subsidized the other reporting that remained the *Times*'s hallmark. The problem was that television was so inherently *entertaining* that newspapers had to become more entertaining if they were to compete with the three networks for the attention and loyalty of Americans. And newspapers found that these sections could generate handsome returns from advertisers.

There is a long-standing debate about whether fluff and trivia were introduced to news that had been mostly serious or whether there was a long-overdue expansion of the definition of news to include things that had been neglected. In fact, it was both. The new coverage of health issues and the nation's changing culture and habits was a breath of fresh air. But a shift toward gossip, sensation, and celebrity was also undeniable. For instance, *Time* magazine's People section became so popular that in 1974 it was spun off as a stand-alone and became one of the most overwhelmingly profitable and most imitated magazines in the world.

By the 1980s, both television and newspapers were facing a new challenge: cable television. In 1970, only about 10 percent of the nation's households had cable, which was mostly a way to give better reception in rural areas where the network signals were weak. Cable in those days consisted of a big antenna on top of the highest available spot, with cables connecting the antenna to subscribers. It was essentially an upgrade of your rooftop antenna or rabbit ears. Cable businesses were generally small operations that made little money and had no great prospects.

But coaxial cable and advances in technology made it possible to feed dozens of channels into a home, rather than the old limit of the three networks, public TV, and a few local UHF stations. Ted Turner's genius was to recognize the potential of what he called a Superstation based in Atlanta, which became TBS and showed the way for cracking the networks' hold on viewership. By the end of the 1980s, over half the households in America were getting multiple channels over their cable connections, and cable had become the norm.

At the same time the news business was changing the focus of news, the relationship of journalists to the sources of news was also changing. During World War II, American journalists had voluntarily submitted to censorship and had worn uniforms. They considered themselves part of the national fight, and if not an arm of government, at least a partner. The concept of the news media as the Fourth Estate of government, complementing the executive, legislative, and judicial, was one that worked in an almost courtly way. For instance, photographers did not take pictures of President Franklin Roosevelt in a wheelchair, which he felt would hurt his image as a strong leader. Nor did it seem peculiar at the time that reporters knew of President John F. Kennedy's sexual escapades in office but did not report them.

That began to change during the civil rights movement. No longer was the government regarded as the vehicle for a solution, as in the Depression and World War II. Now, government officials and politicians often turned out to be the bad guys. Covering civil rights also proved to be a magnet for attracting some highly educated and idealistic reporters to journalism, a field that still was more like *The Front Page* than *All the President's Men*. David Halberstam, for instance, graduated from Harvard in 1955 and became a reporter at the *Daily Times Leader* in West Point, Mississippi, and then moved to the *Tennessean* in Nashville, where he covered the beginnings of the civil rights movement. He was then sent to Vietnam by the *Times*.

If the fight for civil rights cracked the cozy partnership of the press and government, Vietnam shattered it. The publication of the Pentagon Papers in 1971 and the Watergate scandal that soon followed set a new tone, and the message was that the two most establishment newspapers in the country—the *New York Times* and the *Washington Post*—were willing to defy the president and the government. The best of the rest of American journalism followed suit—at least in the newsrooms.

But news was also becoming big business, and the realities of the marketplace were omnipresent. With multiple cable channels came even more choices, and producers of the network nightly news, which had been king, began to notice that people had started watching reruns of *The Mary Tyler Moore Show* instead. Presidential addresses, which had been compulsory fare on the networks, were in competition with scores of entertainment channels. And what had been gavel-to-gavel coverage of the presidential nominating conventions began to be cut back, then slashed.

Technology also had an impact on news. With VCRs, people could tape the program they wanted and watch it whenever they pleased. The remote control made channel surfing a habit, and news programs became capable of tracking their audience segment by segment. The bosses found that policy issues were a turnoff. War was a ratings winner in the early stages, but if the news wasn't good or fatigue had set in, war coverage could prompt an instantaneous loss of audience. Portable satellite dishes and elaborate remote vans made it possible to report live from virtually anywhere in the world, which was enticing, but not good for the quality of news. "Putting someone on the air while an event is unfolding is clearly a technological tour de force," said Ted Koppel, "but it's an impediment, not an aid, to good journalism." Without time to verify and gather contextual information, the "news" could be as misleading as it was informative.

The networks were also under pressure from their corporate owners to maximize profits, as Wall Street had come to expect quarterly gains of media-oriented companies. With the end of the

Cold War, the nation's interest in foreign news, which had always fluctuated, began to wane. The network reaction was to cut foreign bureaus and foreign reporting, which added to the decline in a focus on the world even as the world was becoming ever more interconnected. According to the Tyndall Report, which monitors television news content, foreign bureaus provided only a third as many minutes of coverage for the evening newscasts on ABC, CBS, and NBC in 2000 as they did in 1989, a high point.

By the late 1990s, both newspapers and television were concentrated in larger corporations accustomed to handsome profits and intent on increasing those returns. For television, that meant tailoring news programming to audience preferences. Local TV had all but abandoned covering politics and policy, and was sitting on profit margins of 60 percent or more. Network television news had cut foreign bureaus and achieved other economies by replacing experienced—and more expensive—reporters with younger, cheaper, and less experienced ones. Hard news was mixed liberally with features on medical breakthroughs and human interest on the network news. In a shameful demonstration of journalistic dereliction, the network news programs had all but ignored the debate over the Telecommunications Act of 1996, which was of great commercial importance to their parent companies.

In effect, in the area of public policy and other reported accountability news, television had abandoned the field. Newspapers had changed as a result of the competitive environment, but the iron core of reported news was still an accepted part of the mission of newspapers as they enjoyed profits that were far below those of local television stations but were typically over 20 percent a year, with steady growth. Stock prices of publicly traded newspaper companies were up, and the experts who followed those stocks for Wall Street were generally optimistic about the future.

Then came the Internet and, with it, Epoch IV.

# CHAPTER SEVEN

# Newspapers on
# the Brink

*We can tweak the papers and compete with them, but we can't
replace them.*

—Joel Kramer, editor of MinnPost.com, an online news
organization in Minneapolis

"Do you play golf?" said George Irish, then the
president of Hearst Newspapers, one of the nation's major chains,
in response to my question about his perspective on the newspaper business in these tumultuous times. I responded that I used
to play with my father. He nodded and continued with a note of
pain, "The newspaper business used to be like playing golf on a
par three course where you stood on the tee and you knew the
exact distance to the hole. Now the newspaper business is like
standing on the tee of a par five, shrouded in fog. You can't even
see the green, and overnight they've moved all the bunkers and
sand traps."

He was speaking out of frustration and worry and no small
amount of anguish. The day before, the *San Francisco Chronicle,*

a Hearst paper, had announced that it was cutting a quarter of its news staff. The staff had been extra large because of a merger several years ago with the *San Francisco Examiner,* and Hearst had promised at the time to preserve the jobs. But after losing tens of millions of dollars, the decision had been that cuts had to be made. The news rocked San Francisco and was yet another in what seems an endless series of gloomy announcements that newspaper staffs are being reduced and that newspapers are in deep economic trouble. By early in 2009, Hearst was threatening to close or sell the paper unless it got significant concessions from its unions, and selling was viewed as an unlikely option because almost nobody was buying.

Articles about the decline of the newspaper business are exasperating and infuriating to many newspaper executives. "Every one of the stories talks about Armageddon," said Robert Decherd, the CEO of Belo, owner of the *Dallas Morning News* and other media properties, to a Dow Jones reporter in June 2007. He had just made a presentation to a group of skeptical Wall Street analysts who had gathered to hear the business projections of top executives at newspaper-oriented, publicly traded companies. The overall assessment of the various presentations was described by the Bear Stearns analyst present as "somber" after the "worst monthly revenue statistics since December, 2001." In the 1980s and '90s, these show-and-tell sessions had been opportunities to brag about rising profits and to project a bright future. They now take place amid a trend of declining circulation numbers and sinking advertising revenues that are roiling the industry, and Wall Street has judged the future of newspaper companies harshly. In a slap that is both symbolic and ruthlessly realistic, a number of Wall Street analysts who have made careers following newspaper companies have abandoned ship. John Morton, the dean of newspaper analysts, discontinued his industry newsletter after 30 years with a lament that many newspapers in large markets "have passed the point of opportunity." With newspaper stocks in the basement, investors are few and analysts can't get attention for their number crunching of newspaper stocks. As Peter Appert, an analyst at Goldman Sachs, told Bloomberg News, "Being the newspaper analyst is like being the Maytag repairman."

Unfortunately for the newspaper business, things got vastly worse in 2008 as the economic collapse further devastated newspaper stocks. When Robert Decherd had complained about pessimistic news coverage, his stock had been selling for over $18 per share. A year later it had dropped nearly 90 percent to around $2.50. Similarly breathtaking declines have been inflicted on all newspaper stocks, even the most celebrated. By October 2008, Washington Post Company stock was off about 63 percent, the New York Times Company was down 58 percent, and the Gannett Company, which is the nation's largest chain of newspapers, had been off as much as 80 percent before rallying a bit. These public companies complained that their stock prices were hammered more than their declines in profitability deserved, which was true. But it is undeniable that the newspaper business is fighting for its life, and the 2009 recession has only made things far worse.

Despite the gloomy trends, I believe that the nation's newspaper companies—be they public or private—are going to survive, and eventually thrive once again. My concern has never been that the business will fail. The industry has a history of being slow to react to challenges such as cable, but when roused it is resourceful, since it is run by people who are determined to find a way to keep the business alive and healthy. It may not ever be as healthy in terms of profit as it was in the lush 1980s, but I have been too long in the newspaper business to believe it won't find a way to survive in some form.

Unfortunately, I am not nearly so confident that the business that survives will have news as its central mission—or not in a way that will serve the public interest. The great problem for the nation's newspapers is not whether they can save themselves, but whether they can do so without losing their meaningful public service mission. They have been businesses built around reporting and providing news that their communities want and *need*. I fear that newspapers are trending toward becoming businesses built overwhelmingly around what people *want*, and all but abandoning anything that does not make money or draw eyeballs. But what newspapers will be in the future remains in play and undetermined, which is why it is important to understand the dilemma they face and the choices they must make.

When I started hanging around the *Greeneville Sun* in the 1950s, the business side of newspapers was much as it had been at the turn of the century. Most retail businesses were locally owned, and people shopped downtown. Virtually all advertising was what was called ROP—run of paper—meaning that it appeared in the pages of the newspaper rather than as a preprinted insert, and advertising rates increased at a modest rate. Large newspapers operated basically the same way, with big department stores as their prime retail advertisers. As a kid, I had a paper route, and subscribers paid me 30 cents a week to have a copy of the *Sun* delivered to their door. On my route, virtually every house I passed took the paper, though I occasionally got stiffed for the 30 cents.

My grandmother had two children: Alex, for whom I am named, and Martha Arnold Susong, my mother. My Uncle Alex fled Greeneville as soon as he could and lived his life in New York as a banker. My father, John M. Jones, comes from Sweetwater, Tennessee, a similar small town about a hundred miles southwest of Greeneville. His family was in the textile business, and my father—the oldest son—was expected to join the family firm. Instead he joined an uncle's paint company, married my mother, and had my older brother, John Jr. Then came World War II, and he volunteered for a group that later became known as Merrill's Marauders, the precursor to today's U.S. Army Rangers, whose mission was to go behind Japanese lines in Burma and attack them. Amazingly, he survived and returned in 1945 with every intention of going back to the paint business.

By then my grandmother had survived W.R. Lyon and other competitors, the Depression, and the war, but all those battles had finally caught up with her. She was weary and not well, and she asked my father to come to Greeneville to help her, just for a year, so he could see whether the newspaper business appealed to him.

He knew no more about newspapers than my grandmother had known in 1916, but he was intrigued. After only a few months, he fell completely in love with being a newspaperman and agreed to stay permanently, but not as an employee. He bought the stake in the paper that had belonged to my great-grandparents, which had come in exchange for their financial help when my grandmother had bought the *Sun* decades earlier. John M., as my father is called, and Edith then began a partnership that was to endure in uninterrupted harmony for nearly 30 years.

The *Greeneville Sun* of the 1950s and '60s was a paper of its day, for better and worse. The worse was its acceptance of racial prejudice as simply the way things were. Relative to many other parts of the South, there were few blacks in Greeneville, because a century earlier the small-scale farming economy had not lent itself to slavery. Even so, race was the issue of the era, and my family was conservative, which is to say they believed that separate but equal was the best arrangement. I felt differently, and segregation was the crucible of my life politically. Though I wish the *Sun* had been one of those brave Southern newspapers that championed equal rights for black Americans, I am proud that when the civil rights movement came, my father and grandmother were instrumental in ensuring that Greeneville became an integrated place without the violence and insults that plagued so much of the South.

Greeneville was a tranquil hamlet where I was given almost total freedom to wander and roam from the time I was eight, with the understanding that the town and everyone in it was watching over me. On Saturdays, the downtown was packed with people, some still traveling in horse-drawn wagons, the women wearing sunbonnets. A line of farmers, many without a full set of teeth, would line the courthouse lawn. Almost always there would be a preacher thundering damnation and brimstone, but no one seemed to pay him much mind. On Sunday, we went to church and then to lunch in the Brumley Hotel's dining room, where they served hot rolls and fried cornmeal mush along with fried chicken.

But there was also a frisson of potential violence that was always near, though out of sight. My father bought a .38 caliber pistol and kept it in a filing cabinet at home after a man walked into his office and casually pulled a gun while warning him not to run pictures of strikers bashing some cars in a local dispute. As it happened, the photographer had been so nervous that he had forgotten to take the lens cap off his camera.

In 1966, when she celebrated her fiftieth year in the newspaper business, my grandmother expressed her thanks directly to the people who had supported her all those years. "The people of Greene County are MY people," she wrote. "Shoulder to shoulder, we face the past, the present and the future in a world of fear, confusion and challenge. Thank you, my good comrades, for my golden yesterday and the shining faith I hold for tomorrow." In the summer of 1974, she put her final Cheerful Chatter on the hook and left for a doctor's appointment, where she collapsed. She died at 84, and it was the only time I have ever seen my father weep in my entire life.

I have described this long family story because I believe that the past is very much alive in the present, and my own journalistic journey—including my prejudices and values—were shaped by that story.

I remain a one-fifth owner of the family business, along with my brothers and sisters, and the *Greeneville Sun* and other small papers we own are still a family affair. We, as a family, have no wish to follow the trend and sell. I think that there are a lot of reasons for that. The most important one is that the *Sun*, for us, is like a living, breathing family member, as palpably part of us as another sibling. The thing that always struck me as I watched other families sell their papers over the years was that they were giving up not just a business but a way of life. The "public service" mission that has gone along with newspaper publishing is the thing that sets it apart from other businesses, and to trade that opportunity for mere money was something that never struck me as a sensible bargain—rather like knowing the price of something but not its value.

If newspapers lose that sense of obligation and stewardship to the communities they serve, then the survival of newspapers is of little importance, because they will be just another business. Reporting the important news—telling the hard truth, even while you love your community—has been the principal demonstration of a covenant that newspapers have with their readers. The erosion of that commitment would be a betrayal, whether at the *Greeneville Sun* or the *New York Times* or at any newspaper anywhere. The world of my forbears is gone, but the principle of service upon which they devoted their lives to newspaper work still endures at many newspapers. But it is a concept that I fear may well be passing.

The newspaper business became handsomely profitable even in small towns in the 1960s. The big advantage a newspaper had by then was that radio and television had made it very difficult for more than one newspaper to operate profitably in a town—or even in most cities. The weaker of two competing newspapers could not do well, and most of them were absorbed into the dominant paper. The surviving newspaper could do very well indeed, with a monopoly not on advertising but on *newspaper* advertising, which was thought to be essential by local merchants. Even though there was plenty of competition for advertising from local radio and television, the single newspaper in a town was always the main provider of news.

It was this opportunity to have an effective monopoly that attracted Warren Buffett, the legendary investor who looks for such monopolies as opportunities to make lots of easy money. His company, Berkshire Hathaway, purchased the *Buffalo News* in 1977 and proceeded to make a fortune on it. But now is a very different time. In a letter to Berkshire Hathaway shareholders, Buffett gave his assessment of the plight of newspapers in his usual blunt fashion. He said that when he bought the *Buffalo News*, "No paper in a one-paper city, however bad the product or however inept the management, could avoid gushing profits."

It was more complicated than that. What had happened in the 1960s and '70s was that newspapers changed from being relatively simple businesses that could be operated by people with average management skills into businesses that were far more challenging.

Linotypes were being replaced by computers, and the old hot-metal rotary presses—which were essentially 19th-century technology—were quickly being replaced by offset presses that could print in color with far better reproduction. The genteel local advertising business was also going away, as local retailers were acquired by larger regional or national operations or were put out of business by Kmart or Wal-Mart. The decision of whether to buy advertising was suddenly being made by people in other cities. What had been vibrant downtowns in the 1950s were ghost towns by the end of the '60s as businesses moved to the bypass. What's more, watching television had become the national pastime, and suddenly people weren't reading a newspaper the way they once had.

Families owning newspapers, many of them multigenerational, were faced with a challenging new world. Their newspapers provided a comfortable living for the most part, but hardly great wealth. With the world changing, they needed to upgrade their newspapers technologically, which required a major investment and often meant taking on significant debt. It was a transformative phase in the nation's newspaper landscape that is little understood. The shift from family-owned to chain-owned papers is usually attributed to greed or family strife. In fact, I believe that many of those families simply didn't know what to do when faced with the daunting capital investment and changed environment that suddenly confronted them. They were overwhelmed and worried by the complex demands of this new environment. Some of them were scared and almost paralyzed with indecision. And then along came eager buyers.

Newspaper chains and entrepreneurs like Mr. Buffett recognized that these people were sitting on a potential goldmine that they had neither the will nor the expertise to exploit. It was like picking low-hanging fruit. In these decades, hundreds of family owners sold out for what they considered stunning prices—three or four times annual revenues, even if there was little apparent profit because of payrolls padded with family members and a neighborly reluctance to raise advertising rates. The new owners brought the paper up to date technologically, modernized the design, and—most important—raised advertising and circulation rates far more aggressively than the former owners had dared. Merchants had nowhere else to go with their display ads if they wanted to reach a community's mass audience, and rates went up fast and kept increasing. Neither radio nor television had an effective method of advertising jobs or used cars or real estate, so the paper's classified ad pages were ripe for higher rates. The influx of money swelled the news budget as well.

These were golden years for newspaper profitability, and this period of great prosperity lasted until relatively recently. Even though there were cyclical dips and competitive struggles, the newspaper business was viewed as not only bountifully profitable, but as one that could reliably post increased earnings year after year. For instance, the Gannett Company's pride was many years with an unbroken string of quarters in which it reported ever-increased earnings. The stock of Gannett and other public newspaper companies soared, and the profit margins that they considered standard were well in excess of 20 percent—far higher than those of most public companies. When John Carroll was editor of the *Lexington Herald-Leader*, a paper in Kentucky owned at that time by the Knight Ridder chain, the profit margin was 35 percent. And Knight Ridder had a reputation of spending generously on news. Thomson Newspapers was based in Canada and specialized in buying small-town American papers, then squeezing them hard. The company's head, Lord Thomson, told colleagues that a profit of 45 percent was not too much, but that anything over that would be "gouging." The times were so good for newspapers that it sometimes seemed they didn't know what to do with the money. When Carroll left Lexington to become editor of Times-Mirror's *Baltimore Sun,* the paper's softball team had just returned from a tour of Russia. Among publishers, the most sought-after compliment was to be thought a "good operator," meaning that you made a lot of money while also running a good newspaper.

Being a good operator became the standard for the entire newspaper industry. Many of the newspapers that were part of privately owned chains, such as the Hearst and Park Communications groups, adopted the ever-increasing profit expectations of the publicly owned chains—or even exceeded them. Newspapers that remained in family hands were also not immune from the view that an acceptable bottom line is at least 20 percent, though family operations were more likely than big chains to be satisfied with somewhat less.

But all newspapers expected double-digit profits, and Wall Street got used to those quarterly earnings increases and those fat profit margins. The good operators had faced challenges, even in these salad days. Retailers began to eliminate the expensive advertising that appeared on the pages of the newspaper itself, and substituted less profitable preprinted inserts that were put inside the paper. With consolidation of retailing, the remaining merchants became aware of their power to demand discounts from the official numbers on the newspaper's rate card. Direct-mail companies such as Advo began distributing the inserts of grocery store ads and coupons for less than the newspapers charged. And newspaper circulation, which had been declining for years, began to dip in ways that endangered the claim that ads in newspapers reached the whole community. Total weekday circulation had been over 62 million in 1990, after a long period of slow decline. By 2000, the number had dropped below 56 million. Newspapers responded by creating so-called total market coverage services, which meant that every household got the preprints, either in the paper or in a plastic bag hung from a doorknob. They began to hawk subscriptions with special deals through telephone solicitations to keep their numbers from falling further.

In the late '90s, the trends were disturbing, and there was some dark sense brewing that the Internet was going to be a new kind of threat. But the newspaper business, which had prospered so well for so long, was complacent and confident. Advertising related to the dot-com boom was fattening the bottom lines of many newspapers, though few seemed to think that the technology they were touting was a danger. For instance, classified advertising had remained strong despite fledgling efforts to attract classifieds to the Web.

Then came the reckoning, and it has shocked the newspaper industry like a category four hurricane that had been thought to be only a troublesome tropical storm. Suddenly the newspaper industry found itself in Epoch IV, with digital technology wrecking the economic model that had worked so well for so long. With daunting challenges and no clear sense of the future, the nation's newspaper owners feel not unlike those families who in the 1960s had found themselves unsure what to do. And they too are scared.

There is a great irony to the bashing that newspapers have been getting in the business press. To read many of the articles, it would seem that the nation's newspapers are in imminent jeopardy of closing their doors, unable to escape the ravages being wrought by the Web. It is true that some newspapers—especially large metropolitan papers—are losing money or are slashing staff and other expenses to stay in the black. The rest of the newspaper business is still profitable, though the trends are grim and the cyclic punishment of the broad economic downturn makes everything far worse. The problem at this moment for the papers whose stock is publicly traded isn't just one of making a profit. The problem is making enough profit to satisfy Wall Street and also to pay off the huge debt that many newspaper companies carry from their purchase of more newspapers. The McClatchy Company and Tribune Company both carry staggering debt loads, and most other newspaper companies are also weighed down by debt. While owners may long wistfully for a return to the profits of the golden days, the realistic ones know that survival is the focus now. With an overall decline in revenue, a 20 percent profit margin may well be necessary to generate the cash to pay the debts and also make the necessary investments in new media and other new businesses that newspapers hope will eventually replace some of the revenue that has been lost. The result has been an orgy of cost cutting in the newsroom to help keep profit margins at that high level.

With revenues dropping, the only way to bolster profits is to cut expenses, and they are lopping off anything that doesn't clearly add to the bottom line. Accountability news, alas, does not come attached to a clear base of advertisers, like sports and entertainment news. At many newspapers this has resulted in a tug-of-war between the newsroom and the publisher's office, with editors in the excruciating position of trying to do a credible journalistic job with fewer people and smaller budgets.

The most depressing scenario for the future of newspapers is a concept known as "harvesting," which is a business euphemism for stripping the carcass of every bit of flesh and then abandoning the pile of bones. It is a strategy designed for industries for which there is no prospect of salvation, and it is nasty. Assume that you own a business that still has some loyal customers and makes a profit, like most of today's newspapers. But then suppose that you see the trends as so bad and the future so bleak you have concluded that your business is doomed in the long term. Business school logic would be that the company should be "harvested." For newspapers, harvesting might work this way. In the first years, the industry-standard 20 percent profit margin might be greatly increased through cutting news staff—especially the most experienced people, who would likely be the highest-paid. You would shrink the space for news, get rid of health insurance and other perks, and narrow the size to save on paper. You could save money by forbidding travel to cover news, require the remaining reporters to do multiple stories to make up for those who were laid off, cram the paper with cheap syndicated material and wire services, avoid coverage that might anger advertisers or readers, and squeeze every dime you can out of the operating budget. The newspaper would still be produced. Its news columns would still be filled with words on paper that would look like news. But the enterprise that had been a living thing would essentially be a zombie, the living dead.

Over time, readers would stop subscribing and advertisers would go elsewhere, but for a surprising length of time, the pure inertia and goodwill of an established local newspaper would keep it going. And then that final momentum would slow and the inevitable end would be at hand. The rationale is that the owner would have made a lot of money rather than presiding over a fruitless, expensive effort to save the paper by investing in it, which would be foolish.

For a certain kind of owner, this turns failing businesses into an opportunity. When you see financiers who have no history of investing in newspapers suddenly become buyers of distressed papers, the suspicion is quickly aroused that there is a harvesting strategy in play. This was the case when, in 2006, Avista Capital, a private equity firm, bought the Minneapolis *Star Tribune,* one of the nation's most respected newspapers, but one that falls into that especially vulnerable category of midsize papers with high overheads. The purchase prompted immediate speculation that the *Star Tribune* was to be harvested, though Avista denied it. "The idea that we bought this paper with a quick exit in mind or that we are going to be cutting costs left and right is not who we are," OhSang Kwon, one of Avista's principals, told the *New York Times.* "We are patient, long-term investors." But in the first months of Avista ownership, many veteran reporters left with buyouts, about a third of the newsroom was reassigned to other beats, and the new publisher warned of deeper cuts to come. In May 2007, more than a hundred *Star Tribune* employees staged what they called an act of mourning across the street, complete with black armbands and signs urging passing motorists, "Honk if you care about news." Mr. Kwon's explanation of the actions was to say that the near and medium term at the paper was "more negative than we expected." There are continuing rumbles within the industry that the *Star Tribune* is in steep, perhaps terminal, decline. The *Star Tribune* filed for Chapter 11 bankruptcy in January 2009, prompting a frenetic local effort under way to prevent its ultimate failure. In March, Platinum Equity, an equity firm with no publishing experience, bought the *San Diego Union-Tribune,* arousing fears of another Minneapolis scenario.

Newspapers like the *Star Tribune* have been hit especially hard by the changes wrought by Epoch IV. But is the newspaper business as a whole dying? Some very smart people have begun to write its epitaph. In his 2007 report to shareholders, Warren Buffett painted a grim scenario. "When an industry's underlying economics are crumbling, talented management may slow the rate of decline," he wrote. "Eventually, though, eroding fundamentals will overwhelm managerial brilliance." He says this even though his newspaper, the *News*, has high penetration of its market and is Buffalo's leading online site for news. "The economic potential of a newspaper Internet site—given the many alternative sources of information and entertainment that are free and only a click away—is at best a small fraction of that existing in the past for a print newspaper facing no competition." Buffett added that he loves newspapers and "will stick with the *News*" because he believes that a free and energetic press is a key ingredient for maintaining a great democracy. But should the *News* "face an irreversible cash drain," then all bets are off.

Panic is not too strong a word for the collective mind of the newspaper industry. For several years the nation's newspaper publishers have been looking over their shoulders at the Internet, fearful of what it might mean to the newspaper business that has been so good for so long. But for many it has been like standing on the streets of Pompeii watching in trancelike denial as Vesuvius belched smoke before erupting. The wisdom of the industry is that those newspapers that do not act fast may be buried in the ashes of their once-unassailable newspaper monopolies. Newspapers are trying to cope with their revenue problem with three basic tactics: reinventing the newspaper both online and on paper to keep old readers and attract new ones, creating totally new products—most of which have nothing to do with news—to generate new revenue, and cutting costs to the greatest extent possible. None of these tactics are apt to bolster accountability news.

Every newspaper in the nation is experimenting with how to fashion a Web presence that will solve the thus far intractable difficulty of replacing online the revenues that are being lost in the print edition. The best thing about online advertising is that it is extremely profitable because there is no expense for paper, ink, or distribution. The bad thing is that online advertising, relative to ads in the printed paper, is far cheaper to buy and hence generates far less gross revenue. Online ad rates are calculated in a variety of ways, but they allow payment based on the number of people viewing the ad or even whether the person bought something after seeing the ad. Newspaper print advertising rates are based on the total audience for the newspaper, which is less efficient for the advertiser but much more lucrative for the newspaper. In economic terms, each seven-day subscriber to the print edition of a newspaper represents ad revenues many times that of a person who visits the paper online, where only actual views of ads are calculated in setting the rate. This is why newspapers are frantically trying to shore up the circulation for their print product. The hope for newspaper owners is that a way will be found to make online revenues grow both in quantity and in how much can be charged for Web advertising, and that the golden moment will come when the print version revenues will stabilize and online revenues will be sufficient to start posting overall revenue growth. For a few years, online advertising revenues grew impressively at newspaper Web sites, but that growth has slowed or even declined in recent years. and the income produced online still lags far behind the level needed to replace the revenues lost in the printed version.

If the newspaper industry has a religious faith in what will stave off disaster, it is "hyper-localization," which is based on the theory that each town's newspaper is uniquely well equipped to provide local news. Newspapers from the *Boston Globe* to small-town dailies have embraced this concept, and the result has been traumatic in some respects. The *Globe*, which serves a sophisticated city and has had a distinguished history of foreign reporting, closed all of its foreign bureaus, eliminated the position of foreign editor, and gave its front page a strongly local cast, whereas before it usually featured reporting on international and national issues. Since 2000, the *Globe* has won five Pulitzer Prizes, two of them on the national issues of President Bush's use of signing statements to bypass provisions of new laws and one on stem cell research. In 2003, the *Globe* won the most honored Pulitzer—for public service—for its "courageous, comprehensive coverage of sexual abuse by priests, an effort that pierced secrecy, stirred local, national and international reaction and produced changes in the Roman Catholic Church." Two others were for criticism, at a first-quality level. In each case, the Pulitzers reflected an expansive vision of the paper's mission. There is grumbling at the *Globe* that in the future, such ambitious journalism may be in shorter supply.

For small papers, the hyper-localism movement has been led by young innovators and true believers such as Rob Curley. A lover of newspapers, Curley is passionate about giving people what they will find interesting and—most important—will read. For instance, he believes local papers should cover local T-ball leagues and other peewee sports with the passion and depth—and resources—that a big city paper would devote to a major-league franchise. The thrust of hyper-local coverage is that nothing is too small or insignificant to cover, and the more names and pictures you can get into the paper, and especially onto the Web site, the better. And it works. The *Greeneville Sun* discovered that inviting people to post pictures they took of the local Christmas parade drew a very large number of eyeballs to the paper's Web site.

Another key piece of newspaper strategy is the belief that the content provided by the news staff may not be the material that prospective readers value most. Complementing the hyper-local thrust is a parallel one to draw people into the site by inviting their comments, pictures, votes, questions, opinions, and suggestions. The appeal of "reader content" is that it not only engages and entertains, it is also free to the newspaper. Essentially, newspapers are finding that they can boost their Web site traffic by offering content that costs them nothing in reporter salaries. Increasingly, this content is in the form of video clips, with the paper serving as a local version of YouTube in which people post short videos of themselves or others and those coming to the site, then view what has been posted. The video can be a birthday greeting or a rant, a reminiscence or joke, a heartfelt comment on an issue or a critical analysis of a local coach. The important thing seems to be that you are, in a sense, on TV—or at least you have your thoughts and words before the public. There are endless variations, but the point is that hyper-localization and reader engagement have emerged as essential innovations for newspaper Web sites.

While there is nothing wrong with either of these, they tend to divert resources from covering other, more important news. In most newsrooms, the staffs are not growing but shrinking. This usually means that some things are not getting covered. Particularly in danger of being put on the no-longer-important list are things that many readers may find boring, such as coverage of water boards and county commissions and, in particular, state and regional government and politics. The foundation of the reinvention strategy is that newspapers are trying to win people who have stopped reading newspapers by offering them what will bring them back to the fold. In a sense, this is just a variation on what has long been the newspaper strategy of offering a big package so that everyone can find something they want. But when it comes to Web advertising, the content that attracts a crowd is the content that also attracts the advertising. In the past, readers who bought the paper for sports coverage contributed to paying for the coverage of city hall whether they wanted that or not. Now, the city hall reporting is increasingly apt to be judged on the basis of how many online eyeballs it can attract, and if T-ball is getting far more hits, the newsroom resources are almost irresistibly going to be directed toward T-ball.

The second prong of the newspaper industry's strategy to rescue itself is the creation of entirely new products to attract people who don't read the newspaper in print or online, and most likely cannot be won. One of the shrewdest "good operators" in the newspaper business is Dean Singleton, whose passion for newspapers began when he was a paperboy in Texas and has propelled him to the head of his own newspaper chain, MediaNews Group, which is the nation's fourth-largest newspaper company, with 57 daily newspapers, including the *Denver Post*. "Wall Street is convinced that the newspaper business is over," said Singleton, "My contemporaries at newspaper conventions are literally scared to death."

But if there is a survivor among newspaper publishers, it will probably be Singleton, who has embraced the hyper-local approach at his newspapers and their Web sites. He has also been aggressively pursuing the invention of "products," such as magazines aimed at young people or tourists or any other niche that will make his company money. The key demographic is the young, but they are also the most problematic for newspapers. After years of trying to win young readers with experiments in content, promotion, and design, there is strong evidence that suggests that the generational willingness to read newspapers is essentially fixed. Newspapers almost certainly cannot win young people much beyond a modest level of readership, no matter what they do. This clear-eyed pessimism has had the effect of forcing newspapers to see the problem in a different light. They are no longer focused on saving their newspapers by attracting young readers, but have begun to create products having nothing to do with news that they hope nonreaders will embrace and that will be optimized by being local.

While the Internet is still an evolving frontier, it is now a huge marketplace where commerce takes place and people—especially young people—spend a lot of time. One of the things that the early Web pioneers got wrong, though, was a presumption that geography no longer mattered. The Web does make geography irrelevant when it comes to connecting to the Web and using it to take you to whatever Web site you wish to visit, anywhere in the world. And distance is not a factor when it comes to buying online. But that does not mean geography doesn't matter in some situations. Newspapers, which are inherently geographical, saw great promise in creating new geographically focused sites that would appeal to distinct local audiences. But it isn't that easy.

Take the saga of Dean Singleton's venture designed to appeal to Denver's 21-to-34 age group, which had turned away from his newspaper, the *Denver Post*. The idea was to create something utterly apart from the conventions associated with a family newspaper, and the result, in 2005, was *Bias Magazine,* a cheeky name that mocked the whole issue of bias by claiming it. The concept sounded like a natural. Young people in Denver were focused on having a good time, so the new Web site, Biasdotcom.com, declared its solidarity with the youth culture by creating a section it called "shit to do." Entertainment advertisers were expected to come running. Similarly, the *Post* had a well-established relationship with Coors beer, and Coors became one of the major advertisers. The concept was for a Web site and a magazine, both swollen with advertising aimed at a new, savvy young audience drawn to its own generational voice and snarky attitude. For instance, *Bias* launched a campaign to have the third Friday in October declared St. Hooky's Day, "in honor of the laziest person we could find."

When Dean Singleton told me about the venture, he seemed a bit embarrassed. The fact that the *Denver Post* was the parent of the new magazine was kept as quiet as possible. This was both out of a wish to protect the image of the *Post* and, perhaps more important, to project the image of *Bias* as a real outlaw. Certainly, the Web site made vulgarity a staple, and every effort was made to be shockingly naughty. For instance, one "shit to do" entry pledged "I will make sweet love to you, baby, after I rub you down with only the finest Swedish massage oils. Or maybe some Crisco if I got it." In other words, a lot of it was stupid, and its Web-savvy peer group wasn't hesitant to say so. One particular enemy, *Denver Westword,* a rival for the young audience, reviled *Bias'*s layout as "assembled by a four-year-old with motor-control issues" and dismissed its content as "a weak grab bag of forced irony mostly contributed by unpaid Bias members." Indeed, part of the plan was that the audience would contribute to the content. *Westword* added that "When it comes to writing that's lousy but free, Bias shares conceptual ground with YourHub.com, a venture being heavily pimped by the dailies," referring to the *Post'*s more conventional effort to attract reader content. The young audience did not appear, and finally the experiment of *Bias* was abandoned and the Web domain name was sold. If you visit the site now, you find one devoted to right-wing criticism of "media bias."

The economic model for a site such as Biasdotcom.com is a beauty for the owner. If the site can be established and become profitable, the potential profit margin can be extraordinary. Web sites such as this have no costs for paper, ink, or distribution, which are major expenses for print businesses. Once the investment is made to create the Web site, content is relatively cheap, as much of it is audience-generated or from young contributors who have lots of opinions and like to vent them. The advertising revenue may not be huge, but an extra-high profit margin can make it a significant contributor to the bottom line. Singleton, who is aggressively moving into creating new Web and niche businesses, said that while only a modest percentage of the company's total revenue comes from online businesses, the extra-high profits being earned mean that online is making a disproportionate contribution to the company's total profit. This sector of his business is growing at 50 percent a year, and despite the disappointment of Biasdotcom he expects online to provide a significant amount of MediaNews's profits by 2010.

Singleton is part of the vanguard of this kind of thinking in the newspaper business, and the industry is embracing the concept like converts at a revival meeting. Newspapers of all sizes are suddenly hoping that they may have an advantage, at least for a moment, in establishing online niche businesses and publications that can win the growing audience that has spurned or abandoned them. Newspapers have the existing infrastructure to establish and support new online businesses. They already have relationships with advertisers, and want to offer them new options for the ad dollars now leaving traditional media for new media. In addition to advertising-driven ventures on the Web, newspapers are plunging into an array of businesses that in some way connect with what they already do. For instance, they are selling photographs and offering copies of old articles from their archives—for a fee. They are looking at ways to make income from the elaborate delivery operation that puts newspapers on doorsteps but can also deliver other things. My family has branched into the business of creating books of coupons for discounts at motels along the interstate highways of the Southeast. The motel owners pay to have their coupons in the books, which are distributed by the tens of thousands at welcome centers. We are also trying to persuade local merchants and institutions to let us create enhanced Web sites for their businesses—for a monthly fee.

All these new ventures have two significant differences from what newspapers do now. First, they will not be local monopolies, but they will try to thrive in an intensely competitive environment that does not have barriers to entering the fray. Anyone can start a new Web business, but newspaper companies believe that they can still be dominant in their markets and that this will be the road to growth. There will almost certainly be some difficult years as newspapers make the transition and their traditional business continues to decline. But though revenue from the Web for newspapers has slowed, the optimists in the industry believe that there is a golden future a few years away.

The second thing that is different, of course, is that the new businesses will have almost nothing to do with serious accountability news. As the ancillary businesses displace the traditional one as generators of profit, the "business" of newspapers may well shift steadily away from the model founded on delivering news.

Those in the newspaper industry who still embrace this traditional vision of newspapering say that these new profits will help replace the profits that are being lost and are needed to fulfill the news mission. Perhaps in some public spirited newspaper companies that will happen. But the newspaper business is increasingly run by people who view a public service obligation to high-quality news coverage as a romantic notion.

The more likely scenario for newspapers is that news budgets will be squeezed hard in the coming years, and, even more importantly, resources that would in the past have been used for serious news will be diverted to something quite different—the creation of "content," meaning whatever will draw eyeballs.

The third leg of the newspaper industry's strategy for rescuing itself is cutting costs. In hard times, newspapers have always cut budgets, including news budgets. But something quite different is under way as a result of the changes wrought by Epoch IV. It costs a lot of money to create a new online presence, reinvent the print newspaper, and expand into ancillary businesses, and newspapers are trying to do all of that even as their basic business is hurting. This doesn't include servicing the debt that many newspaper companies carry. There is also huge pressure to keep profit margins acceptably high to pay dividends to shareholders and keep the share price from sinking further. Every newspaper balances all these factors in its own way, but the trends seem clear: the commitment to serious news is being overcome by a hunger for "content" directly linked to advertising revenues and "unique monthly visitors," the metric that is often used to measure the success of a Web site.

The most obvious signal of the erosion of a commitment to serious news is the depressing reports from all over the country of news staffs being slashed. The Project for Excellence in Journalism provides an annual "State of the News" review, and by its careful count the total number of journalists is in steady decline. But as Jack Shafer, the media critic at Slate.com, has pointed out, high-quality journalism can be done by small staffs, and many of the newsroom staffs had been at levels created during the fat days of the 1980s and '90s. While that is true, I think it misses a larger point about what is happening in newspaper newsrooms.

The people who are being encouraged—or forced—to leave include many of the best and most experienced journalists, who have grown depressed and despondent about their futures. These are the people who are most likely to command other options, such as becoming the press officer at a local college or some other better-paying, more secure job in corporate public relations. Those who remain on the reduced news staff are increasingly being asked to provide all the manpower for the new Web site, the new hyper-local focus of the paper, the new advertising-driven special sections, the new niche publications, and ancillary businesses. Newspapers, in other words, are trying to reinvent and significantly expand, but with a reduced staff. Reporters are increasingly expected to file stories to the online version of the paper, to generate podcasts for an audio audience, to write for cell phone news distribution, to carry a digital camera to generate video for the Web site, and to blog and interact with readers hungry for direct contact with them. And they are increasingly asked to cover the minutiae of local life as newspapers seek to be encyclopedic in their hometown coverage, and to report stories without really being able to explore them in any depth. That takes time and focus, and both are in short supply at many newspapers. Many editors and publishers are struggling to keep alive a sense of the mission that was their reason for entering the newspaper business, but the riptide of demands in this unsettled period makes it a constant battle.

Some professional journalists have a sense that they are like polar bears pacing back and forth in high anxiety as the ice around them melts away. Mordant humor has become a newspaper staple. In 2007, Bill Shein of the *Berkshire Eagle,* one of the nation's most respected small papers, was prompted to write a sarcastic article headlined "Last Newspaper Reporter Fired" after the *Los Angeles Times* announced the elimination of yet another 57 jobs. "In what Wall Street cheered as a long-overdue and welcome cost-cutting measure, the very last newspaper reporter in America was fired yesterday," Shein wrote, "capping years of newsroom cuts and officially eliminating basic newsgathering as a journalistic function." He added that the last reporter, Ted "Inky Fingers" Mandersoll, had spent the last three months with no salary, but "earning a dollar for each 'qualified lead' produced via dating-service and mortgage-refinancing ads that accompanied the online version of his news stories."

Shein, clearly warming to his subject, then described how "with no reporters to pay, America's media organizations are likely to invest even more resources in upbeat, news-free, advertiser-friendly features" such as a "colorful American Idol daily feature, with tie-ins and contests. Puzzles. Lots and lots of puzzles. Dramatically expanded auto-trader sections, some of which may approach 1,000 advertising-heavy pages a day. Page after page of 'advertorials' promoting the products and services offered by the subsidiaries and 'marketing partners.' " And "lots of full-page advertisements touting the latest 'scientific breakthroughs' in weight loss... hair growth, collectible coins..." What was left would be "bias-free, fact-free, content-free, wholly irrelevant material."

Shein's satire reflects a growing anxiety among journalists that the very profession is in danger—at least as it has been practiced. As newspapers all across the country struggle with keeping their values and also staying solvent, the battle in newsrooms is against a creeping fear. David Shribman, executive editor of the *Pittsburgh Post-Gazette*, has been one of those who have sought to rally the troops against the pessimistic belief that newspapers are headed for oblivion. The *Post-Gazette* is just the kind of midsized paper that has been clobbered by the Web. The paper, which traces its lineage to 1786 and was one of the first papers to print the brand-new U.S. Constitution, has been owned by the Block family since 1927. It boasts on its Web site, "This newspaper puts the public welfare above any special interest," and it has a distinguished history of living up to that claim. It is now trying to honor that legacy while also staying afloat financially. After several brutal years, Shribman's perspective is that of a battered realist.

For two years, the paper actually lost money because of the very difficult environment and economy, he wrote in an e-mail. There were layoffs and renegotiated contracts with unions. The *Post-Gazette* is aggressively experimenting with both its print and online editions, such as introducing locally produced crossword puzzles and huge new graphics and asking local writers to produce novellas on deadline. But the core of the mission remains "putting out a very good, very serious—and thus old fashioned—newspaper." In a gesture bolstering the sense that the best traditional values were intact at the *Post-Gazette,* Shribman "reinstituted courtesy titles, tightened up on the war on bias, and has been a warrior against split infinitives and dangling participles."

But in a poignant coda, he concedes, "We have had terrible staff losses, but probably no worse than anyone else. Harder still than the staff losses has been the erosion of faith in our business.

It has enduring worth, and it will endure. It is noble and enno-
bling. It is terribly hard right now to focus people on these things,
especially when people are leaving and the circulation and revenue numbers are falling, but the truth is that we got into this business the way people go into marriage—mostly as young people,
for better and for worse, and with great hope and idealism. We
need in our business a reaffirmation of vows. I make that vow
anew every day."

But the people who will determine the future of newspapers
are probably more in sync with Dean Singleton's perspective when
he spoke in 2008 about what was coming. He said that newspapers
had thrived despite radio and television and that U.S. newspapers
in their printed form still reach over half the adults on a daily
basis. With newspaper Web sites, that audience expands further,
and such sites reach 37 percent of all Internet users.

But while the average newspaper still makes a profit of nearly
20 percent, Singleton said that he thinks 19 of the 50 top metro
papers are losing money and that this number will continue to
grow. "Too many whining editors, reporters and newspaper
unions continue to bark at the dark, thinking their bark will make
the night go away. They fondly remember the past as if it will suddenly reappear and the staffing in newsrooms will suddenly begin
to grow again. Well, as a former journalist, I also wish for the past,
but it's not coming back. The printed space allocated to news and
newsroom staffing levels will continue to decline, so it's time to
get over it and move to a print model that matches the reality of
a changing business."

He said he saw great opportunity in wireless technology. He
said he had identified 25 categories of niche and local publications, from home and design to weddings. And as for news, his
formula was—to my ear—both realistic and chilling. Newspapers
can survive "if we print what our readers—not what we—want; if
we discard our arrogance and old ideas; if we let our readers participate." But the "old newspaper model, without major changes,
is destined to fail. Paired with a revolutionary new model, we can
succeed. If we fail, democracy fails."

Singleton made his predictions in June 2008. When the economy tanked in October, the newspaper business took a particular battering, and the news seemed to get worse and worse. In late October came the news that the *Christian Science Monitor*, a venerable and respected paper, was abandoning print and would become the first national paper to do so. John Yemma, the paper's editor, said that he was "making a leap that most newspapers will have to make in the next five years." Only shortly before, the *Newark Star-Ledger*, the dominant news organization in New Jersey, announced it was cutting its news staff by 40 percent. Gannett, the nation's largest newspaper company, announced layoffs of 10 percent of its work force, up to 3,000 people. And the *Los Angeles Times*, which had become the poster boy for such cuts, said there would be yet another, which would bring the news staff to about half of what it had been a few years ago.

David Carr, a business columnist in the *New York Times*, wrote a cri de coeur headlined "Mourning Old Media's Decline," in which he observed, "New Jersey, a petri dish of corruption, will have to make do with 40 percent fewer reporters at the *Star-Ledger*, one of the few remaining cops on the beat." He argued that it wasn't that the newspapers didn't have an audience. It had a huge audience. But it was increasingly an audience that read the Web edition, where advertising sells for a fraction of what it brings in the print edition. It was advertising in the print paper that had been paying for those reporters, and both the ads and the reporters were disappearing.

"At the recent American Magazine Conference," Carr concluded, "one of the speakers worried that if the great brands of journalism—the trusted news sources readers have relied on— were to vanish, then the Web itself would quickly become a 'cesspool' of useless information."

"That kind of hand-wringing," Carr added, "is a staple of industry gatherings. But in this case, it wasn't an old journalism hack lamenting his industry. It was Eric Schmidt, the chief executive of Google."

CHAPTER EIGHT

# THE NEW NEWS MEDIA

*I think the model of the future may be political news as a video game.*

—Nicco Mele, founder and president of EchoDitto,
a leading Internet strategy consulting company

THE HEADLINE ON THE COVER OF THE *AMERICAN Journalism Review* said it all: "Adapt or Die." In a frenzy of change, every sector of the traditional news media has been trying to solve the riddle of how to remain solvent and relevant. There have been many "new media" moments for news, when some new technology came along and overturned what had been the accepted way of doing things. Radio allowed President Franklin Roosevelt to speak with Americans in a totally new way. His famous "fireside chats" were revolutionary because he was able to speak in a personal, even intimate, way to a nation that had always before heard its presidents orating with dramatic flourishes. Similarly, in the early days of television, news was delivered with almost funereal seriousness. When Chet Huntley and David Brinkley adopted a more personal style for their newscast, it was an instant hit and changed TV anchormen into welcome friends with whom people forged personal relationships. In both cases, there were voices of resistance that argued that such changes were catastrophic. The presidency was going to be undermined, they said, by Roosevelt's undignified familiarity, and the news was too serious to be treated casually. Needless to say, the doomsayers were wrong.

Some people see the anxiety about today's new news media in much the same light. Samuel Popkin, a professor of political science at the University of California, San Diego, terms the traditional media's resistance to replacing hard news with drama and human interest as "cultural protectionism," and as futile in the face of the public's taste for soft news as were those voices protesting Huntley and Brinkley's conversational style. Certainly, the traditional media must literally adapt or die, as what is now being born is a new style of news, delivered and consumed differently. What is still uncertain is whether the core values of journalism are going to survive in this new world. And perhaps it is also uncertain whether they truly need to survive and whether we can have a vibrant democracy undergirded by an informed citizenry without traditional news. "What makes the old standards of excellence so self-evident that alternatives are barely considered?" argues Professor Popkin. "Some people are learning more from soft news than they ever did from hard news," referring to people who more or less ignore hard news. While I agree that people can learn from every form and style of news, I believe that eroding the iron core of hard news is a bad thing. I look at the new news media from that perspective, and what I see is that the kind of news I believe to be the essential foundation of all the other kinds is increasingly being framed as the last gasp of old elites who are rapidly being pushed from the stage. Some cheer this as both inevitable and a long-overdue comeuppance to journalists who presumed to make news judgments based on their own standards and traditions rather than the public's preferences. In the world of the new news media, the vast, capricious, empowered, technologically savvy, media-insatiable audience will decide what happens to news, and no one knows where that is going to lead.

Good journalism on the Web is a wondrous thing. Using all the tools that the Web offers—words, sound, video, links, limitless data, search, graphics, interactivity—has produced an intoxicating ferment of creative journalistic thinking. If journalism is essentially storytelling, the potential is now comparable to a child being presented with a superdeluxe box of crayons that makes the old, limited array of colors look paltry. Good "new" journalism can take news to a level that none of the older forms of media can match.

For instance, I recently saw a piece of reporting by some creative journalism students that would have been a cause for pride on the Web site of any news organization. The objective was to probe the way corporations and the government observe and monitor us, an issue that is of significant public policy importance as we enter a world where virtually every transaction is captured as data. The students decided to track an average person—as it happened, a schoolteacher—during a normal day and to try to identify every moment when she entered some database or digital record. It was essentially a television report, with a camera following her as she went to the dry cleaner, shopped for food, and did other normal activities. The sharp-eyed students were on the lookout for the ubiquitous hidden cameras that tracked her movements as though she was in a spy movie. And each time she made a purchase or used a credit card or had a transaction of any kind, they identified the database that captured her action. But because of the Web, they were able to go far deeper, while still keeping the narrative engaging. With a click, viewers could delve into the database and see how each piece of data was used, sold, and otherwise manipulated. This novel feature required a great deal of hard reporting and digging that would have done honor to any dogged journalist on the trail of a story. There were links to related subjects and to more information on a host of themes and issues raised by the report. Furthermore, provision was made for reacting to the story online, which allowed people to offer thought and further information and to express their own concerns. It was first-rate journalism, using the powers of Internet technology.

It was also, in my experience, not typical of news on the Web. Without question, there is some dazzling work being done, but the culture of the Web favors news in small bites—increasingly, just enough news to fill the screen of a cell phone. By that standard, this was boringly long. It was also essentially objective in its approach, whereas the Web prefers attitude and edge and opinion. It was on a subject of importance, and the Web tends to favor novelty and entertainment value over substance that may take some effort to digest. News on the Web is almost entirely chosen by the viewer. You have to seek it out, which means that you can easily miss important stories or avoid troubling ones. Print newspapers had offered a smorgasbord, but you had to cast your eye over a range of information that included some hard news. And both television and radio news gave no choices other than to change the channel or station. On the Web, you get the news you want, and what Americans seem to want, when it comes to news, is a lot of Britney Spears and much less of the Iraq war.

A 2007 study of young Americans and news found that most young adults do not have ingrained news habits and do not spend focused time on news the way older adults do. "They aren't acquiring the news habit," according to Harvard professor Thomas Patterson, the author of the study. Young people spend huge amounts of time using media of all kinds, but even when they say they are paying attention to news, the study found that they know very little about it. For instance, the study found that most of them did not know that Condoleezza Rice was secretary of state. In earlier studies, the news habits of young people and adults were much closer, in part because reading the newspaper or—especially—watching the nightly television news was a family affair, and everyone watched the same television. Now, young people have not only their own televisions but their own computers, cell phones, iPods, BlackBerries, and other devices that allow them to be completely independent in their choices. And news has not fared well. Young people especially spurn newspapers in printed form and seem to have almost an aversion to what they perceive as a communications medium of the past. In those surveyed who were

18 to 30, only 16 percent said that they read a newspaper every day, and the number of newspaper-reading teenagers was an even worse 9 percent. For adults over 30, the number was 35 percent. Numbers like these have propelled newspapers into a headlong plunge into Web journalism and a fevered effort to put young journalists to work producing online journalism that will appeal to their generation—which turns out to be a complex and daunting challenge if you also seek to preserve traditional journalistic values.

The Internet media landscape is far too changeable and dynamic to try to define, and even the direction of its evolution seems as uncertain as a hurricane's path. Sometimes it looks like a battlefield or, perhaps more accurately, a free-for-all, with little certainty as to who will emerge still standing.

But before taking an overview of what seems to be happening with news, it is essential to view online news in the context of the entire World Wide Web, of which it is hardly the dominant part. The economic model for traditional news has collapsed not just because of other sources of news, but because there is so much more competition for time and attention—most of it on the Web or through digital cable TV. Rather than a handful of choices or even several dozen, digital cable offers hundreds of channels, each calculated to catch a narrow slice of the overall audience. My cable service offers scores of movies on demand at no extra charge, and scores more through HBO and other premium channels. It seems easy to imagine that the time will soon come when virtually any movie or television program will be readily available on demand, which will be a stunningly seductive invitation for me to distract myself. To add to the potential for wasting time, this unlimited access to movies will not be limited to the large plasma TV in your living room, but will also be available on your office computer and cell phone. Indeed, although the Web is often lauded for its contribution to knowledge and efficient communication, I suspect that some day we shall find that the net impact has been a colossal number of wasted hours. Dan Okrent, the first public editor of the *New York Times,* jokes that he may be responsible for more lost man-hours of working time than anyone in history because of his invention in 1980 of Rotisserie League Baseball. It was at a New York restaurant called La Rotisserie Française that Okrent conceived the idea of creating fantasy baseball leagues based on real players who would be drafted and traded by "owners," who would then compete based on the actual performance of the players. The Web made it possible to follow in minute detail every player in major league baseball, and has probably been responsible for billions of lost dollars in time spent "managing" one's team while supposedly working. The concept has now spread to other sports and is so enticingly irresistible to those caught up in fantasy sports that some businesses have installed software that entraps employees doing it on the job. Good luck.

But fantasy sports is just one of a legion of such entertainments that the Web facilitates. There is, for instance, pornography, which was the business that was the commercial driving force behind much Web innovation. Elementary video amusements like Pong have morphed into vivid, sophisticated, often violent games that have become a gigantic business and require special devices such as Sony PlayStations, which retail for hundreds of dollars and are highly coveted by kids. With your PlayStation 3, you can launch games such as *Call of Duty 3*, which places up to 24 game players in the middle of the Normandy invasion, where they try to destroy each other with hand-to-hand combat, booby traps, and as much realism as is possible to simulate. "If you've seen Saving Private Ryan, you know what you're in for," wrote one reviewer who had given the game the highest rating on Amazon.com. "Head-throbbing noise and death all around you." The word "game" in this context has taken on a whole new meaning, and it is easy to understand that kids find it irresistible to enter—and then remain in—a virtual world of huge excitement without actual blood.

And for adults, there is the phenomenon of creating a whole fantasy identity and life online at such sites as Second Life (www. secondlife.com), where you are invited to be the person you choose to be through the creation of an avatar, an alternate "you" that buys real estate, has romantic adventures, and lives a whole other life. The lure of virtual reality is compellingly real and seductive, and technological advances are making it increasingly difficult to tell reality from fantasy. Now news is part of this virtual world. The Intelligent Information Laboratory at Northwestern University has unveiled News at Seven (www.newsatseven.com), which it describes as "an automated system combining 3-D avatars, images, video, opinion and generated speech." The idea is that you can instruct the site to assemble the news you want—from updates on your friends on their social network site to sports results from your hometown paper's site to the latest from Afghanistan—all delivered by two avatar anchors who will argue with each other and exchange jokes and banter, just as if they were real. "News At Seven isn't just the future, it's the future of the future," the Web site modestly asserts. That proved to be, for the short term at least, an overstatement. The My News portion of the site has advised would-be viewers that it is "currently disabled," though work is under way to relaunch. Nevertheless, the prediction about the future of the future may be on the money: news as a video game.

Then there is YouTube, which is its own vortex of fascinating enticement, capable of capturing endless hours as one wanders through the corridors of video clips, my all-time favorite being a piano-playing cat. The material on this site ranges from crude homemade videos of teenagers acting silly to the hottest new embarrassing footage taken by cell phone camera of a celebrity's cellulite. But that doesn't actually begin to capture what is there. For instance, in the category of music, imagine you are an Elvis fan. If you search for the category Elvis, what emerges is over 52,000 video clips of everything from his classic performance of "Jailhouse Rock" to the worst imaginable Elvis imitators. Prefer Ethel Merman or Pablo Casals? They are there doing "There's No Business Like Show Business" and Bach, amid dozens of other clips. Hungry for more Britney Spears? There are 130,000 clips to peruse, some of them X-rated. And there is similar fodder for virtually any interest or notion. Both Barack Obama and John McCain used YouTube to spread their commercials and campaign pitches. Every minute, the site uploads 13 hours of video from all kinds of sources.

Then there are the dating sites like Match.com and social networking sites such as Facebook and MySpace, the limitless pools of information available through search engines such as Google, and portal sites like Yahoo and AOL that provide an array of services from shopping to networking to instantaneous updates on your investment portfolio. Young people have gone beyond e-mail communication to text messaging through their cell phones, but still are able to do homework, watch TV, and carry on simultaneous conversations with multiple friends through instant messaging. I've seen my teenage niece do it with aplomb, while also talking to me. And through the Web there is access to millions of Web logs, or blogs, that offer commentary on everything from presidential politics to Barbie dolls. Virtually every business and institution needs a Web site, and increasingly it appears that every individual will have one, just as they have a telephone number and an e-mail address. In other words, Americans have walked into a cavernous room spread with a buffet of media choices ranging from the equivalent of haute cuisine to Elvis's favorite peanut-butter-banana-and-bacon deep-fried sandwiches. Imagine facing such a choice. Do you eat sensibly? Based on our national history of succumbing to temptation despite our knowledge of what we *should* be eating, it is easy to imagine the media equivalent of chronic obesity. We seem poised to be a nation overfed but undernourished, a culture of people waddling around, swollen with media exposure, and headed toward an epidemic of social diabetes. It is in this environment that accountability news must find a way to survive.

In the past, when there has been a dramatic change in the news landscape, the losers and winners have been apparent. In the early '60s, the television networks moved aggressively into nightly news, which proved devastating for the nation's afternoon newspapers. While there had been nearly three times as many afternoon papers as morning papers when television made its move, in two decades many of those afternoon papers had closed their doors and a majority of those remaining were published in the morning. Similarly, the nightly network news hit its peak in the late 1970s, but cable made it possible to choose reruns of syndicated programing instead of news at 6:30 P.M. Then came CNN and other cable news channels that offered news at any time. From 1980 to 2000, the nightly news lost almost half its audience.

Now, because of the Web, there is disruption of a different magnitude, and every traditional form of news is affected by what the economist Joseph Schumpeter called "creative destruction." With the Web still in its infancy and new wonders of digital technology coming every day, it may be foolish even to try to explore the impact of the Web on news. But in 2007 Thomas Patterson examined recent online news trends for the purpose of "peering into the future of news in America," an effort whose assessments he characterizes as "speculative." Nevertheless, his work provides a snapshot of what seems to be happening, and what it shows is frightening for much of the traditional media. Overall, online sites connected to traditional news organizations are growing more slowly than virtually every category of nontraditional news sites, including aggregators, blogs, search engines, and service providers. The message seems to be that the institutions that have provided much of the iron core of news are falling behind in the race to win primacy on the Web. This is particularly true of print media, which is to say the nation's newspapers. Though they have enduring strengths, all but the biggest brand-name newspapers, such as the *New York Times* and *USA Today*, face a daunting challenge.

There are roughly half a billion Web sites worldwide, and that universe is expanding, which creates ever more competition for time and attention. The Internet began as a way for university researchers and government agencies to share information via computer, but it evolved into the World Wide Web, which is open to all and allows everyone to communicate. In short order, the Web became a mass medium, though one whose nature was to fragment the mass audience of the traditional media. It is ironic that the Web, which is usually touted for its power to diminish the power of established media, has effectively concentrated that power into even fewer institutions. If there are winners among traditional media on the Web, it is the brand names that have national stature and are now the destination of choice for most Americans seeking news. CNN (www.cnn.com) is the biggest of all news Web sites, with www.nytimes.com the leading newspaper Web site, followed in the top tier by a handful of other brand-name sites. And when it comes to advertising, Google and a few other giant sites soak up almost all of it, leaving the other online sites to fight over relative crumbs.

When it became clear that the Web represented the future, print-based news organizations grudgingly entered the online sphere, which was relatively easy because they could simply post material from their print product on their Web site. Or at least part of the paper version's content. Newspapers from the start were caught in a frustrating dilemma. Overwhelmingly, the culture of the Web is that content is free. If newspapers put the content of the newspaper online for free, they would encourage subscribers to drop their subscriptions and undermine the circulation of their print version. If they charged for content, the prospective audience would avoid them and go instead to other sites where content was free. That would lessen the online traffic around which they hoped to build new advertising sales. The result for many years was a half-hearted compromise in which the online content was free, but included only a smattering of the print product's news. Some newspapers decided to charge for the online product, or to offer it free only to paid subscribers to the print edition. As a sense of panic has overtaken the industry, most newspapers have abandoned charging for content and steeled themselves for the unhappy reality that they are indeed undermining their print circulation. A print subscriber's value in terms of advertising revenue he generates is about ten times the value of an online reader because Web advertising is so relatively cheap. But the wisdom of the industry is that the most important thing is to grow an online presence, which represents the future. In this context, for the nation's newspapers, Web site growth is essential to replace the advertising that is being lost from the print edition.

Taken as a whole, traditional news organizations seem to have hit something of a wall in their search for vibrant online growth, and certainly the nation's newspapers—the source of most reported news—are not expanding online the way they did in the first blush of the Web explosion.

Search engines and Web portals such as Google and Yahoo and AOL are all major providers of news, but very little of it is originated by them. They are "free riders," who get the benefit of offering their audience a range of reported news that has been generated by newspapers and other traditional media. But the originating news organizations get little if any enduring traffic to their own sites. In the case of Google News, which has been surging in growth, you search for news on a topic and are offered dozens or even hundreds of articles on the subject, most of them from newspapers. You may then call up the newspaper article, which is on the originating newspaper's site. But the visit is a short one, and the person calling up a particular story is unlikely to form any loyalty to the newspaper. Instead, the loyalty is to Google News, which sells vast quantities of advertising based on its voluminous Web traffic. Google, in other words, makes money from the news article while the newspaper does the work.

This "free rider" syndrome is also at the heart of the portion of the burgeoning blogosphere devoted to news and public affairs, because almost all of their commentary is based on the traditional media's reporting. Technorati, a Web site that tracks the blogosphere, estimates that 120,000 new blogs are created every day, adding to the more than 70 million blogs now glutting the Web. Of the several million blogs that in some way focus on public affairs, most are in what is called "the long tail" of blog sites that get little or no traffic. But a few bloggers have become as powerful at shaping public discourse as the most influential op-ed columnists. The phenomenon of blogging began around 1997 with a few outspoken folks who found that they liked being able to write just what they thought, publish it by posting it on their Web site, and—if they were lucky—have it circle the globe in a flash through links to other sites that, in turn, linked to yet more sites. This viral spread of information through linking is one of the Web's greatest powers, and it has led to worldwide exposure of everything from torture in Iraq to the secret ending of the final Harry Potter book before it was published.

The so-called blogosphere includes everyone who creates a Web log, or blog, which is merely a site where an individual's views are expressed on the Web. Some make it possible for visitors to respond to their commentary, and some do not. But the important thing for news is that a cadre of bloggers has passionately entered the public sphere on all sides of political and social issues, and what they say is now read by a lot of people. At their best, these bloggers act as a kind of truth squad for the traditional media, assailing them for ignoring important stories or getting something wrong. Many of them like to think of themselves as heirs of the highly partisan and joyously irreverent pamphleteers of the 18th and 19th centuries, who thrived before the days of objective journalism. They generally disdain the notion that they are journalists in any traditional way, but frame their work as a breath of fresh candor, untouched by editors and unrestrained by conventions of mainstream journalism. The blogosphere can be an exciting place to visit, and also an ugly one; obscene and viciously insulting posts can be brutal. But blogging has become a place where people go to see what's up, who's saying what about whom, and it is one of the Web's significant additions to the big conversation that is needed in a strong democracy.

That said, the irony of the blogosphere is that only a handful of bloggers have significant followings and those tend to be early-middle-age white men such as Josh Marshall of Talking Points Memo (www.talkingpointsmemo.com), Andrew Sullivan of The Daily Dish (www.andrewsullivan.theatlantic.com/the_daily_dish/), and Markos Moulitsas of Daily Kos (www.dailykos.com). There are exceptions such as Arianna Huffington of The Huffington Post (www.huffingtonpost.com), who is in her fifties but has the energy and ambition of a Web-savvy teenager and has created a site packed with diverse opinion from a host of bloggers. Michelle Malkin, a strong conservative voice, has two successful blog sites—michellemalkin.com and Hot Air (hotair.com). At the height of the presidential campaign, political sites like Politico.com and RealClearPolitics (www.realclearpolitics.com) and, of course, Drudge Report (www.drudgereport.com) were buzzing with activity, and Tina Brown's The Daily Beast (www.thedailybeast.com), which was launched in the heat of election fever, made a huge splash by publishing an Obama endorsement by Chris Buckley, son of the late William F. Buckley, a conservative icon.

But the vast majority of political bloggers remain in the crowded ranks of those bringing up the rear like an army trailing for miles behind a small cluster of generals. And while a few of the top bloggers and blogging sites may make a profit, they are far more likely to be passionate but penniless. I teach at the Harvard Kennedy School, and one of the students recently told me he never went to mainstream media Web sites for news, but only to bloggers. He had started his own political blog and intended to do it professionally. I first asked him where he thought the news he got on blogs was actually produced. I then asked if he thought he could support himself by blogging, and he told me he was already making money. "But I have four other jobs," he added.

For the most part, political and news-related bloggers are parasites, just like Google News. They do not report news but comment on the iron core of reported news that newspapers and other traditional media are still churning out. Indeed, if there is any group that feeds on the work of newspapers, it is bloggers. As long as there is a strong body of news, this symbiotic relationship works well, as the traditional media increasingly consult the blogosphere for tips and ideas that then find their way into the mainstream.

Aggregators and portals dwarf even the largest news organization Web sites in their Web traffic, which means that the free riders are using content that they don't create to build juggernauts of Web advertising power while the originators of the content are struggling. Google, Yahoo, and others are increasingly cited in national surveys as relied-upon news sources, though they are merely the vehicle for distribution of news they don't create. Similarly, a group of specialized aggregators has emerged that uses artful software to search the Web and gather all the news on their particular topic in one place, where viewers can—as with Google News—call up the original story, then leave that site to return to the aggregating site. Such aggregating sites have been staggeringly successful. For instance, Digg (digg.com), a site that allows viewers to comment on and rank the various items it aggregates, had under 2 million unique visitors in April 2006, but that number has doubled and redoubled and redoubled again. And other such parasite sites are doing as well or better.

One of the big ideas of the Web era is the emergence of "citizen journalism," which is a concept that has risen out of the power the Web creates for any individual to be part of the journalism universe. The essential idea is that anyone can be a journalist and publisher by creating something that looks like journalism and is "published" by posting it on the Web. Citizen journalism takes place when soldiers post from Iraq, or when people caught in New Orleans during Katrina post firsthand accounts of the mayhem and also post photographs taken on the spot. Twitter is now a news vehicle in that its ultrashort electronic posts—or tweets—can carry information—though not much of it. It is citizen journalism when a nonjournalist with expertise in a given field posts something on a news site that reflects his special knowledge. It is citizen journalism when nonjournalists go to water board meetings and send the local newspaper an account of what happened. And such citizen journalism is increasingly finding its way onto newspaper and other traditional media news sites as part of the reader-generated "content," which is becoming a significant portion of what appears in news organization Web sites. To my dismay, such material often has more credibility and is of greater interest to readers than what is produced by professionals. My frustration is not based on scorn for nonprofessionals but on the unhappy fact that the professionals often can't find a way to produce something as interesting, readable, and credible.

There are many strong advocates of citizen journalism as an answer to the problem of a shrinking iron core. Indeed, newspapers are increasingly inviting citizen journalists to cover government and school board meetings and the like—the very things that newspapers are increasingly finding they don't have the professional staff to cover. The hyper-localism of many papers requires that everything be covered, and a convenient and inexpensive way to do it is to recruit unpaid volunteers—citizen journalists—who will do the job as best they can. Some of them can do the job as well as any professional, and follow the same ethical standards of impartiality. But this arrangement can be exploitative, and it is unreliable in the long term. It is also my experience that nonjournalists, meaning unpaid nonprofessionals, generally come to this role with definite views. When I was covering school board and county council meetings as a young reporter, there were always one or two people at every meeting who were vitally interested and would be just the sort to declare themselves citizen journalists. They were often intelligent and informed, but they all had a point of view that was firmly in place, and I would not have wanted to depend on them for a dispassionate account of what transpired.

But there can be no doubt that there is a powerful mechanism in play with the concept of broadening the sources of knowledge and expertise that traditional news organizations bring to reporting the news. One of the most innovative efforts to marry participatory journalism with traditional reporting is under way at Public Insight Journalism, the brain child of Michael Skoler, whose credentials as a traditional journalist span radio, print, and television. Skoler has become an evangelist for what he terms "collaborative journalism." He has assembled—and vetted—65,000 individuals who have expertise in particular areas and are eager to be sources for traditional journalism. In a sense, Skoler's approach is to create a vast rolodex of people who know what they are talking about and can be tapped for their knowledge, their ideas, and their guidance on what the important issues are.

But more than creating a model for broader-sourced reporting, Skoler's view is that the traditional media need collaboration with their readers and viewers as a way to start repairing the deep, long-term trend of diminishing trust in the mainstream media. "You listen to people who listen to you," Skoler told an audience of traditional journalists in October 2008, "and journalists have not listened to the public for ages."

In a sense, some aspects of contributory journalism have long been a staple of traditional journalism, but submissions by nonjournalists have been screened through the reporting and editing process. Letters to the editor are a venerable version of citizen journalism, and have been one of the best-read parts of newspapers. And such letters can be as persuasively powerful as anything in the newspaper. Early in his ownership of the *New York Times*, Adolph Ochs editorially opposed women's suffrage, but he published scores of pro-suffrage letters. When the Nineteenth Amendment passed and was ratified, the leaders of the suffrage movement credited the *Times*'s letters pages as critical to their success. But letters to the editor are edited, as those who write them know all too well.

Similarly, most reporting is a process of tapping the knowledge of other people with expertise in some specific area. To journalists, these "citizens" are sources, and their contribution may be an eyewitness account of Hurricane Katrina, a scientist's authoritative analysis of how much mercury is safe to consume, or a willingness to tell all—not for attribution—about the governor's slush fund. Journalism depends on journalists finding such sources, but traditional reporting also requires checking what they say, testing it against other accounts, and seeking confirmation that the eyewitness was actually in New Orleans when Katrina happened, that the authoritative scientist is not a crackpot, and—especially—that the anonymous source is credible.

One of the greatest boons to journalism in the digital era is that it has expanded the potential that those with expertise will come forward on any given subject. In a celebrated incident in 2004, *60 Minutes* aired an investigation by Dan Rather that asserted that

President George W. Bush failed to fulfill his duty as a member of the Air National Guard. As proof the show offered typed military documents from the 1970s. Later that same night, the documents were challenged in an obscure blog on the basis that the typeface was inappropriate for that era. Soon a blog-driven search was on for other examples of 1970s typewriting and military documents, and experts in this arcane subject seemed to come out of the woodwork. While some so-called experts seemed suspect, others were genuinely authoritative, and their skepticism undermined the credibility of the documents. This contributed to discrediting the investigation and led to a humiliating CBS apology and Dan Rather's early retirement.

If the Web has demonstrated anything, it is that many people want to speak, and the surge in citizen journalism is part of this torrent of communicating. But treating journalism as an avocation has dangers. My primary fear is that it will supplant professional reporting for economic reasons. Citizen journalists get paid little or nothing, which makes them very appealing to the nation's floundering newspapers. On the one hand, this means that people who want to perform journalism for the fun of it or as part of their sense of citizenship are apt to be exploited. But from the news consumer's perspective, they may also be replacing people with professional experience and training. Advocates for citizen journalism argue properly that the place for citizen journalism is as a complement to professional journalism, an added value that expands the range of voices and perspectives. I agree with that. But citizen journalism is inherently a personal medium attracting highly motivated people who have a strong perspective on what they are writing about. And I fear that this self-created content will become a staple in covering issues of politics and policy, as those same subjects are increasingly neglected by news organizations.

Not surprisingly, newspaper reporters and editors are extremely nervous, and many of them feel that something is in jeopardy that goes beyond their obvious self-interest about losing jobs and the power that goes with their work. Certainly that self-interest is there. But in my experience, most journalists chose the profession because they are highly motivated to do something that they regard as important, and—yes—to be able to make a living at it. They are, to my mind, much like people who choose to become teachers. Both groups have educations that would make other options viable, and both have chosen relatively low-paying work that has other rewards. The notion that journalists are obsessed with losing the power that goes with their jobs is mostly nonsense. They worry about losing a paycheck and, with few options in journalism, also losing the profession to which they have devoted their lives. Certainly newspaper journalists like to do meaningful work, and there is a measure of prestige to a byline. But there isn't a lot of glamour attached to the journeyman journalist's work. Watchdog journalism is mostly a matter of showing up for the meetings that are the meat and potatoes of governance and poring over documents. Nevertheless, professional journalists have the bolstering belief that what they do *is* important. And they believe it is a job that needs to be done by people who are trained and are themselves held accountable by their peers, their editors, and the public.

One of the endless arguments now taking place in journalism circles is about how to define what a journalist is. Anyone can write something and send it into the world—indeed, send it around the world—via the Web. But is that journalism? Not to me. It is not journalism when someone uses a cell phone camera to capture a brutal crime or to catch a celebrity in an embarrassing moment. That's taking a picture. Nor is it journalism as I define it when people on the scene in natural disasters or war zones give first-hand accounts of what they see. It is valuable firsthand testimony, but it is not journalism. When a newspaper invites its Web audience to contribute ideas and knowledge about the newspaper's investigation of a controversial construction project, it is inviting them to be *sources* for journalism, but they are not practicing journalism. The concepts of citizen journalism and soliciting reader input are hot at newspapers, which are looking for ways to engage people as well as to capitalize on the expertise that is undeniably out there. But that is not journalism as I see it.

There are those who are worried that the very *profession* of journalism as it has been known is passing, to be replaced by a combination of advocacy, public relations, and individual voices whose freedom to speak as they please—and entertainingly—will be what attracts them to the field. Should that prove to be the main form that news takes, we shall be the poorer for it.

Counterbalancing these negatives in the new news media are the spellbinding infusion of expertise from interested citizens, the prospect of restoring the connection of trust that iron core news must have to perform its function, and the hope that a new model will take advantage of the technology, harness the exploding creativity of the Web, and preserve the values that have been essential. There is also the possibility that serious journalists may be able to do their work as independent contractors, supported by fans of their work, like music groups. The music business spawned the notion that it took only a "thousand true fans" willing to pay $10 a month to support a musician, and there is some thought that a vein of high-quality journalism in the future might work the same way. Some reporters are already seeking donations to pay for trips to trouble spots, but whether this is a viable model for the long term remains to be seen.

At the end of the day, though, saving the iron core of news depends on answering one daunting question: "How do we pay for it?"

# CHAPTER NINE

# SAVING THE NEWS

*The thing that has not speeded up is the capacity to actually think through something.*

—Ellen Goodman, November 2008

THE TOWN OF IDAHO FALLS IS TUCKED INTO THE southeast corner of Idaho, an area known for its striking natural beauty, Republican politics, and powerful ties to the Mormon Church, which dominates the region even more than it does Salt Lake City, about 200 miles to the south. The local paper, the *Post Register*, has been owned for four generations by the Brady family, a clan of Irish Catholic Democrats who have thrived despite being routinely bashed by locals who consider them liberal papists.

In February 2005, the *Post Register* began publishing a six-part series of articles based on hitherto secret court documents revealing that local Boy Scout officials had ignored repeated warnings about an Idaho Falls scout leader who had eventually been convicted of pedophilia. The first story was an account of 14-year-old Adam Steed, who had been one of the scoutmaster's numerous victims. It told how this boy and his family had demanded the scoutmaster be stopped, and instead of being praised had been shunned and disparaged.

Just like Adam Steed, the *Post Register* was vilified for dragging such dirty laundry into the light, and the series prompted a withering assault from the Boy Scouts, the Mormon Church, and some of the most powerful people in Idaho Falls, including, of course, advertisers. In Idaho Falls, being a Boy Scout is almost a second religion, and the Mormon Church is the organization's principal backer. The paper had taken on the most sacred of cows.

At a small paper, the damage from angering powerful people can be felt quickly, and in this case the stakes were particularly high because nearly half the paper's ownership is held by 140 employees—many of them Mormon—who count on it for their retirement. Talk radio hosts assailed the paper as anti-Mormon, and calls and e-mails poured in accusing the paper of Mormon-bashing. Advertisers canceled their business, vowing never to return. One outraged citizen began buying full-page ads in the Sunday edition, where among other things he noted that the principal reporter for the articles was gay, implying that the series was vengeance for the anti-gay stance of the Mormon church and the Boy Scouts. People started harassing the reporter, ringing his doorbell at midnight and the like. His partner of five years was fired from his job.

Even so, as executive editor Dean Miller wrote in his account of those difficult days, the reporter pressed on, and the staff remained solidly behind what the paper was doing. Publisher Roger Plothow, who grew up a Mormon and was an Eagle Scout, wrote an open letter proclaiming the articles a victory for open public records. The newspaper company's president, who was Plothow's boss, published his own open letter proclaiming his support of the Boy Scouts and expressing "regret at any negativity," but he did not stop the ongoing investigation. The series had emboldened other Boy Scouts who had been abused by a dozen other scoutmasters to come forward, though the local Boy Scout organization had declared that there had been only one. No one named in articles published by the *Post Register* asked for a correction, retraction, or clarification, as much of the information had come from deposition transcripts that had been in secret lawsuit files. One of those exposed was a vicious child rapist who had been reported to the Grand Teton Council of the Boy Scouts in the 1980s, convicted in Utah, and was now at work for the Council. Two weeks later, the paper documented another pedophile in the Council, whose criminal file had been sealed and hidden. Ultimately, the Utah legislature unanimously passed a law to do away with the statute of limitations on child molestation.

The *Post Register* is a newspaper with a circulation of 26,000 and a news staff that has some veterans, but is mostly a cadre of recent journalism school graduates. Working there is considered an entry-level spot in the journalism hierarchy, but the news staff was passionate, led by people who believed in the journalistic mission, including a publisher who backed them to the hilt. One of the sweeter rewards for their work was a spike in circulation at a time when most newspapers were reporting steady declines. "Publishing uncomfortable truths needn't be an act of hot-blooded courage," Miller wrote in his account. "It should be a cool-headed exercise in focus: Find the civic heart of a story, steer a steady course to it, and serve the public's legitimate interests in openness and justice."

I tell the story of the Idaho Falls *Post Register* to help answer a critical question: does news really need saving? The argument of this book is that news of the sort that the *Post Register* provided to the citizens it serves is the news that feeds our democracy and is vital to our character as a self-governing nation. There is a great deal that powerful people and institutions seek to keep hidden, and far more that would be hidden were it not for the vigilance of a watchdog press corps. Indeed, far too much goes unwatched and unreported as it is; the act of saving the news should, in fact, include a goad and a prod to news organizations to be more rigorous. While Web-based organizations can break news, it has been the best newspapers that have done the deep reporting. In this time of transition, when so much is unclear and uncertain about the future of news, there are reasons to be hopeful and—even more important—there are actions to be taken. But there isn't much time.

To roam the Web is to wander in a world so dazzling in its breadth and innovation that there is a kind of vertigo of head-shaking wonder at the speed with which it has changed our world. No one can doubt that the world of the future is going to be centered on the Web and digital technology, and that saving the news has to begin by recognizing that. This does not mean that there will be no printed news or books, but the world has already changed for most Americans into one that *requires* interaction online, and that requirement will only increase. Saving the news in no way means damming up the current that is running so very strong. The current can sweep away everything in its path, or it can be guided like a river shaped by levees so that it irrigates the land instead of destroying it. The market doesn't care where the Web goes, as long as it results in profit. I have lost any illusion I may have had that the market is always the wisest arbiter, and I think that in the case of news, a purely market-driven future will damage or even destroy the iron core.

That said, I also believe that an enduring solution for preserving the iron core of news and traditional journalism standards has to be a commercial one. Katharine Graham, the legendary publisher and owner of the *Washington Post*, famously observed that the best guarantee of first-class journalism is a strong bottom line. A marginally profitable news organization is too weak to withstand the kind of punishment that comes from publishing news that makes powerful people mad. The more tenuous the news organization financially, the more timid and vulnerable to self-censorship. The Idaho Falls *Post Register* probably could not have taken on the most powerful institutions in its town, and weathered an advertising boycott, without a sound economic foundation. Similarly, a financially successful news organization can afford to pay the wages and health care benefits of the caliber of journalistic talent that is required for serious news reporting. A news organization that is losing money has few choices, and, while hard times can be endured for a while, a business that is chronically only marginally profitable is likely doomed.

I define "saving the news" as finding a commercial model that will sustain professional journalism focused on serious news, conducted with traditional values and standards for a broad audience in towns and cities throughout the nation. This does not necessarily mean saving newspapers, though they remain the greatest source of the kind of accountability journalism I want saved. If newspapers as a species die, that will simply be reality, and we shall have to figure out how to save the news without newspapers. But I have not given up on newspapers, and I think they have a future, if only they can endure long enough to find it. Those who sound the death knell for newspapers liken their plight to that of silent movies when the talkies began to appear. I see them as more like the railroad industry in the face of airplanes, automobiles, and interstate highways. Railroads were forced out of the city-to-city passenger business, which they had once dominated. But the industry survived by hauling freight and now trains move about two-thirds of the total tonnage in the country. Newspapers have to find a way to haul freight.

The first challenge for the nation's newspapers is to figure out a way to stay in business in the face of the worst economic downturn since the Depression. Newspapers were already reeling from epochal technological change when the economy collapsed. In December 2008, as it became clear that advertising was falling off a cliff and revenues were plummeting, many newspapers found themselves in a triage situation, killing parts of themselves to keep the rest alive. Cost reduction, which had already cut away much of the fat, now began to slice off muscle and bone. The few remaining cities with competing papers saw the weaker go down, such as the *Rocky Mountain News* in Denver and the *Post-Intelligencer* in Seattle. The *Detroit News* and the *Detroit Free Press* tried a different tack, preserving their reporting strength but eliminating home delivery several days a week. Everywhere, newspapers were demanding concessions and enduring painful layoffs. At our family paper, we had the first layoffs in our history, and it was excruciating. Ultimately, the downsizing may prove to be a blessing in that the industry has to reinvent itself on a lower cost basis if it is to survive, and such wrenching changes tend to happen when extinction is the alternative. The newspaper industry that emerges will be leaner and, when the economy turns and some of the lost advertising returns, the new revenue will have an outsized reviving power like food to a starving man. The result may be a surge in profitability and a chance to face the more daunting challenge of secular change.

Newspapers are in a situation in which, as my grandmother would say, the rabbit has to climb a tree. But the change is of a magnitude that many newspaper owners have even now not fully grasped. It is not unlike the moment when rock and roll with its pounding rhythms and speed blew away the quieter popular music of Frank Sinatra and Bing Crosby. That was a generational change. Today, the nation's newspaper newsrooms are largely occupied by people for whom the Web is familiar but not ingrained. They are not trained to be the journalists of the future, who will have to be able to report with shrewdness, write well, and also have a facility with working in a 24/7 news environment, shooting videos, creating audio reports, blogging, interacting with readers and citizen journalists, coming up with dazzling graphics, and adapting to a cascade of ever-newer Web applications so they can create journalism for everything from the print newspaper to cell phone screens, Web television, and podcasts. Similarly, on the business side the environment is fiercely competitive, and will only grow more so as Web-based rivals multiply without the barriers to entry that printing presses and broadcast licenses represented. In the 1960s and '70s, family newspaper owners were undone when printing technology changed and people began leaving newspapers for television. Those who preferred not to assume the risk left the business. Compared to the fear and trauma of what lies ahead for newspapers now, that transition was simple. This time around, the change is so extreme that no one really knows what is coming or who will survive.

In November 2008, in the midst of the worst fall for newspapers in memory, 50 senior newspaper executives from most of the nation's leading newspaper companies gathered behind closed doors at the American Press Institute outside Washington, D.C., to try to figure out how to save their businesses. It was billed as a "Summit on Saving an Industry in Crisis," and the participants listened as people like James Shein, a turnaround specialist at the Kellogg School of Management at Northwestern University, led them through the psychological phases of dealing with a faltering business. First, being blind to eroding conditions followed by an inaction bred of denial and finally to "faulty action" in hope of a quick fix, such as slashing costs by dumping the reporters who are the chief creators of the only product that will potentially save their businesses. Full-blown crisis is next, followed by "dissolution." It was not a cheery message, and the advice seemed to be essentially to do *something* productive and imaginative, and if that doesn't work to try something else. According to Shein, "Ready, fire, aim" should be the operating principle. Though there was a lot of discussion about research and development and collaboration, the only action taken by the group was to agree to reconvene in six months.

But the hardy newspaper owners who suck it up and move into the future still have some significant advantages. The commercial lesson of the Web—at least so far—has been that established brands have the advantage. The most frequently visited news-generating Web sites belong to CNN and the *New York Times*. Local news organizations are known and familiar, though the trends suggest that this head start may carry them only until competition stiffens. They have a chance, though, to adapt.

So, what should forward-thinking owners of news organizations be doing now? They should recognize that these are hard times unlike anything seen before. They are going to have to spend some serious money, endure smaller profits, and have the faith that the future will reward them. They should start by recognizing that they have two businesses rather than one. The print newspaper is one thing. The Web newspaper, to my mind, must be viewed not as a complementary or ancillary product, but as something utterly different: a separate business and a separate news organization.

This is *not* the way newspaper owners see things, for the most part. They are dealing with the Web by tasking their reporters and ad salesmen to serve both the print and online products, which I believe is a strategy that is unlikely to succeed as the Web picks up speed and sophistication and diverges more and more from the old established media genres. The Web is going to be a medium of its own. Thinking that a successful hybrid can be manufactured by print journalists and ad salesmen used to selling space and inserts is like asking Sinatra to sing "Blue Suede Shoes." He can do it, after a fashion, but it isn't what he *does.* It isn't his authentic self. Newspapers—the printed ones—have an authenticity that is their greatest strength, and a Web newspaper must have the same. They both reflect a specific culture that needs, in both cases, to be respected. You can't do either on the cheap and get away with it for long. This is a concept that some of the best newspapers have already grasped, and they are infusing their Web sites with a sensibility of their own. Not surprisingly, washingtonpost.com and nytimes.com are leaders in this, using the reporting of the newspaper staff as a point of departure for a new environment that has the multiplatforms of the Web.

But even these sites may not prove to be sufficiently appealing to an audience that is steeped in the culture of the Web, which is faster, more irreverent, more subjective, cruder, more experimental, and geared to an audience with a short attention span. When news sites offer up expansive online databases and scores of links to deepen reporting, they are serving a traditional news sensibility, not the sensibility of the Web. The daunting question then becomes whether traditional news organizations should move so far outside their traditional culture that they have a real chance of capturing the attention of this new Web-centric audience. And if they do, will they have to leave behind the standards of journalism that have been at the heart of their value system? The state of newspaper Web sites now is one that could be considered newspaper-plus, and the sensibility remains, despite a Web presence, very much that of a traditional newspaper.

My sense is that this will prove to be a transitional stage, and the Web will continue to establish its own standards and practices and culture, just as television did. In the 1950s, when TV was young, the style of television news was largely stiff and serious, with radio and print reporters going before the camera. But as time passed, television news developed into a medium with its own style and limits. For instance, in the early days, TV news judgments were similar to those of print, and there were a lot of talking heads. But TV's power came to be recognized as moving pictures. And that realization has evolved into a widely observed principle of television news that if there are no good pictures, TV doesn't do the story. That is why you rarely see a public policy question explored in any depth on TV, and why you see so much junk that has the virtue of great video.

The important point is that each of the traditional forms of media has a culture of its own that needs to be respected, and the traditional way of dealing with news may not lend itself to the Web. National Public Radio (NPR), for example, would not seem an apt prospect for a Web site that tried to offer written news, video, and such. Its Web site will probably be an alternate delivery system, with some interaction, some video, and added bells and whistles that are appropriate. But should NPR try to become both the *New York Times* and ABC News? It does not seem a sensible strategy. Similarly, every news organization will have an alternate delivery system on the Web, with the additions and gizmos that a Web audience now expects. And this will gradually—or perhaps not so gradually—evolve into something quite apart, with an identity that will be more brotherly than complementary, and with a largely separate staff.

This means that the print version of newspapers must find its own way to survive, and I believe it will—or at least that it can. No one really knows what the bottom is in terms of circulation and advertising for newspapers, but there seems every reason to think that it has not yet been reached. The instincts of a lifetime spent in print journalism tell me that the best guarantee of reaching a stable and sustainable level of both advertising and circulation is to publish a newspaper that is strong, brave, and rich in quality and in personality. It should have reporters and editors whose job is to publish the most innovative, most provocative, most interesting news it can find, and trust that readers will find that indispensable.

A newspaper should be distinctive in its sense of place and character, reflecting its town and region and tailoring itself to its readers without pandering. And if those readers want to read the newspaper's articles online, they can. But the job of reporters will be to report and write, not to try also to be a Web jockey. If there needs to be a cell phone–sized version, let a specialist in cell phone–sized news write it, not a newspaper reporter. And if reporters want to expand into Web journalism, they should not allow that to interfere with the main job of reporting.

One of the most fearlessly experimental—not to say wacky—approaches to making this community connection has taken place at the *Las Vegas Sun* under the direction of Rob Curley, the passionate proselytizer of hyper-local coverage. His vision is that the *Sun*'s mission—and business—is building a community, which requires something as tailored to the individual town as a bespoke suit. When Curley arrived in June 2008, he arranged coverage of all the football games at each of the city's 35 high schools, with four cameras and an individual Web page for every single player. "It was crazy overkill," he said, "and we couldn't get anyone to look at it." The population of Las Vegas has doubled over the last decade, and high school sports have little traction where it wasn't unusual for kids to attend several different high schools over four years. He tried jazzing up the paper's stories in the online version with gorgeous graphics and all kinds of extra features. Traffic went down. Then he started measuring everything and learned that, in Vegas, the things that get the traffic are breaking news, University of Nevada at Las Vegas sports, and anything to do with the gaming industry. This time, traffic jumped 400 percent in six months. The print version of the *Sun*, which is owned by Greenspun Media Group, is now an eight-page, advertising-free journalistic product inserted into the *Las Vegas Review-Journal*, its senior partner in a joint operating arrangement. But with a twist.

"We got rid of the reporters," said Curley, who is president and executive editor of Greenspun Interactive. The paper then hired a group of high-profile journalists from major papers like the *Los Angeles Times* and assigned them to write enterprising "holy crap" stories about local issues. "Not what the city council did, but the how and why of it," Curley said. The plan now is to launch an exhaustively researched online operation that will provide the ultimate in targeted, hyper-local information "right down to what third grade teacher in your local elementary school does the best job at teaching girls science." As to whether all this will attract a big online audience, Curley said he hasn't a clue.

In a more traditional style, it was the guts and commitment of the *Times-Picayune* in New Orleans in the aftermath of Hurricane Katrina that turned the citizens of that city back into newspaper readers. It was this kind of focused, brave work that made the *Post Register* in Idaho Falls a circulation winner. When the *Lexington Herald-Leader* in Kentucky published a probing examination of unethical athletic recruiting by the University of Kentucky, the town was up in arms because basketball in Lexington is a religion. There were threats and boycotts, and also a strong surge in circulation. Newspapers that tell people what is going on have an indispensable role in a community, and they also, I believe, have an enduring place as a medium—even with the young. Typically, people get interested in news when it begins to matter to them, which is when they take on the responsibilities of adulthood. We are living at a time of extended youth, with people in their thirties sometimes still thinking of themselves as kids. But eventually those kids will mature, and news will be more important to them, although newspapers may not be their medium of choice; my students who don't like newspapers find them boring and intimidating.

But many of us find newspapers a warm and comfortable medium, and as such, able to command a sustainable audience, just as books have done. There is a sensual pleasure and satisfaction to reading a newspaper while sipping a morning coffee that I believe will prove as enduring as the quiet solace of a martini in a chilled glass. And newspapers in their printed form are a symbol of community in a way that Web sites are not...at least not yet. The *institution* of a good newspaper is the beating heart of a community, and it embodies something living that goes beyond black type on compressed wood pulp. As I think back on the newspaper I have known longest— the *Greeneville Sun*—I remember an engagement with the town that all newspapers, including that one, should seek to recover and renew.

Among the happiest memories of my childhood were the sultry August evenings every other year on which the *Sun* threw a party for the whole county—an election party! In the 1950s, the most important election in our world was on the first Thursday in August on alternate years, when the primaries were contested for various state and local offices. In our county, which hadn't sent a Democrat to Congress since 1881, winning the Republican primary for local offices such as sheriff was tantamount to being elected. And, similarly, the winner of the statewide Democratic primary signaled almost certain victory. Politics in Greene County had long been a bruising spectator sport, so it was not surprising when people began to gather outside the *Sun* on election night to get the most recent returns. Over the years, as the crowd grew, my grandmother began piping out recorded music. By the late 1950s, the *Sun* election party had become a huge affair, with Main Street closed in front of the paper, a flatbed truck straddling the street, and live country music. The service clubs sold hot dogs and drinks. My grandmother and father would function as generals, guiding the tabulation of the returns as they were reported, precinct by precinct, reading them out from the stage between songs, which always included Tiny Day, our sports editor, moaning a lovelorn ballad called "Foggy River." Those August nights, with cheering and jeering and—it seemed—the whole county in attendance, are a piece of America that has been lost to technology. With television, the returns were available at home, and the custom died out.

My father and grandmother seemed to treat their work as a daily joy. My father rose at 6:30 and went directly to the office, returning about 8:00 for breakfast. He came home most days for a quick lunch, and was there for supper until the phone rang, which it inevitably did. His phone number was in the book. My grandmother's routine, on the other hand, was to make breakfast last most of the morning. She had a gallbladder problem that robbed her of her appetite, so in her later years, she mostly pushed food around on her plate. But each morning, as she sat at the breakfast table, a stream of people would come in the door to say hello to Miss Edith, sometimes bringing personals that she would then batter out on her old typewriter in the little room off the kitchen. Other people brought gifts like quail, one of the few foods she fancied, or just dropped in to chat. She was clearly respected and loved, and she respected and loved the people of her native soil in return.

I think that what newspapers have to rediscover is this kind of connection to the people they serve. I suspect that at one time or another everybody *did* get mad at my father for what was in the paper. But the bond of trust and affection was also there, as it was at the Idaho Falls *Post Register,* and restoring these bonds is essential if newspapers are to save themselves. Perhaps the Web will facilitate a restoration of close ties, but I believe that it will more likely come from something that is based not so much on the Web's interaction as on demonstrating commitment to a community, presenting a distinctive personality, and reflecting a genuine affection for the people it serves. Perhaps it is counterintuitive given the open forum of the Web, but these things— to my mind—show themselves more persuasively in print than online.

Ironically, though the overall circulation of the print edition of newspapers has been in steady decline, their "total audience," which includes the online version, is significantly up at many papers. Newspapers are much underappreciated as a refined, evolved technology that is portable, recyclable, and cheap. The human eye scanning a page of newsprint is faster and more effective than reading online will ever be. A newspaper is also a phenomenal bargain in that it is the distilled product of hundreds—even thousands—of man-hours spent gathering, editing, designing, and displaying the information that its skilled professional staff believes would be of most value to its readers. But none of this will matter if newspapers don't report real news and tell stories with imagination and candor. In other words, newspapers must do something that people find valuable, which means in this era of so many alternatives they must be focused and concentrate on job one: quality. This has long been the mantra of Arthur Gelb, former managing editor at the *New York Times*, who I think has the most fertile and imaginative journalistic mind of his generation. "Good stories!" he would bellow in exasperation as he read of yet another news organization's trendy experiment in trying to attract a crowd. "It is all about good stories!" Then you surround those good stories with strong headlines—which is an art in itself. And you edit the stories so that readers don't have to read ten paragraphs before they find out what happened yesterday. The fad of beginning every article with a long, meandering anecdote has begun to rot. Gelb would say that being first on the Web with a story is someone's job and a service to readers, but that the print newspaper is worthy of being created by its own standards and rules and made into a polished and exciting package.

This kind of thinking goes against popular wisdom in the newspaper industry, which is a business that has long been plagued by ambitions that were too low and a yearning for a quick fix to win reader's hearts and loyalty. In 1982, *USA Today* began publishing with a policy of having no articles so long as to jump inside the paper from the front page, save for one piece deemed the "cover story." Short articles that did not have jumps became the industry's mantra, and story length was considered the key to flagging confidence. Readers said they didn't like jumps, so there should be no jumps. I recall covering a newspaper publishers' convention for the *Times* in the mid-1980s when Tina Brown, then the hot and trendy editor of *Vanity Fair* magazine, was asked to speak. Ms. Brown told the hotel ballroom filled with middle-aged-plus white men that their problem was not story length or anything like that. She said people would read stories of any length if they were good and interesting. You should mix it up, she said.

But then she added, "Your biggest problem is that you edit your newspapers for men when you should edit them for women." An audible groan echoed through the room as the publishers geared for a feminist rant, but Ms. Brown was on to something far more important than urging stories about babies and diets. "Men want to know what happened," she told the publishers. "Women want to know what *really* happened." When I heard that, I knew she had put her finger on the key to the whole issue: newspapers—indeed, all news organizations—have to assume the burden of telling readers what *really* happened, and if they do, they will be performing an essential service. This is not the same thing as offering up hyper-local coverage of every Kiwanis Club speaker, garden club event, and fund-raising car wash. That kind of coverage can succeed for a while, but at the cost of becoming a journalistic eunuch for which no ambitious journalist would be willing to work.

The same journalistic chops will work for the online version of the newspaper, but for that you need journalists who are authentic to the medium. News organizations have a great opportunity now to create online journalism that will incorporate all the tools and culture of the Web and make the kind of connection with young people and Web users that is possible only when an authentic contemporary sensibility is recognized. Online news consumers are going to want all of what the Web offers. And there is no reason to think that those who read print newspapers will not also go online for news, and vice versa. Print newspapers and their brother publications online do different things and satisfy in different ways, and if that is recognized, they can both thrive. What can't thrive is the muddled half measure.

There is a value system embedded in this solution to the problem, and it is rooted in a choice that owners may not be willing to make. It puts the public service mission of delivering high-quality news above the commercial strategy, which is an expensive risk to take. Some news organizations have invested heavily in quality only to see their circulations fall. But the key consideration isn't whether quality will stem circulation losses, but whether it will make possible a stable circulation base upon which to build an enduring business. Without that commitment to quality—in many cases, a quality that newspapers did not have because they didn't have to—the circulation declines cannot be stabilized.

This means lower profits, perhaps permanently lower profits. But it also means that newspapers would have two high-quality businesses with built-in advantages, and if the print newspaper can ask only for stability, its brother enterprise, the online paper, has the potential to grow by leaps and bounds—but only if it is authentically online in its sensibility and culture as well as in its variety and technological innovation.

The business problem that newspapers must solve is one of producing more revenue, which has become doubly difficult in a deep recession. With the print product attracting fewer advertising dollars, and with online advertising on newspaper Web sites flattening, the solution is one that has thus far defied the best minds in the business. One line of thinking is that newspapers made a fundamental mistake when they decided to give away their news online rather than to charge for it as they do the print product. This is the view of such towering industry figures as John Carroll, whose rationale is that the only thing newspapers offer that is unique and valuable is their news. He imagines a stunning moment when the largest newspapers would all decide to start charging for their news, which may well be a flight of fancy. Such a move, if it should happen, would undoubtedly depress the number of visitors to their Web sites, and traffic is the only thing that Web advertisers respect. I think a shift to charging for online news is unlikely, more's the pity.

That said, I think there must be new ways for those generating news to be paid for their work, and there is a feverish effort to "monetize" news. One key objective is to wring money out of Google, which pays nothing for its use of the material it aggregates on GoogleNews. There are efforts to explore micro-payments for news or to create tiers of service online, with a free once-over-lightly rendition of the newspaper's content and a fee for the complete package. In the spring of 2009, the New York Times Company threatened to close the *Boston Globe*, which it owns, unless the *Globe*'s unions agreed to $20 million in cost reductions. The prospect of losing the *Globe* shook Boston to its bedrock and prompted an outpouring of anguish at the thought that such an appalling thing could happen. The embedded message in many of the letters and postings was a new awareness of what life in Boston and New England would be like without the *Globe* and, in some cases, a willingness to pay more to keep the paper alive. As newspapers fail and some cities see these institutions go dark, a determination may be born in other cities not to let it happen. It was the destruction of Pennsylvania Station in New York that shocked that city into preserving its architectural heritage. That said, a Pew Research Center in March 2009 found that less than half the Americans surveyed said that losing their local newspaper would hurt civic life, and only a third said they would miss reading it should it disappear. Similarly, I attended a class focused on the future of newspapers in which young people were asked what they would pay for arts coverage or the crossword puzzle or the other bits and pieces associated with the newspaper package. The numbers weren't high. I found myself wanting to ask how much they would pay to have someone watching city hall on their behalf or doing investigative reporting to expose malfeasance.

I think the revenue solution is one that will solve itself, in the sense that it will be what it is. With an improved economy and an array of schemes to enhance revenues online that have little or nothing to do with news, the nation's newspapers will find a new set point of operational viability and a new level of profit. But if they abandon their news-gathering and community-enhancing mission, I believe they are doomed. It is only by serving the public that they will survive in the long term.

As news organizations of all kinds scramble to find new solutions, the nonprofit and governmental sectors are frequently cited as critical players in assuring that serious news coverage continues.

In the *Nation*, John Nichols and Robert W. McChesney laid out a detailed proposal for an extensive government subsidy of news that would offer "hard-hitting reporting" that would draw all Americans into public life. They suggested, for instance, a tax credit for the first $200 spent on daily newspapers, which they acknowledge would be hard to sell politically. I think a commercial answer is the only enduring one, but nonprofits have a lot to offer, especially in the short and medium terms, and government too may have a role to play, especially for broadcast television.

Part of the problem is motivating owners of television stations to invest in quality and accountability news. Government offers an appealing carrot and stick. The stick could be wielded by the Federal Communications Commission; broadcasters could be required to fulfill a more rigorously enforced obligation to perform public service in return for their broadcasting licenses. Congress could also be more generous with public broadcasting. The First Amendment makes it impossible for government regulation to impose standards on print, but a demonstration of public service seems a reasonable quid pro quo for those who have made billions on public airwaves.

The public could also assert an obligation of public service on nonregulated media businesses, including newspapers. The carrot of such an obligation would be that putting the public interest first could be turned into a marketing tool. The ultra-competitive media environment has created a premium for any advantage that can be exploited to differentiate one news organization from another. One way other industries have found to do this is through something that has to some extent been forced on them by the advent of transnational businesses. Traditionally, businesses have had an economic obligation to their customers, their employees, and their owners and a legal one to the governments in the countries in which they operated. But if they paid taxes and behaved as required, they were thought to have done all that was asked. In recent years, however, a concept known as corporate social responsibility has arisen, which can be defined in many ways but which essentially means that corporations have a responsibility to the society in which they live. It is under the umbrella of corporate social responsibility that Coca-Cola underwrites education programs in undeveloped countries where it is selling its products. It has no legal responsibility to do this, but by doing so it is signaling to its employees and customers that it is going the extra mile in earning their trust and their business. This is a concept that has made inroads in the oil business, among car manufacturers, and in other industries, but not—so far—among media businesses. The media, which have an obvious social responsibility, have steered clear of anything that would add an extra burden of obligation to the society in which they function, in the sense of having an obligation to preserve a news operation of a certain size and focus. The public-spirited fundraising efforts for charity at Christmas, spelling bees, and other such worthy endeavors are valuable but don't represent the heart of the newspaper's mission.

It seems to me that if any business has a corporate social responsibility, it is the news business, and this translates as an obligation not to abandon the public service role that has been woven into the history of the traditional news media. This is not a burden that is mandated by law, but it is a duty most news organizations claim. By embracing the concept that there *is* a corporate social responsibility, a news organization could set itself apart, just as the *Guardian* has done in Britain. For several years, the *Guardian* has been publishing an audit that it calls "Living Our Values," which is designed to measure the newspaper's exalted principles against its performance. The *Guardian* is owned by a nonprofit trust and is a special case, but it is also a model of how a news organization can define itself not just as a business but morally, and by doing so enhance the business. It is a model that some smart news entrepreneur will seize and use to set his business apart, thus inspiring imitators. Or so I hope.

As the fortunes of traditional news organizations have declined, nonprofit models have been put forward as ways to preserve the essential role of accountability news, in whatever journalistic form. Each has its strengths, but all seem to me to be flawed as solutions that could be broadly applied and would endure.

For instance, foundations have been discussed as possible owners of newspapers, which might work in a few cases. But it seems unlikely that many foundations would wish to spend their money this way and bind themselves to an ongoing commitment. Indeed, while I am grateful to foundations for supporting the journalistic work of such nonprofit news organizations as *The News Hour with Jim Lehrer*, I am also leery of depending on foundation funding. Foundations frequently change their priorities and direction, and the naming of a new president of a foundation is reliably predictive of a change in what the foundation wishes to do with its money. Most foundations like to use their resources for development of new things rather than ongoing funding of operations.

Indeed, the whole concept of nonprofit journalism has at its heart a vulnerability that makes it inherently unstable. Funders can change their minds, lose their money, get mad, get bored, or simply want to do something different. The Center for Public Integrity in Washington is a nonprofit organization dedicated to nonpartisan, high-quality investigative journalism and has been supported by foundations and other philanthropic friends. The Center's work is recognized for its quality, and it has tackled some of the daunting journalistic challenges that even the best-funded newspapers have avoided, such as meticulous tracking of campaign contributions and how they relate to congressional actions. Even so, the Center struggles to find the funding it needs, as do many other nonprofit news organizations—even the best ones.

Another model is that of turning newspapers into nonprofits, thus reducing the financial pressure on them to produce any profits at all. Again, this is a good model in certain circumstances, but seems unlikely to be one that can be widely imitated. The great success story of this model is the *St. Petersburg Times*, which modestly describes itself on its flag as "Florida's best paper." It is not an idle claim, and the paper has been recognized for decades for its quality and commitment to news. It is owned by an educational institution, the Poynter Institute, that was created for that very purpose. The *Times*'s owner, Nelson Poynter, did not want his beloved newspaper to go into a newspaper chain upon his death, so he arranged for it to pass instead to the Poynter Institute, whose central focus is training journalists. The problem is that Nelson Poynter was able to make this decision because he effectively owned the paper, though there was a minority shareholder. Few newspapers are owned by an individual. Family ownership is now usually several generations deep, with multiple stakeholders who are unlikely to give away what is likely their principal asset. Brandt and Josie Ayers, at the *Anniston Star* in Alabama, elected to give their newspaper—which is recognized as one of the best small papers in the country—to the University of Alabama as a journalism teaching laboratory. Such a gesture is rare.

Another model that has been much discussed is the notion that newspapers will be taken over by local wealthy citizens and run more openhandedly than chains have been willing to do. Effectively, this model involves the return of newspapers from corporate to family ownership, which is what happened at the *Philadelphia Inquirer*, a part of the Knight-Ridder chain that was purchased in 2006 by a local consortium of rich Philadelphians. The nation's journalists are carefully watching the saga of the *Inquirer*, which was once a great newspaper, as its fate unfolds. The business has proved much more difficult than expected, and the owners have stopped paying their debt service, a situation that has become more common as the newspaper business falters in big cities. Warren Buffett has said that the lure of owning the local newspaper will dissipate as newspapers lose circulation and, hence, influence. That is a theory yet to be tested, and I believe the intervention of local owners is something that has genuine promise. In many places, the newspaper is viewed as not nearly what it should be—a beating heart with a faint pulse. New owners are buying potential and trust, and they are on to something. But I fear such local owners cannot outbid a well-financed investor who wants to harvest the paper instead of investing in it. If newspapers start to turn over, I fear that most of them will be purchased by sharp operators who see the chance to make a big profit by slashing costs and building nothing. Or will find no new owner and go dark.

There is also what could be called the "billionaire model" in which some of the extremely wealthy people in America decide to spend some of their billions to buy existing news organizations or endow nonprofits. My personal fantasy—and it is very much a dream—is for *The News Hour with Jim Lehrer* to turn from an hour-long program of talking heads and analysis into the nation's best television news program, the product of a new news organization dedicated to being the leader at television news. *The News Hour* has almost no resources for reporting news, which is why it is what it is. But imagine if Warren Buffett and a group of others who had the means created a $2 billion endowment to fund what was intended to be the most outstanding television news in the world. The income from such an endowment would provide $100 million a year for reporters, editors, and other professionals who could mount a worldwide effort at television news that would inspire viewers and embarrass every other television news operation. The best television journalists would flock to PBS, hungry for the chance to use their skills and energy. Good television— meaning television that is both compelling and engaging—is hard to make, and expensive. Think of *60 Minutes* combined with the probing reporting of a troop of Christiane Amanpours and no commercials. Good TV is powerful and would draw an audience. Just as important, it would put pressure on the network and cable news operations to shift their focus from endless hot air and political screaming matches to covering the news. Because it is on PBS, *The News Hour* is available on every television set in the nation and on every cable system, and if it became a beacon of high-quality reporting, the entire news establishment would be shocked and awed. And with the principles of Jim Lehrer as the guide, the news organization would also bolster the best standards of journalism. If one were looking for a way to change the world with $2 billion, it seems to me the money could not be better spent.

Other possibilities are that Google or Yahoo will move seriously into news, though they have not indicated they will. Google has gone into partnership with some newspapers to facilitate selling newspaper advertising, which may help newspapers financially if it proves effective, but gathering news does not seem to be of interest. Bloomberg Financial News could blossom into a full-service news organization, but its owner, Mike Bloomberg, who is also mayor of New York City, is more focused on politics than news.

There are also new ventures springing up, mostly on the Web. Many of these have been experiments in citizen journalism, and it is yet to be proven that a news business staffed by volunteers can succeed as a business that actually returns a profit of any consequence. But the Web has awakened so much energy and pent-up desire to communicate that such ventures will keep appearing. Other approaches to Web-delivered news are more seriously commercial, many of them tapping the ranks of laid-off reporters or working reporters who have grown discouraged and frustrated and are looking for a way to do the work they love and also make a living. The theory goes that by uncoupling the printing press and dependence on ink and paper, the costs for news delivery go down precipitously and an audience can be found online for serious news. The greatest strength of such ventures is their low cost structure.

But their limitation is embodied in the story of the Idaho City *Post Register*. An article in the *New York Times* headlined "Web Sites That Dig for News Rise as Community Watchdogs" told of such new ventures as VoiceofSanDiego.org, which offer "a brand of serious, original reporting by professional journalists." The article described the passion of the reporters, the quality of the reporting, and the sense of mission and public service that is in the DNA of such upstart news organizations. But deep in the story there was also a confession by some that their work hadn't had the impact it might have had if it had appeared in the local newspaper. I fear that excellent work without the amplification of a broad-reaching local news organization may be underappreciated and easier to ignore, which is another reason I hope the big megaphone that newspapers represent will survive.

The most encouraging thing about journalism is that young journalists are excited by the Web, as are some not so young ones. The nation's journalism schools are in a quiet debate over what they should be teaching young journalists at such a time. Some argue that the key is and remains an ability to report and write with clarity and skill. Vartan Gregorian, chairman of the Carnegie Corporation, asserts that the future's journalists must have more specialized knowledge than ever before and in partnership with Alberto Ibargüen, chairman of the John S. and James L. Knight Foundation, has launched an effort to deepen journalism education. For instance, the Columbia Graduate School of Journalism has expanded its curriculum to provide a second year of in-depth emphasis on such things as law and business in the belief that it is the minds of journalists, not their facility with the tools of the trade, that will be their argument for relevance. At the Medill School of Journalism at Northwestern University, the curriculum has been revised dramatically to prepare journalists for an online world with an emphasis on marketing. When others protest that marketing should not be part of newsroom decision making, Dean John Lavine responds that great journalism is worthless if no one sees it. Critics respond that making marketing central will open the door to making news decisions based on what will sell rather than what is important. Being sensitive to marketing and ignoring marketing priorities are both essential, as every sensible journalist knows, and the hard part is finding the right balance.

The Knight Foundation, which is dedicated to journalistic priorities, is helping uncover all kinds of new models for news that will engage and also stay true to the essentials. The most encouraging aspect of Knight's enterprise is that new ideas poured in when they offered funding for pilot projects, which is a demonstration that news remains exciting as an ideal and a vocation. People want to *do* news, and this time of transition has been a catalyst for creativity after far too long when the traditional media were too comfortable. Being terrified has prompted more energy and innovation in the news business than ever.

One of the most exciting new media news organizations is GlobalPost (www.globalpost.com), which has the great power of being a commercial rather than a nonprofit model. Phil Balboni, its cofounder and CEO, is one of the nation's most respected television journalists and the founder of New England Cable News, a regional news organization that is both serious about news and very successful as a business. GlobalPost is intended to provide international news, something that has been hit particularly hard. In his model, reporters are paid a modest salary but are given stock in the company. He has been swamped by applications for the reporting slots, and if he is successful at turning GlobalPost into a strongly profitable business, he may inspire similar domestic efforts. Certainly, the passion is there.

It is an exciting moment for news, and a frightening one. I come back, at the end, to my certain belief in the importance of journalism to our nation and to the regard I have for my fellow journalists. I urge them to keep the faith and to take comfort from their own idealism and that of their colleagues. I believe that journalism is an honorable profession and, at its best, a public service as valuable as that provided by teachers in the classroom or soldiers on the battlefield.

Saving the news requires many things. Organizations such as the Online News Association and the Center for Innovation in Journalism are striving to encourage both quality and productive change. We Media, an organization that focuses on participatory journalism, proclaims that we are at the beginning of "a Golden Age of journalism—but it is not journalism as we have known it." Its vision is that in a dozen years, half the news will be produced by "citizens" rather than professionals.

I admit that that is not my idea of a Golden Age scenario, but if news is preserved, I shall be happy to applaud. My own view is more in line with a dozen questions about the future of news posed by Bill Kovach, a distinguished journalist and founder of the Committee of Concerned Journalists, in the *American Scholar*. They were all profound questions focused on the uncertain survival of "the kind of independently verified information that emerged from the Age of Enlightenment." He asked, "How can journalists use interactive technology to help citizens participate in verification and discussion?" adding a quote from the philosopher Hannah Arendt that "freedom of opinion is a farce unless factual information is guaranteed."

And he ended, "Will the public realize that the news they now acquire for free will rapidly diminish in quality and value if a new way is not found to fund its production by careful practitioners?"

My nightmare scenario is one of bankrupt newspapers, news by press release that is thinly disguised advocacy, scattered and ineffectual bands of former journalists and sincere amateurs whose work is left in obscurity, and a small cadre of high-priced newsletters that serve as an intelligence service for the rich and powerful.

So how can the news be saved? Journalists must hold fast and persevere. Owners must do the right thing. And citizens and news consumers must notice and demand the news that they need. We may be headed for a world in which there is a yawning disparity in accurate knowledge just as there is in wealth. The elite will be deeply informed, and there will be a huge difference between what they know and what most other Americans know. We could be heading for a well-informed class at the top and a broad populace awash in opinion, spin, and propaganda. The Obama campaign demonstrated that politicians don't really need to go through the filter of the news media to win power, and it is sure to be a lesson that others learn well. Indeed, the Bush administration pioneered the concept. Ron Suskind, a celebrated journalist, put his finger on this line of thinking in an article in the *New York Times Magazine*. He recounted how the Bush administration had not liked an article he had written, so he met with a senior advisor to President Bush, who expressed the White House's displeasure. The aide told Suskind that journalists were "in what we call the reality-based community," which the aide defined as people who "believe that solutions emerge from your judicious study of discernable reality." Suskind began to respond that that was the essential point of journalism, and the aide abruptly cut him off. "That's not the way the world really works anymore. We're an empire now, and when we act, we create our own reality. And while you're studying that reality—judiciously, as you will—we'll act again, creating other new realities, which you can study too, and that's how things will sort out. We're history's actors... and you, all of you, will be left to just study what we do."

America has been a place where difference in knowledge—like difference in wealth—was not a yawning chasm and where a "reality-based" press was, for all its shortcomings, premised on the belief that reality is something all Americans should know about. A successful news media that does its job for all the nation's citizens is the engine for the news that nourishes democracy. To demand that news organizations perform this service is a part of the legacy of American democracy as much as are the principles of tolerance and the pursuit of happiness. If the iron core should gradually rust away, Americans will have squandered part of their birthright. Surely we shall not allow that to happen.

# INDEX